READING AND WRITING FOR CHANGE

READING AND WRITING FOR CHANGE

Theories and Tools for Confronting Power

Amelia Walker

BLOOMSBURY ACADEMIC
LONDON • NEW YORK • OXFORD • NEW DELHI • SYDNEY

BLOOMSBURY ACADEMIC
Bloomsbury Publishing Plc, 50 Bedford Square, London, WC1B 3DP, UK
Bloomsbury Publishing Inc, 1359 Broadway, New York, NY 10018, USA
Bloomsbury Publishing Ireland, 29 Earlsfort Terrace, Dublin 2, D02 AY28, Ireland

BLOOMSBURY, BLOOMSBURY ACADEMIC and the Diana logo are trademarks of
Bloomsbury Publishing Plc

First published in Great Britain 2025

Cover design: Matt Thame
Cover image: *Foster Tree I* by Kendrea Rhodes, 2024, mixed media

A catalogue record for this book is available from the British Library.

Library of Congress Control Number: 2025936832

ISBN: HB: 978-1-3504-5039-4
        PB: 978-1-3504-5040-0
        ePDF: 978-1-3504-5041-7
        eBook: 978-1-3504-5042-4

Typeset by RefineCatch Limited, Bungay, Suffolk
Printed and bound in Great Britain

For product safety related questions contact productsafety@bloomsbury.com.

To find out more about our authors and books visit www.bloomsbury.com
and sign up for our newsletters.

For Sue Page, who taught me the power of story,
and so much more.

CONTENTS

PART ONE WRITING, KNOWLEDGE, POWER 1

PART TWO CANONS, PUBLISHING, AND THE MYTH OF LITERARY MERIT 65

ACKNOWLEDGEMENT OF COUNTRY

This book was written on Kaurna Yerta, the lands of the Kaurna people. I pay respect to Kaurna Elders, past and present, and to all Aboriginal and Torres Strait Islander peoples, as well as First Nations peoples from other places. Sovereignty was never ceded. This always was, and always will be Aboriginal land.

TABLES

AUTHOR BIOGRAPHIES

Amelia Walker lives and writes on the lands of the Kaurna people, where she lectures at the University of South Australia (soon to be Adelaide University). She has published five poetry collections, most recently *Alogopoiesis* (2023). Her creative writings appear in journals including *Antipodes*, *Plumwood Mountain*, *The Tiger Moth Review* and *Social Alternatives*. Her academic writings have been published in *New Writing*, *TEXT: Journal of Writing and Writing Courses*, *Transnational Literature*, *The Journal of Autoethnography*, and *AXON: Creative Explorations*. She is also co-editor of *Ludic Inquiries into Power and Pedagogy in Higher Education: How Games Play Us* (eds. Walker, Grimmett & Black, 2025).

Paul Collis is a Barkindji man, born in Bourke in far western New South Wales on the Darling River. Paul worked in Newcastle for much of his young adult life in the areas of teaching and in Aboriginal community development positions. He has taught Aboriginal Studies to Indigenous inmates at the Worimi and Mount Penang juvenile detention centres, and in Cessnock and Maitland prisons. Paul has a Bachelor of Arts degree and a doctorate in Communications. He lives in Canberra and works as a creative writing academic at the University of Canberra. *Dancing Home* is his first novel and won the national 2016 David Unaipon Award for a previously unpublished Indigenous writer and the 2018 ACT Book of the Year Award.

PREFACE

Since childhood, I have taken to words on paper as a means of voicing issues for which no hearing seems otherwise available, regardless of how loud I shout with my actual voice. The first story I ever wrote, in kindergarten, was about a group of peahens who staged a coup against a domineering peacock. The peacock symbolized a group of boys who bullied me and my female friends: I may not have known the word *gender*, but already I knew gendered injustice. As I grew older, I experienced additional injustices based on social class, sexuality and more. I was a scholarship student at an elite school, and although my own family were hardly poor, richer students snubbed me for my working-class habits and shabby dress. Meanwhile, I was gradually realizing that I was bisexual and queer – in a strongly religious environment, far from easy. Problems of pollution, extinction, climate change and other environmental injustices increasingly worried at me, too.

Inspired by George Orwell's case for 'political writing' – writing that seeks 'to push the world in a certain direction, to alter other people's idea of the kind of society that they should strive after' (Orwell, 1946: para. 9) – I spent my teens and twenties continuing to write about things I thought were wrong with the world, and the ways it could change to be better. Unlike Orwell, however, I gravitated towards poetry as my main creative writing practice alongside fiction and creative non-fiction. And I believe political writing can take many styles beyond those Orwell advocated. In this book, political writing indicates all practices of creative writing oriented towards calling out problems and sparking change. Creative writing indicates a broad range of practices including but exceeding poetry, fiction, creative non-fiction and hybrid writing. My usage encompasses oral literature, theatre and visual poetry (which may incorporate or solely use non-alphabetical symbols) in addition to writing in the sense of words on pages or screens. Alongside Orwell, my other early influences for political writing were Grace Nichols, Kamala Das, Allen Ginsberg, Diane Di Prima, Langston Hughes, Audre Lorde, Shelton Lea, Gwen Harwood, Oodgeroo Noonuccal and Adrienne Rich. Later, I would become (and remain) enthralled by living writers including John Kinsella, πo, Charmaine Papertalk Green, Natalie Harkin, Quinn Eades, Andy Jackson,

Dominique Hecq, Dan Disney, Paul Collis and Taslima Nasrin – to name but a few – all of whom demonstrate not only how powerfully creative writing can speak out against injustice to promote change, but the wide variety of traditional and experimental forms and styles political writing can take.

As a young writer, I achieved a reasonable modicum of what I counted as success. My poems were published and picked up for use in Australian schools in the late 2000s and early 2010s. I was invited to perform at literary festivals in Australia and overseas, and established a small business offering writing workshops for schools and community groups. I focused on arts education and community art with disadvantaged groups around topics of injustice and pushing for change. The workshop business thrived, giving me the confidence to walk away from the sensible nursing career I had pursued upon the advice of school careers counsellors who warned me writing would never provide a stable income. In my late twenties, I enrolled to study creative writing at university, as I had wanted to when I left school, slowly earning my way from a bachelor's degree towards a PhD. Following conferral, I gained a lecturing position and relished the opportunity to explore political writing in a new context of undergraduate teaching where we could delve into issues of greater complexity than it had been possible to confront in high school and community workshop settings.

The title doctor and publication credits brought me the social voice and capacity for influence my younger self had craved. However, at the same time I was starting to realize these long-held dreams, my actual writing output was dwindling and my confidence plummeting as I found myself increasingly questioning my ability to produce ethically viable political writing. This was not impostor syndrome or self-sabotage. The doubts seeding in me were real, important ones, the growth and negotiation of which across the past decade brought me to write this book and revive my political writing practice in more cautious, critically considered ways.

Before entering academia, I had always perceived myself as an underdog. As a girl and a woman, my lot in life seemed unfair compared with the better circumstances awarded to boys and men. That I wasn't from old money and forged my first career emptying bedpans made some people think they had the right to say they were better than me. I couldn't do heteronormativity, no matter how hard I tried. Plus, I had an invisible disability, in the form of bipolar disorder, and the gross stigma that carries. All these things placed me 'below the line' of privilege, so to speak – privilege being a set of unearned invisible benefits people glean via contingencies of identity and circumstance (McIntosh, 2020: ix). But one of the quirks about privilege is, it's much easier for people to recognize when they *don't* have it – whereas those who benefit from privilege will typically accredit their good fortune to aptitude and hard work (McIntosh, 2020: 22).

Privilege is intersectional across multiple axes of social experience (Collins et al., 2021). In addition to those I have already indicated – namely gender, social class, sexuality and disability, all of which disadvantage me – axes of privilege include but exceed race, Indigeneity, body size, spirituality, language, nationality, age and neurotype, across all of which I am advantaged or 'above the line' (McIntosh, 2009: ix). Even across the axes where I initially perceived myself as disadvantaged, I've come to recognize that I was always more privileged than I thought – for instance, as an able-bodied person who never needs think about ramps or accessible toilets; as a cis-woman not subject to the discriminations faced by trans people of all genders; and as someone who, notwithstanding mental illness, has a more-or-less neurotypical mind when I'm well – which is most of the time.

Intersectionality theory (Collins et al., 2021) helped me recognize that my privileges far outweigh my disadvantages. This fed – and still feeds – my doubts around my capacity to produce ethically viable political writing. For people who bear privilege are liable to act insensitively, unaware of how their / our assumptions bear on those not privileged in the same ways (McIntosh, 2009: 13–14). Most of all, I worry about white privilege, which seems to bear a special level of force in western cultures such as that in which I live – one that in my experiences tends to override or compensate for lack of privilege in other areas. The theory of intersectionality arose, after all, largely as a response from Black feminists frustrated by white feminists' failures to recognize or redress racial privilege (Collins et al., 2021). I am not only white, but a non-Indigenous Australian person living on stolen never ceded land where Aboriginal and Torres Strait Islander people – regardless of their visible skin colours – continue suffering injustices wrought by ongoing violences of invasion and colonization, in which dominant versions of white feminism have often been complicit (Moreton-Robinson, 2000). Though this situation is one I abhor, I must face the fact that my ancestors were implicated in colonial violences, thanks to which I live with multiform benefits – many of which are so deeply ingrained in the norms of my society, I may not even realize what they are.

And so arises this troublesome question: what if my attempts to practice and teach political writing wind up inadvertently supporting the very injustices I seek to undo? There are countless examples of creative writers from backgrounds of privilege who have attempted political writing with what appear to be basically good intentions, and whose lack of awareness around their privileges has proven majorly problematic. In the 1970s, Thomas Keneally believed his historical novel *The Chant of Jimmie Blacksmith* (1978), about Aboriginal bushranger Jimmy Governor (1875–1901), was an act of solidarity with First Nations people. In 2017, Keneally officially apologized for the book, recognizing that he had misappropriated and misrepresented a story that was not his to tell (Zhou, 2017). Another example is American white feminist Mary Daly's *Gyn/Ecology: The Metaethics of Radical Feminism* (1978), which depicted 'women of color as powerless victims' (Glassman, 2012: 1), prompting Audre Lorde to respond with an open letter reflecting on the hurt the book caused her and other Black American women whose experiences Daly 'trivialized and ignored' (Lorde in Glassman, 2012: 1). Fatemeh Fakhraie's expresses similar sentiments in 'Open Letter to White Non-Muslim Western Feminists': 'Don't ignore the fighting we do for ourselves. We can – and do – speak for ourselves. So stop speaking for us' (Fakhraie in Glassman, 2012: 1).

This book reflects my efforts to work with and beyond the challenges of political writing from fraught standpoints such as my own. Through my work with creative writing students and correspondences with writers and educators across the world, I know that the issues I confront are not unique to my own scenario or the Australian context, but globally pertinent to readers and writers across diverse backgrounds and situations. Because questions about privilege and power matter for both the production and interpretation of creative texts of all kinds, this book presents theories and tools applicable to politically oriented textual analysis or reading as well as writing. I recognize, however, the substantial nature of my objectives. It would be contradictory to my intersectional politics to presume any one book or person might manage to provide all the answers (much less someone from a fraught subjective standpoint such as my own). I emphasize, this book is not claiming to answer everything. Rather, it raises possibilities for ongoing consideration as part of what must necessarily be a collective effort and a dialogue between readers and writers from multiple backgrounds bearing multiple points of view.

FOREWORD

Amelia Walker is a dear friend to me, although I do not remember how long ago it was that I met her; I rarely mark time with, or by a calendar date, or year number.

When I met Amelia that first time, a deep respect for each of our work, our writings, was held by both for the work that we'd written, and a strong friendship was made. The friendship I share with Amelia is so strongly held by me that I often refer to her as my Yaapa. That word, Yaapa, means sister, in my grandfather's language.

And, until *very* recently (just a couple of months ago), I knew that Amelia was a very good poet, and it was her poetry that I admire so much. I had only seen Amelia's poetry in text format and/or heard her read some of her poems at various poetry conferences that we'd attended.

I was truly surprised when her manuscript arrived in the post, for I did not know that Amelia is a theorist writer, who writes powerfully and beautifully. I was surprised when Amelia told me she was writing a book on communications. Amelia's book is a stunning surprise to me, for I had been expecting it to be a book of poetry, or, that is would be a book about poetry.

Reading and Writing for Change is a complete masterpiece.

In the opening chapter, Amelia writes herself into the complexities of identity and politics, bringing in that chapter a history of herself and also, a history of her family. These are brave acts for an author to 'play themselves' in their writing.

Amelia then moves quickly onto speaking about power and language. And Amelia also speaks about the power and privilege that comes with speaking – to have voice in the political sense.

It was Fanon who said, 'mastery of language affords remarkable power'.

Amelia's book is an exacting work in style and content. Chapters mirror each other in style, and each covers a new aspect of communication, mirroring one of Stuart Hall's famous works, *Representation*. Hall would write the key words of the chapter, an overview of what the chapter was going to do, and then write it, leaving the conclusion to bring it all together. It makes the ideas, readable and available, like a manual for contesting and assuming power.

Amelia is a great poet. *Reading and Writing for Change* is a surprise, containing both creative and theoretical delights for students and their teachers alike.

Running and walking are both methodical actions in much the same way as writing. The runs and walks that open each chapter are models for that, and they bring the reader into a new/a different landscape. That's what makes the ideas feel real. Your mind is emptied of other things, totally concentrating with, and on the words. Don't miss this one. *Reading and Writing for Change* is an exciting read that engages the reader in the very political moment of ideas and practises of identity and the political in our contemporary lives.

Paul Collis

ACKNOWLEDGEMENTS

I extend special thanks to Uncle Ivan-Tiwu Copley OAM, respected Kaurna and Peramangk Elder, for discussing the 'walking/writing' sections of this book, and assisting me to improve them in many ways. Any errors or shortcomings remain, of course, my own.

I likewise thank Uncle Kym Kropinyeri, respected Ngarrindjeri Elder. Your guest lectures for 'Power of Story' are the highlight of our course. The insights you share have opened my eyes to oh so much.

For similar reasons, thank you Paul Collis, for learning, friendship, kindness, collaboration and conversations that I treasure deeply. To know and spend time with you is a valued honour.

This book was completed while on Professional Experience Program leave granted by the University of South Australia. I am very grateful for the opportunities this provided for focused reading, writing, reflection and rewriting. I also thank the University of South Australia for supporting my 2023 travel to London for conferences and workshops that vitally nourished my thinking around the issues this book probes.

I have also benefited from informal support via collaborations, conversations, reading group meetings and general kindness from many writers and academics I am privileged to call colleagues and friends, at my own university and beyond. Special thanks to Susan Luckman, Corinna Di Niro, Pablo Muslera, Bronwyn Lovell, Frances Wyld, Kit MacFarlane, Chrisanthi Giotis, Phil Van Hout, Domenica Panagaris, Dominique Hecq, Ali Black, Helen Grimmett, Karen Sinclair, Cassandra Loeser, Dan Disney, Cassandra Atherton, Jen Webb, Julia Prendergast, Quinn Eades, Deb Wain, Shane Strange, Kimberly Williams, Paul Magee, Nigel Krauth, Antonia Pont, Craig Batty, Aidan Coleman, Jaydeep Sarangi, Zinia Mitra, Emily Orley, Mia Lindgren, Georgia Philips, Matthew Hooton, Hossein Asgari, Gemma Parker, Kendrea Rhodes, Barrina South, Samantha Faulkner, Autumn Royal, Phil Day, Xavier Hennekinne, Cameron Raynes, Kath Dooley, Susannah Emery, Michele Jarldorn, Jessica White, Stuart Richards, Jess Pacella, Sam Whiting, Kim Munro, Catherine Campbell, Matthew Rofe, Robert Crocker, Elliott Mundy, Chloe Cannell, Simon-Peter Telford, Dante De Bono, Stef Rozitis, Sophia Booij, Anne

Brady-Clark, Rebekah Clarkson, and all the CCRWC crew. And thank you to Lucy Brown from Bloomsbury, for believing in and supporting this idea.

On a more personal note, I thank my partner Daniel Pitman for boundless understanding, patience and laughter through the madness (and messiness) of growing a book and a baby all at once. Huge thanks also to my parents Sabrina and Charles for love, support and encouragement throughout my life. And, though you're not here yet, thank you Fox, for kicking whenever I needed to leave the desk and stretch my legs, and for keeping me focused on the better worlds for which it's worth writing.

NOTE ON TERMS AND CAPITALIZATIONS

Writing this book, I grappled hard with decisions around respectful language use. Questions about 'First Nations' versus 'Indigenous' versus 'Aboriginal' proved especially tricky, because the myriad global cultures, knowledges and peoples these labels potentially indicate are incredibly diverse. Different groups, and individuals within groups, often bear vastly differing positions about which terms are preferred and which are considered offensive. I decided to follow the patterns of the writers and theorists whose works I cite in various chapters and contexts. As a result, language shifts across the book. For instance, in chapter two I cite Aileen Moreton-Robinson (2015a), who uses 'Indigenous', so I do the same. In chapter three, I cite a resource that discusses 'Native Americans' (Eason et al., 2018), so I also use that term when paraphrasing that article.

To emphasize the diversities within 'First Nations' and related descriptors, I where possible, name the specific group to which a writer or theorist belongs (e.g. 'an Anishinabekwe scientist', 'the Ngugi/Wakka Wakka culture', etc.). Otherwise, I try to reflect preferences associated with the relevant context. For instance, if discussing Australian situations, I am more likely to refer to 'Aboriginal and Torres Strait Islander peoples' in line with Reconciliation Australia (2021) advice, or 'First Nations people' in line with the move made by the First Nations Australia Writers Network (FNAWN). 'Peoples' is pluralized to recognize and respect the vast number and diversity of distinct cultural and language groups these terms indicate. For international contexts, I tend towards 'First Nations' for general discussions, as this currently appears to be accepted in more places overall, and 'Indigenous' for research contexts, in line with the field of Indigenous Knowledges. I use the term 'non-Indigenous' to indicate those of us born into colonial privilege on lands not our own, or in colonizing nations like Britain and France. Following advice from Uncle Ivan-Tiwu Copley, I specify 'non-Indigenous Australians' when referencing the Australian context. I use 'non-Indigenous' in isolation when referring to two or more global contexts or within direct quotes from other sources.

Similar questions arose around discussions of disability, neurodiversity and madness. Some people prefer person-first language (e.g. 'person with a disability') and some prefer identity-first language (e.g. 'disabled person' or 'neurodiverse person' – or more ideally, naming the specific disability or form of neurodiversity, e.g. 'deaf person' or 'autistic person'). Again, I have aimed to follow the leads of the authors I cite and/or the dominant preferences of the specific group most relevant to the context. My own preference as a person with an invisible disability in the form of mental illness is for person-first language. When discussing my own situation, I typically write of 'living with bipolar' or 'living with madness' to emphasize that those of us who bear such diagnoses can still live rich lives. I use 'madness' as a self-empowering term, in line with its reclaiming by the mad pride movement (Rashed, 2023).

I likewise use 'queer' as a self-empowering term reclaimed from previous negative implications (Hanman, 2013). To me, queer indicates a standpoint – a 'perspective on social reality as well as a moral or political commitment' (James et al., 2023) to 'think[ing] across boundaries, beyond what is deemed to be normal, to jump at the possibilities opened' (Hanman, 2013: para. 11). Queer is not, in my usage, a synonym or umbrella term for the LGBTQIA+ community broadly, because not all LGBTQIA+ people embrace queerness. I use the LGBTQIA+ acronym to indicate a loosely associated group of people with differing yet often connected experiences around issues of gender, sex, and sexuality. LGBTQIA+ includes but exceeds lesbian, gay, bisexual, transgender, queer, intersex, asexual and aromantic people, with the plus gesturing towards the many members of our community who don't neatly identify with any of these labels but nonetheless connect with the same concerns, and towards LGBTQIA+ allies, too.

The phrase 'beyond-human being' is one I use frequently throughout this book, sometimes alternating with 'beyond-human actors', 'beyond-human kin' and similar variations. Beyond-human being here indicates basically everything that is not a human being – for instance, plants, fungi, soil, bacteria, rocks, waterways, landforms, buildings, machines, the weather and animals other than humans (for I class humans as animals). I prefer the term beyond-human over nonhuman because the latter potentially suggests othering, lack and negativity, whereas beyond-human bears positive valences via humble recognition of life forms and phenomena that exceed human comprehension. I use 'being' because I am convinced by arguments that sentience is not the sole domain of animals like humans but exists in different forms for different beings we tend to callously write off as 'things' (see discussion in Rose, 2017). The two words are hyphenated to indicate relationality and blurring of perceived boundaries. My occasional use of the phrase 'beyond-human actor' is prompted by the adoption of Bruno Latour's 'actor-network theory' (2011) into posthuman literary studies, which emphasizes the need to push beyond-human anthropocentrism by paying attention to 'the interconnectedness of human and nonhuman life and . . . necessity of factoring in nonhuman forces' (Burger et al., 2021: 2). Usage of 'kin' is primarily inspired by my colleague France Wyld (2025), alongside other theorists in whose works it indicates human interconnectedness with and responsibilities to fellow beings and the earth (Todd, 2015; Haraway, 2016; Rose, 2017).

International readers may note that I sometimes use what may appear odd capitalizations. For instance, the word 'country' is sometimes capitalized, sometimes not. Country with capitals indicates the sacred relationships First Nations Australian peoples bear with lands, skies and waterways. This is distinctly different from western cultural ideas about lower-case 'c' countries as bordered nations between which to stage wars or enter economic partnerships. Capitalization versus non-capitalization of this word indicates the meaning I intend in the given context. Similar practices apply with 's/Story' 'u/Uncle', 'a/Aunty' and 'e/Elder', among other terms. I also tend to capitalize terms like 'Black', 'First Nations', 'Indigenous' and 'Aboriginal' as markers of respect. I do not capitalize 'white' or 'western' because, as a person of white western enculturation, I feel we have disgraced ourselves through violence and must work to earn respect. On this note, whiteness is not defined by skin colour, referring rather to a position of hegemonic privilege.

MAP OF CHAPTERS

To put this book's arguments into practice, each chapter opens with a **'Walking / writing'** vignette or poem based on my musings while hiking in national parks and former mine sites. These sections unpack challenges of political writing related to my fraught subjective situation as a non-Indigenous Australian writer born and living on stolen, never ceded land. They contextualize where, when, how and why this book was written. In line with practices of creative criticism, each vignette or poem also provides an oblique way into that chapter's main questions, themes, and theories. Some also serve as examples of techniques discussed in the chapter bodies. Following each vignette, a **'Compass'** section provides a more conventional chapter overview. At the end of each chapter, a **'Re-orienting'** section reviews key points and signposts next steps. Because this book seeks to offer not only theories, but practical tools readers and writers can put to work, its chapters are supplemented by three **Praxis** modules. These offer prompts and frameworks for hands on experiments in creative writing and literary analysis to consolidate and extend ideas from the main chapters. The experiments are suitable for both formal and informal group learning and independent practice.

This book's discussions proceed across three parts. **Part one** (chapters one to three) extends the lines of inquiry opened by the preface regarding challenges of political writing from fraught standpoints such as my own. It contemplates links between writing, knowledge and social power in the form of uneven power relations across intersecting axes of identity. **Chapter one** explores critiques of white western literature by First Nations writers and thinkers. These explorations raise a need to unsettle dominant attitudes of extreme individualism and human exceptionalism in western cultures, and renew recognition of creative writing's connections with knowledge, place, and relationality. In **chapter two** I consider how creative writing's connections with knowledge in turn connects with power. This includes writing's capacities to become complicit in maintaining established scenarios of injustice, as well as its potentials for questioning these scenarios and promoting change. Chapter two establishes the book's approach to power as relational, and definitions of associated terms including discourse, ideology, capital, intersectionality, privilege, hegemony, resistance, and agency. **Chapter**

three then raises representation as re-presentation as one way creative writing is implicated in power relations. Representation as re-presentation indicates processes via which textual portrayals of people, places, and beyond-human actors affect the material worlds where they are read (Hall, 1997). Problematic representations include normalization of inequality, negative misrepresentations, tokenism and erasure. Yet representation simultaneously offers scope for intervention by politically oriented readers and writers – strategies for which chapter three provides via discussion of theories about round versus flat characters, backdrop versus integral settings, and interplays of presence with absence. **Praxis module one** follows up with writing and analysis experiments based around these concepts.

Part two begins from the observation that mainstream writing and publishing have long borne representative imbalances through which people bearing privilege have been afforded more frequent and positive representations, while those denied privilege have been subject to misrepresentation and/or erasure. As privilege is associated with white western cultures, this representative imbalance of human power relations goes hand in hand with re-presentation of white western ideologies that privilege humans above beyond-human being, which normalizes disregard for the environment and beyond-human life. Seeking to grasp how creative writing's representative imbalances arose in the first place, **chapter four** probes the social, cultural and material circumstances that shaped the western literary canon. This includes exploration of the canon's historic relationships with social institutions of religion, education, imperialism, and the mainstream western publishing industry. **Chapter five** then considers critiques levelled at the canon, efforts made to reshape it, and how creative writers have negotiated its legacies. **Chapter six** follows by examining changes to the publishing industry in the twentieth century and since, particularly how reviewers and activists are using social media to demand change.

Efforts to transform the literary canon and the publishing industry have contributed significantly towards addressing creative writing's representative imbalances. However, towards the end of part two, I venture that these approaches are limited because they focus primarily on *who* writes about *what,* with scant attention to *how* – to the formal and stylistic devices writers employ, and the gatekeeping operations mobilized via purportedly apolitical ideas about so-called literary merit. This focus drives **part three**, which explores how textual aesthetics may be considered a mode of content that affects representation as re-presentation of aesthetic preferences tied with the values and interests of various social groups. To frame this argument, **chapter seven** notes differing definitions of aesthetics, and theories about its political valences. Chapter seven also surveys historical approaches to textual aesthetics as sites for pursuing social equity, including Marxian and anarchist perspectives. Problematically, both have proven co-optable towards commercial and totalitarian agendas, indicating that no intrinsic political force universally attributable to any given writing style or set of techniques. Politically oriented writers and readers must continually and critically rethink textual aesthetics in relation to context. **Chapter eight** poses conceptual metaphor as a useful site for orienting these considerations. Conceptual metaphor bears a broader definition than linguistic metaphor, which chapter nine clarifies before elucidating ways in which conceptual metaphor may operate via micro-textual elements of figurative language (including but exceeding linguistic metaphor) (Lakoff & Johnson, 1980/2003). **Chapter nine** then considers conceptual metaphor at macro-textual levels of form and structure. I use the hero's journey and arc narratives as examples of how macro-textual conceptual metaphors can reflect and reinstate ideologies that support the interests of hegemonically dominant groups – even when these formal patterns are used to represent groups historically subjugated within those hegemonies. **Chapter ten** then considers alternative approaches to form and structure including ecologically inspired patterns, braided narratives, short story cycles and experimental approaches to poetic traditions of sonnets, villanelles, ghazals and pantoums.

Following part three, the **Concluding reflections** collate key points from across the book. I open with a 'walking/writing' poem much older than those presented across chapters one to ten, noting how I and my writing have changed through the processes of writing and researching for this book. These musings frame my recommendations for creative writers and readers seeking to produce and/or analyse writing in politically oriented ways. A key final emphasis is on the necessarily ongoing nature of the inquiries this book pursues – in particular, the fact that my recommendations for political reading and writing offer but one contribution to what must necessarily be a polyvocal dialogue articulating multiple points of view.

PART ONE

WRITING, KNOWLEDGE, POWER

1 WRITING AND KNOWLEDGE

Walking/writing on stolen Country

There are kangaroos all through this park,
but I never see them here.

Here the grey-green gumtrees part:
colonial walls of stone stand crumbling,

a grain at a time, flanked by lurid blooms
and emerald leaves:

agaves, chestnuts, lilies, figs,
a palm tree shooting high

like Babel, exploding into spiky fronds
that pierce and rip the hurting sky.

A sign explains, this site is a ruin:
the nursery closed in 1932, hit by storms,

flooding, then fires.
But what was here before?

What was ruined for these stone walls to rise?
The sign says nothing, not of this

nor of the wars yet unfolding beneath ground
and above, between roots and in shades of green.

Today I set out at sunrise to hike at the national park near where I live. This is my usual routine, weather permitting. Following the low price of living at suburbia's endpoint, closeness to nature was the biggest drawcard for my partner and I when we moved here, just over a year ago. Then, I saw the park as a space of wild beauty – somewhere I could lose myself amid gumtrees, kangaroos and hilltop views across the city, right out to sea. I've since come to understand it differently – a place of hurt, wounded by violences in which I as a white person, born on but not from this land, am implicated.

This is Kaurna Yerta, the lands of the Kaurna people, known in contemporary colonial terms as the suburb Tea Tree Gully, South Australia. The park I hike in is named Anstey Hill. At least, that's what the entrance signs declare. No doubt it has other, older, more fitting names. George Alexander Anstey was born in London in 1814. He migrated with his family to Tasmania at thirteen, and at sixteen fought with the British in the Australian Frontier Wars, which are now increasingly recognized as an act of attempted genocide against the First Nations peoples of this land. Anstey moved around, but ultimately settled here, farming sheep and grapevines for viticulture (Payne, 2014–17) – agricultural practices that have destroyed local ecosystems and contributed to climate change (Pascoe, 2014/2018, p. 10).

Why name a place after someone like that?

Beyond the entrance, hallmarks of colonial violences abound. Like a wooden home bored by ravenous white ants, the landscape remains gutted by 1800s mineshafts, where silver and quartz were torn from the earth. One edge is bordered by a barbed wire-topped fence adorned with *Danger: Keep Out* signs. The teenager-sized holes in the fence I first observed at least twelve months ago still haven't been patched. The signs' purpose is, I deduce, primarily to avoid public liability claims for drownings in the water-filled pits of the former Highbury open-cut quarry. The quarry closed operations in 2009, when the flooding of the pits became too costly to manage in comparison with profits. The accidental man-made lakes now sit like necrotic ulcers in hacked-up flesh, green-black and unhealing.

The main park's trails are made of sand and dolomite quite possibly mined from the quarry next door, or others nearby. The trails are named, well-marked with interpretative signage calling attention to sites of claimed significance. Many tell tales of so-called settlers or pioneers, depicted as brave, heroic figures. For instance, this morning's hike took me past the ruins of Newman's Nursery, the signs at which describe it as '[a]n innovative importing and exporting business' that at its time represented '[t]he model nursery: one of the finest in the state' (Anstey Hill Recreation Park, n.d.). Founded in 1854 and devastated by floods in 1912, then later bushfires, it's a world-renowned site for ghost hunters, some of whom travel great distances hoping for a glimpse of Mary Newman, the daughter of the nursery founders, who died tragically at a young age (Hall, 2014). I'm unsure about that kind of haunting, but the ruin's vibe definitely strikes me as eerie. Crumbling roofless walls of one-time greenhouses and homestead rooms overrun by vines and succulents remind me of post-apocalyptic filmscapes. Maybe that's not so far from the truth: Australia's invasion by the British in 1788 was in some senses already the end of many worlds and ways of life (Polak, 2020). These ruins are deemed a heritage site. Yet they're barely new compared with the 60,000 years or more of history here prior to that. While the rest of the park is mostly gum trees and scrub, of grey-green and silver hues, the plants surrounding the old nursery are lurid shades of lime and emerald. There are mulberries, figs, agaves, mulberries, even palm trees – in the eyes of the Newmans, exotic specimens gathered from around the world to beautify the new colony, but from a current-day view, feral pests against which local conservationists wage constant battles to protect the fragile ecosystems this park otherwise sustains (Taplin & Symon, 2008).

The nursery signs say nothing of the problems introduced plants wreak, instead telling of the Newman family and their business, particularly the family matriarch, Margaretha Newman, who was 'reputed to be the oldest native-born woman in South Australia' when she passed away in 1983, aged ninety-four (Anstey Hill Recreational Park, n.d.). This wording jolts me. Women gave birth and were born on this land for tens of thousands of years before Margaretha. What the sign means is, she was the oldest woman of non-Aboriginal descent, implying that the Kaurna people didn't really count. It's a brutal evocation of the shameful *terra nullius* myth that was used to justify British invasion (Vincent et al., 2014, p. 19). Finding such attitudes still displayed in public like this shocks me, though I shouldn't be surprised. I grew up in the 1980s, barely a decade after the referendum that led to Aboriginal and Torres Strait Islander peoples being granted the vote – though still not fully recognized in the Australian constitution (Copley, personal communication, 14 June 2024). At school, I learned barely anything about First Nations cultures beyond falsehoods that have since been disproven, most of which are too offensive to relay. Just last year, another referendum was held. Had it passed, Aboriginal and Torres Strait Islander peoples would have gained an official 'Voice to parliament', meaning a greater say in decisions affecting their lives (Davis & Williams, 2023). The referendum didn't pass. The Voice that could have been was suppressed by non-Indigenous Australian voters – shouted down and spoken over in a fashion resembling that in which the park signs' colonial tales overwrite those stories associated with this place since time immemorial.

Invasion also echoes through the park's ecosystems. The area around the nursery is the most obvious example of introduced plants displacing local species, but problems are evident throughout. Olives, blackberries, Salvation Jane and Scotch Thistles run rampant. The last of these twists my insides into particularly sharp knots. I am half-Scottish. The rest of my ancestry is Irish, Welsh and German-Lutheran – all people who were also forced off their lands, in different ways. Some came here as convicts, some as refugees fleeing persecution and some for economic survival. This ancestry doesn't, however, mean my ancestors weren't complicit in the invasion. Nor does it lessen my own implicatedness in the ongoing colonial violences and racial injustices of contemporary Australia. Much as Noel Ignatiev (1995) has argued in the American context, once the Irish and other formerly-oppressed groups hit Australian soil, we 'became white' – joined those who had beaten us, colluding with the British to become like them and share in their domination, participating in colonial violence against both others and ourselves as we willingly surrendered our languages, legends and identities in exchange for the privileges that come with assimilation into the status quo. The difference white privilege makes in this country is observable via my maternal family line's fast ascension from working to middle class: my grandmother was a child servant who received barely any schooling at all; my mother was the first in her family to complete high school and study a teaching degree; I hold a PhD and lecture at a university, a position that I love made possible by opportunities for which I am endlessly grateful. Yet I know, all this comes at grave costs. The privileges I was born into were woven through violence, theft, rape and subjugation, through the forced removal of children from families, the tortures and abuses suffered by those children in cruel institutions, the anguish of bereft parents, and millions more brutalities. This is why I sometimes hate myself, why I'm frightened of how my white-western enculturation conditions my thoughts and attitudes even though I don't want it to, of the potential violences I perhaps don't recognize in my everyday words and actions, of the unwitting impacts even the simplest of my gestures might cause.

The Scotch Thistle thrives in all kinds of conditions. In Scotland – a land I've never set foot on but dream about – the thistle is a sign of anticolonial resilience, of survival despite the odds. Here, it's just one more pest the invaders brought with them. The very resilience for which the thistle is elsewhere celebrated is part of what makes it such a problem. Scotch Thistles bloom brilliant purple for a few brief weeks, like glistening amethysts, set in green. They then fast turn to brown dry spikes that sit for months, spitting seeds into the wind, spreading ever more of themselves. Like rabbits. Like cane toads. Like me and all the other non-Indigenous Australians, clueless how to live in harmony with this place. The Traditional Owners were here for more than 60,000 years. They understood how to source food sustainably, when to burn forests to spark renewal and prevent larger-scale fires in the long-run (Pascoe 2014/2018, pp. 161–2). We've been here barely over 200 years, and made a complete mess: flooding, droughts and out of control flames are the results and evidence of just how badly we've got it all wrong (Yunkaporta, 2020).

Compass

The preface relayed the uncertainties I feel about producing and teaching political writing as a person whose invisible privileges render me unwittingly susceptible to re-perpetuating the forms of violence I aim to undo – challenges neither unique to me, nor to the Australian context, but relevant for many writers and readers worldwide. In grappling with these challenges, I take passionate interest in the creative and scholarly writings of First Nations thinkers globally, reading in search of insights about how to write in allyship rather than inadvertently causing more harm. This has helped me perceive many problems of the white western culture in which I have been raised, leading me to reflect on implications for politically oriented reading and writing. This chapter arises from these reflections and recognitions. I begin by discussing Tracey Bunda's juxtaposition of Ngugi/Wakka Wakka Story against white-western notions of narrative (Phillips & Bunda, 2018). I then consider approaches to storytelling and other modes of creative writing from First Nations cultures around the world, observing that while all are unique, a common theme is linkages of creative writing with knowledge, particularly knowledges of place and relationality. This prompts me to reconsider my received understandings of story, narrative, poetry and creative writing broadly. Word etymologies indicate that western cultures historically recognized stronger links between creative writing and knowledge than we currently do. I pose a need to restore this recognition, and to learn from First Nations writers and thinkers about how writing might help us mend severed connections with Earth and each other. This includes discussion of two dominant attitudes in western cultures: extreme individualism, and human exceptionalism. Both foster problems of inequity among humans and human exploitation of beyond-human being. My suggestion is that practices of reading and writing to ignite writing-knowledge-place-relationality connections in western cultures could contribute towards redressing extreme individualism and human exceptionalism to promote more harmonious interactions both amongst humans and of humans with beyond-human kin. However, I by no means suggest creative writing as a sole solution. Contemporary problems are complex and bear no singular answer. Rather, creative writing could form one part of what must necessarily be a connected and ongoing collaborative effort across many scholarly fields and creative practices.

The Story/narrative split

Dominant western cultures have long split the arts from the purportedly more serious activities of scientific research and 'productive labour', disregarding creative and playful practices as 'frivolous' and 'meaningless' while overlooking the opportunities creativity offers for learning (Rapti & Gordon, 2021, p. 2). In *Research Through, With and As Storying*, Louise Phillips and Tracey Bunda (2018) contest this hierarchical split, arguing for the important roles storytelling and other creative acts can play in academic research. In their account, the arts/ sciences split is reflected and supported by a split between narrative and storytelling (Phillips & Bunda, 2018, p. 4). There has since the 1970s at least been a 'narrative turn' across many academic fields that, though happy to pose narrative as a source of knowledge and a process of inquiry, steer far clear of the terms 'story' and 'storytelling' (p. 4). For the primarily white western academics dominating these fields, the term narrative better serves 'in appealing to the inclinations of adults in realms of power, prestige' (Sobol et al., 2004, cited in Phillips & Bunda, 2018, p. 4). Bunda contrasts the western theorizations of narrative with her own Ngugi/Wakka Wakka culture's treatment of Story as 'the communication of what it means to be human, that tells of emplaced, relational tragedies, challenges and joys of living' via creative practices including those 'spoken, gestured, danced, dramatized, painted, drawn, etched, sculpted, woven, stitched, filmed, written … any combination of these modes and more' (Phillips & Bunda, 2018, p. 3).

Bunda's points about Story-knowledge connections in her culture and the relevance these retain in current times are consistent with those of other First Nations Australian scholars including Linda Payi Ford, who writes of how 'metaphors can be drawn from our knowledge systems to inform and guide our thinking and understanding of new endeavours in our contemporary times' (2010, p. 29), and Tyson Yunkaporta, whose books *Sand Talk* (2020) and *Right Story, Wrong Story* (2023) simulate processes of yarning – story-sharing that unfolds 'like conversations but take a traditional form we have always used to create and transmit knowledge' (2020, p. 19). Yunkaporta also emphasizes the importance of Songlines: 'maps of story carrying knowledge along the lines of energy that manifest as Law in the mind and land as one, webbed throughout the traditional lands of the First Peoples' (p. 11).

Songlines form the focus of Margo Neale and Lynne Kelly's book *First Knowledges Songlines: The Power and the Promise* (2020), which configures Songlines as intergenerationally-transmitted stories that might from a western point of view seem to resemble traditional mythology, but which differ in their dynamic, living status as sites of knowledge ongoingly and collectively re-created in adaptation to changing situations and challenges in current times – for 'Knowledge contained in the stories deepens and enlarges over time for those who continue to engage with law and culture on Country' and 'ways of learning are evolving, including access to knowledge in digital forms through Aboriginal managed archives' via which Songlines remain 'never-ending but firm foundations for lifelong learning' (p. 63). Neale and Kelly explain how Songlines 'connect sites of knowledge embodied in the features of the land', often operating as directions for safely navigating long journeys across terrains where food and water can be difficult to find: 'It is along these routes that people travelled to learn from Country' (p. 63). In addition to geographic routes, Neale and Kelly note that the 'information, innovations, stories and secrets' borne through Songlines and Country also include 'medicine, engineering, ecology and astronomy to social mores on how to live, and social organisation, including moiety division and kinship systems' (p. 63).

The interconnections between Story, Country, knowledge and community emphasized in First Nations Australian cultures bear similarities to those described by First Nations scholars from other parts of the world – although it is important to recognize that none of these approaches is identical or interchangeable. Even within Australia, each of the hundreds of distinct groups spread across the continent and its islands bears its own language, customs, values, law, stories and conception of Story. To reductively conflate them into a homogenized mass would be to damagingly overlook the vital differences that characterize and make each one unique. They do, however, articulate on certain general points (Moreton-Robinson, 2016, p. 8). For instance, Anishinabekwe (First Nations American) scientist Robin Wall Kimmerer writes of 'an intertwining of science, spirit, and story', emphasizing how 'old stories and new ones' can help heal 'our broken relationship with earth', providing 'a pharmacopoeia of healing stories that allow us to imagine a different relationship, in which people and land are good medicine for each other' (201, p. xi). From a Māori (New Zealand) perspective, Linda Tuhiwai Smith describes how 'new stories contribute to a collective story in which every Indigenous person has a place', serving 'to connect the past with the future, one generation with the other, the land with the people and the people with the story' via storytelling as 'both method and meaning' (2021, p. 166).

Smith also notes uses of story in cultures beyond her own, including those of Latin America, where '*Testimonio*' represents 'a narrative of collective memory' that 'has become one of a number of literary methods for making sense of histories, of voices and representation, and of the political narrative of oppression' (Smith, 2021, p. 165). Similar story-knowledge connections are also observable in accounts from Indigenous researchers spanning Samoa (Alefaio, 2022), Namibia (Nghikefelwa et al., 2022) and Canada (Barcham, 2023), among other places (Hernández et al., 2021). For me as a person partly descended from the Irish diaspora but raised without any exposure to Irish language or culture, accounts of the Irish seanchaí are particularly interesting. The seanchaí were 'treasurer[s] of the[ir] community's oral arts and genealogies' (Robinson 2003, p. 44), revered by their communities for their 'impressive command of Irish myths, legends, and tales' concerning 'events of the past' (Messenger, 1964, p. 201). Traditionally, seanchaí would host seasonal gatherings, and storytelling was 'institutionalised' as a practice that cohered community connection by reminding people of their shared histories and values (pp. 201–4). The 'dinnseanchaí', were seanchaí specifically knowledgeable in placelore or 'the local micro-geography' (Robinson, 2003, p. 44). Their storytelling was an act of 'attention … appreciation of uniqueness' involving evocation of placenames and stories as a 'creative force' that 'allocates value and, ideally, directs our care' (p. 44).

As a creative writer and educator who has long argued the value poetry and other modes of creative writing offer for engaging multiple intelligences or learning styles across in science, maths and history as well as arts subjects (Walker, 2010), First Nations links between creative writing and knowledge appeal to me. I am cautious, however, to resist temptations towards co-option of these practices into my own, as this could contribute to ongoing processes of colonization via epistemic violences of misappropriation, misrepresentation and misuse (Kovach 2009, pp. 28–9). I abide by the guidelines my colleague Frances Wyld, posed in a presentation directed at non-Indigenous Australian academics interested in engaging with Indigenous Knowledges in our work (personal communication, 31 October 2023). Wyld is a Doctor of Communication and a Martu woman (Traditional Owners of lands in the Pilbara region of Western Australia). Citing Plains Cree and Saulteaux (First Nations Canadian) scholar Margaret Kovach's claim that academics who are not themselves Indigenous can make 'strong allies for Indigenous methodologies' because we 'can assist in making space for Indigenous methods' and 'for the epistemic shift from a Western paradigm that Indigenous methodologies bring' (2009, p. 86), Wyld encouraged us to learn by reading widely and engaging with literature from the field of Indigenous Knowledges. It is important to use Indigenous-authored sources that faithfully represent Indigenous knowledges in accordance with cultural protocols about what is and is not suitable for public sharing. Other sources may problematically misrepresent and/or disrespectfully publicize knowledges that are meant to be kept specifically for specific groups or members of groups. Wyld also raised Aileen Moreton-Robinson's stipulation that 'non-Indigenous scholars can engage with Indigenous analytics but not produce them' (Moreton-Robinson, 2016, p. 4).

From Wyld's talk, my take-home was that as a non-Indigenous Australian, it is ethically important for me to engage deeply and thoughtfully with the available scholarly and creative insights First Nations thinkers offer, but that I should do so with careful respect for boundaries. This, coupled with Yunkaporta's turning of Indigenous Knowledge lenses towards critique of western cultures' problems (2020, p. 22), guides the approach I take here – one of applying what I learn from my readings of First Nations thinkers towards revaluation of my own culturally-formed habits and assumptions. In line with my earlier-stated aim of avoiding the cultural violences towards which writers born into positions of privilege are often prone, I particularly apply my learning towards re-thinking how creative writing is understood across contemporary western societies, and how the insights gained through this process can inform ethically viable political writing.

The next section begins the self-revaluation process by interrogating the culturally received meanings I as a person of white-western upbringing associate with the terms story, poetry and narrative.

Creative writing and knowledge

Story, narrative and poetry are terms I've long taken for granted. The critique raised by Bunda (Phillips & Bunda, 2018) now drives me to reconsider critically what these words mean to me and others raised in westernized cultures. Common dictionary definitions position story and narrative in a tautological spiral: 'story' indicates a 'connected account or narration of some happening', while 'narrative' indicates 'a tale, a story, a connected account of the particulars of an event or series of incidents' (Harper, 2024). In addition to the difficulties of telling one from the other, these definitions are in themselves also vast, loosely bounded ones: as European-trained anthropologist Rodolfo Maggio notes, a story 'can be many things, if not all things' (2014, p. 90). Among a long list of examples, Maggio cites 'account', 'adventure', 'allegory', 'anecdote', 'apology', 'ballad', 'case study', 'chronicle', 'confession', 'contrivance', 'discourse', 'dream', 'epic', 'episode', 'fable', 'fiction', 'faction', 'fantasy', 'gossip', 'histography', 'joke', 'legend', 'lesson', 'lie', metaphor', 'myth', 'news', 'poem', 'poiesis', 'protest', 'question', 'reason', 'rumour', 'science', 'tale', testimony', 'translation, 'truth' and – reflecting the tautologies in the dictionary definitions noted before – 'narrative' (p. 90).

The field of narratology offers a clearer perspective on story, narrative and the relationship between them – albeit a problematic one, for reasons I will shortly explain. I turn to narratology not to uncritically take its terms and methods on board, but rather to grasp how I am already influenced by it, and to trouble that influence's sway. From a classic narratological perspective, 'story' represents what is told and narrative the act, means, style or product of telling (Chatman, 1980, p. 19). Linguists similarly distinguish between 'the *narrated event*' and 'the *narrative event*' (Stapleton & Wilson, 2017, p. 16, original italics). Via this model of understanding, the transformation of a story into a narrative involves decisions about 'where to begin, what events and evaluations to include or emphasize, and where to end' as well as 'the right words and gestures' for conveying these things (Clark, 2011, p. 457). One example of how a story and its narrative as defined by narratology might differ is in the ordering of events – for instance, a story's events might be chronological, but its narrative could relay events in non-chronological order to heighten their impact. Another example is that the ostensibly same story can be told via different media (such as oral storytelling, written texts, films, sound recordings, visual art, theatre and more) and pitched to different audiences via different techniques of genre and style.

The American film and literary critic Seymour Chatman, who was strongly influential on the field of narratology, proposed a three-way split between *story*, *narrative* and *discourse*: 'the story is the what in a narrative that is depicted, the discourse the how' (1980, p. 19). Chatman drew influence from the French Poststructuralist Gérard Genette. Genette posed three uses of the term narrative: one, 'the narrative statement, the oral or written discourse that undertakes to tell of an event or a series of events'; two, 'the succession of events, real or fictitious, that are the subjects of this discourse', including their 'linking, opposition, repetition, etc.'; and three, 'the event that consists of someone recounting something: the act of narrating taken in itself' (1980, pp. 25–6). A similar three-way split is offered by contemporary feminist historian Clare Hemmings, who delineates between stories as 'the overall tales feminists tell', narratives as 'the textual refrains (content and pattern) used to tell stories', and 'grammar' as 'techniques' that 'serve as narrative building blocks' (2011, p. 227).

As a writer and educator, I have long found narratological theory useful for understanding relationships between form, style and content. However, narratology's efforts to code 'a system of analysis that examined both the actual narration and the act of narrating as they existed apart from the story or the content' (Augustyn, 2008, para. 2) seems to have contributed to the splitting of story from narrative and divorcing of creative writing from knowledge in western cultures. Narratology seems connected with the problems Bunda signals when scrutinizing the uptake of narrative in academic fields focused on 'power', 'prestige', 'pretension' and 'over-intellectualization' (Phillips & Bunda, 2018, p. 4). Even from a broadly western perspective, this splitting of narrative from story is recognized as problematic. Creative critic Timothy Mathews emphasizes the dynamic interrelations of form and content, pitching 'Questions about art' (both form and content) as 'questions about life: about the point at which things begin to mean' (2014, p. 1). Mathews ponders the difficulties of ever pinning down 'the line crossed from a transient perception to a moment of wonder or wound' (p. 1). Maggio also notes the difficulties of separating stories from their telling, urging anthropologists to 'refrain from defining a story before its making' (2014, p. 92).

The observable problems and paradoxes of separating story from narrative lead me to wonder when and how this split came about. Etymology offers clues. Until the 1500s, 'story' bore strong connections with 'history': it was used to signify a 'narrative of important events or celebrated persons of the past, true or presumed to be' (Harper, 2024). This usage can be traced from the Old French 'estoire', meaning 'story, chronicle, history', which in turn reflects the Late Latin 'storia', a shortening of 'historia', meaning 'history, account, tale, story' (Harper, 2024). The idea of a true story is a peculiarly English-speaking notion, arising only in recent centuries. Earlier English language uses of story as connected with history appear largely compatible with the Gaelic 'seanachas', which signalled both 'history, antiquity' and 'story, tale, narration' (Harper, 2024). From the 1500s onwards, a shift of meaning began occurring towards story in both its 'literary sense' as a 'tale in more or less imaginative style, narrative of fictitious events meant to entertain' and its commonplace sense as a 'humorous anecdote, incident related for interest or entertainment' (Harper, 2024). By the 1600s, story had also become euphemistic for 'a lie, a falsehood' (Harper, 2024).

As for narrative, it derives from the Latin 'narrare', meaning 'to tell, relate, recount, explain' – or more literally, 'to make acquainted with' – in turn from *gnarus*, 'knowing', and the Proto-Indo-European 'gno' for 'to know', from which the word 'knowledge' also derives (Harper, 2024). Narrative has thus long borne direct connections with knowledge in western culture, which may in part account for why it has to date been more readily adopted into western academia as both a site of study and a method of inquiry. However, story's etymological connections with history indicate that it too bore stronger connections with knowledge in western cultures than are currently recognized. Pertinent to this point is the etymology of 'history' itself: like story, history comes from the Latin '*historia*', which in turn comes from Greek wherein '*historia*' represented 'learning or knowing by inquiry; an account of one's inquiries; knowledge, account, historical account, record, narrative' (Harper, 2024). This meaning evolved from the earlier Greek verb '*historein*': to 'be witness or expert; give testimony, recount; find out, search, inquire', and even earlier, the Proto-Indo-European '*weid*' for both 'to see' and 'to know' (Harper, 2024).

The etymologies of 'story' and 'narrative' suggest that both previously bore strong associations with developing and sharing knowledges in western cultures. For me as a writer whose creative practices primarily include poetry and experimental prose, a question here arises of where non-narrative creative writing practices – such as texts that emphasize a specific image, thought or sensation without reference to events or temporal markers – fit into this picture, if at all. In answer to this question, I pose that they do, for the Proto-Indo European origins of story are not limited to narrative in the sense of relaying things that happened across a given time frame. Witnessing, inquiring, seeing and knowing can involve much more than what happened in what order. It is also worth noting the origins of 'poetry' and 'poet' in the Greek '*poiein*': 'to make, create, compose' (Harper, 2024). *Poiein* is thought to have come from the Proto-Indo-European '*kwei*', meaning 'to pile up, build, make' (Harper, 2024), which suggests poetic making as more than simple fabrication in the sense of fancy: rather, poetry gathers materials found in the world and makes new meaning of them. In this way, 'Poetry, thoughtfully and technically created' can provide 'a notion of reality' that 'allows us to see, more clearly, how in our lived experience the elements of reality are constructed, and how they fit together' (Webb, 2012, p. 10).

It therefore appears that in western cultures creative writing – including storytelling and poetry among other practices – once bore stronger associations with knowledge than we now usually recognize. The next section considers what the lost recognition of these associations means for connections with place and community.

Place, relationality and uprootedness

The section before last surveyed accounts of writing-knowledge connections in various First Nations cultures around the world. Common to most if not all these accounts was the emphasis on knowledges specific to place and relationality – on caring for Earth and living in harmonious relation with both human and beyond-human kin. This contrasts with what seem to be two dominant attitudes in contemporary western cultures: extreme individualism and human exceptionalism.

This section considers each in turn before arguing their connections with contemporary uprootedness and associated problems including social and environmental crises.

Individualism 'emphasizes self-reliance, competition, and the subordination of in-group goals to personal goals', and may be contrasted with collectivism, which 'emphasizes interdependence, interpersonal harmony, co-operation, and the subordination of personal goals to in-group goals' (Marshall, 2008, p. 143). Martin Åberg traces individualism's emergence to the Enlightenment, noting its strong connections with liberalism and 'European modernization', and identifying it 'as the keystone of modern politics as we know it' (2013, p. 155). Lisa Lowe (2015) similarly identifies individualism with:

> branches of European political philosophy that include the narration of political emancipation through citizenship in the state, the promise of economic freedom in the development of wage labor and exchange markets, and the conferring of civilization to human persons educated in aesthetic and national culture – in each case unifying particularity, difference, or locality through universal concepts of reason and community. (p. 3)

Lowe adds that while individualism is associated with 'universal promises' including human rights, 'emancipation', 'civility', 'mobility' and other modes of freedom, it paradoxically depends on 'global divisions and asymmetries … according to which such liberties are reserved for some and wholly denied to others' (2015, p. 3). Individualism is thereby also associated with 'subjection, administration, and governance', and has served as a tool of colonial power through which western cultures have asserted dominance over colonized people (p. 3).

Lowe's critique of individualism aligns with Todd Greene's observation that individualism 'travels in many directions, positive and negative' (2022, p. 69). For Greene, positive examples include individualism's role in social movements focused on 'the many positive freedoms increasing for women, minorities, etc.' and general cultural shifts towards 'a healthier respect for inherent individual differences, and the dignity of such' (p. 69). Greene also notes the dangers in extreme collectivism, citing Nazi Germany and Communist China as examples of how '[n]ations with too much collectivism experience groupthink, the suffocation of the individual spirit, and many other negative consequences' (p. 69). In other words, both individualism and collectivism bear valuable elements when they coexist in moderation, but either one taken to extremes is troublesome. To be clear, my critique of individualism is not an argument against it in outright terms, nor a suggestion to pursue the opposite. Rather, I am arguing that western cultures have currently gone to an extreme version of individualism that causes major problems including those Greene observes in the form of 'widespread self-absorption, and a lack of desire to correct structural problems' (p. 68).

For instance, the '*ideology of full self-reliance*' is a brand of individualism that celebrates the flaunting of wealth on the assumption that any person bearing 'will and determination' can and will succeed – while those who lack wealth 'must be somehow lacking in will and determination' and so deserving of inferior circumstances (Greene, 2022, p. 70). This form of individualism fails to account for the multiple social, cultural and other factors that place people from varying backgrounds at differing levels of advantage and disadvantage for accessing education, gaining employment, entering the investment market and other means towards monetary and other modes of success, and as such has been an ideology predominantly embraced by 'rich white men' (p. 70). '[L]ess rich white men' have meanwhile tended to favour the '*ideology of full self-reliance*', which states 'that even those who do not attain wealth . . . still have cultural value and validation if they are fully self-reliant; that is, if they do not ask for help (or later, go on welfare)' (p. 70). Another more recent variant, embraced by a broader range of the population is the '*ideology of online individuality*', which 'suggests that people can receive value and validation by expressing their "individuality" online', for instance via '[s]elfies, YouTube celebrities, blogs, [and] podcasts' (p. 70). The 'shadowy sides' of extreme retreat into online individuality include '[c]atfishing, online bullying, [and] body image disorders', all of which contribute towards social isolation, anxiety and depression (p. 70).

Overall, extreme individualism encourages people to prioritize their own needs while disregarding others, which promotes competition ahead of collaboration, care and community responsibility, thereby helping sustain inequities of wealth and wellbeing among different members of human societies. Additionally, individualism tends to go hand in hand with disregard for the environment. For individualism is specifically oriented towards human individuals, with 'distinction between definitions of the human and those to whom such definitions do not extend' being 'the condition of possibility for Western liberalism, and not its particular exception' (Lowe, 2015, p. 6). In this way, extreme individualism, as the first of two attitudes that appear dominant in contemporary western cultures, relates to the second: human exceptionalism.

Human exceptionalism indicates 'the belief that humans are categorically and qualitatively different from all other animals, and consequently have more moral worth and more rights' (Cook, 2015, p. 590). Guy Cook identifies human exceptionalism as 'the default view' in the UK and other broadly western cultures, tracing its origins to Ancient Greek philosophy (particularly Aristotle), Judeo-Christian claims about 'divine authority for human dominion over all other species', and the nature / culture dualisms promoted by René Descartes (Cook, 2015, p. 590). While contemporary versions of human exceptionalism have largely if not entirely moved beyond 'the Cartesian view that animals are mere machines', they still pose 'a qualitative difference between humans and all other animals and/ or the uniqueness of certain capacities, such as, for example, language' (p. 590).

Cook's account is consistent with the late Deborah Bird Rose's characterization of human exceptionalism in terms of 'repeated assertions . . . that man is the only animal to make tools; that man is the only animal with language, a sense of fairness, generosity, laughter; that man is the only mindful creature' – all of which, Rose emphasizes, have been 'thoroughly undermined' by research-based evidence that '[o]ther beings also do wonderful and clever things; we are not a unique outlier but rather are part of various continua' (2017, p. 55).

Human exceptionalism encourages people in western cultures to 'act as if the world beyond humans is composed of "things" for human use', thereby contributing to the 'catastrophic assault on the diversity, complexity, abundance, and beauty of life' that is our current era of climate crises, multispecies extinctions, extractivism, and related assaults on Earth (Rose, 2015, p. 55). In response to this scenario, in which western cultures have divorced ourselves from fellow animals and beyond-human beings and entities with catastrophic implications for all forms of life on Earth, Rose advocates that western cultures learn from First Nations cultures about 'multispecies kinship and connectivity' (2015, p. 52). Zoe Todd similarly argues a need 'to examine underlying assumptions about, and responses to, human and non-human relationships' via 'ethical relationality' as a movement to 'envisage ourselves as rooted in reciprocal, ongoing, and dynamic relationships that are informed by Indigenous legal orders and our embeddedness in the meshworks that connect us through an "ecological imagination"' (2015, pp. 249–51). Reflecting human exceptionalism's links with extreme individualism, ethical relationality also involves overcoming western tendencies towards the latter via 'reciprocal discourse' between cultures as 'an ethical imperative to recognize the significance of the relationships we have with others, how our histories and experiences are layered and position us in relation to each other, and how our futures as people similarly are tied together' (p. 250).

The current dominance of individualism and human exceptionalism in contemporary western cultures seems to me both a symptom of and contributor to widespread *uprootedness,* which I define as a severing of ties to place and relationality bearing many worrying consequences. My treatment of uprootedness is based on the separate-yet-similar accounts generated by Simone Weil (1949/2005) and Hannah Arendt (1951/2017), both of whom were Jewish women living at the time of World War Two and the German Nazi Holocaust. Arendt defined uprootedness as extreme loneliness coupled with superfluousness: 'to be uprooted mans to have no place in the world, recognized and guaranteed by others; to be superfluous means not to belong to the world at all' (1951/2017, p. 625). She posed that early twentieth century populations experienced widespread uprootedness due to upheavals including 'unemployment, displacement, homelessness, [and] war' (p. ix). Weil, too, defined uprootedness as a profound sense of disconnection from place, social relationships and purpose or role, noting unemployment as a precipitating factor (1949/2005, p. 42). She juxtaposed it with rootedness, which represents 'participation in the life of a community which preserves in living shape' both 'treasures of the past' and 'expectations for the future' (p. 40).

The factors of precarity and isolation Weil and Arendt separately identified as drivers of uprootedness in the early twentieth century appear rife in contemporary times. Since the turn of the century, there have been multiple wars, environmental disasters, health epidemics and global financial crises, which have together exacerbated worldwide issues of displacement, unemployment, poverty, precarity, social atomization and anxiety. Concurrent with these worsening problems have been resurgences of xenophobic movements such as neo nazi groups, and far-right political parties (Lowe, 2022). This concurrence is consistent with Weil's characterization of uprootedness as 'by far the most dangerous malady to which human societies are exposed' because uprooted people are vulnerable to totalitarian regimes promising security and camaraderie (1949/2005, p. 40). Arendt likewise theorized that uprooted people turn to totalitarian regimes for feelings of place, belonging, purpose, and figures to guide them. In Arendt's account, uprooted people feel excluded from society and unrepresented in official politics, and so 'will always shout for the "strong man", the "great leader"' (Arendt 1951/2017, p. 138). Reflecting the ways in which uprootedness severs people from place as well as each other, contemporary movements of this kind tend to advocate xenophobic violence not only among humans, but against beyond-human being via denial or downplaying of problems such as climate change, pollution and extinction, coupled with advocacy for money-making ventures of animal exploitation, unsustainable agriculture, mining and polluting industries.

As already noted, contemporary uprootedness bears multiple contributing factors and requires multiple forms of address. In line with the arguments of Rose (2017) and Todd (2015), one among those many modes could involve western cultures learning from First Nations cultures about ways to re-establish connectivities both amongst human communities and with beyond-human kin. Both Todd (2015) and Rose (2017) emphasize the role that art can play in this process, which articulates with points from earlier in this chapter about the links in First Nations cultures between creative writing and knowledges of place and relationality. I therefore pose that readers and writers who, like myself, have been raised in western cultures need to think carefully about how connectivities with places and kin (human and beyond-human) manifest – or fail to manifest – in the texts we read and write. What can we learn from First Nations writers and thinkers? In condensed terms, I am proposing that increased recognition of *writing-knowledge-place-relationality* ties in western cultures could help lessen uprootedness and its problems. I emphasize, however, my earlier the point about uprootedness bearing multiple contributing factors and requiring multiple forms of address. I am not naïve or idealistic enough to imagine that practices of creative reading and writing might provide a full solution to the issues this section has discussed – merely a contribution to what must necessarily be a larger set of concerted and ongoing efforts. Nonetheless, the potentials of this contribution generate vital implications for politically oriented reading and writing. These implications form the sites of inquiry to which subsequent chapters of this book attend.

Re-orienting

This chapter has argued a need for contemporary western cultures to learn from First Nations cultures about creative writing's connections with knowledge, particularly knowledges of place and relationality. I have posed that revived recognition of writing-knowledge-place-relationality connections in western cultures might help us redress current attitudes of extreme individualism and human exceptionalism, both of which are associated with widespread uprootedness and the problems it promotes both amongst humans and between humans and beyond-human being. This is certainly not to suggest that creative writing might independently solve contemporary the multiform problems at play. More temperately, I suggest that creative writing has a role to play in what must necessarily be much larger concerted processes involving many disciplines and approaches. Chapter two builds on this chapter's themes by exploring how writing's connections with knowledge in turn connect it with power – specifically, the maintenance as well as troubling of existing power relations both amongst humans and of humans with beyond-human being.

2 WRITING AND POWER

Walking/writing through fields of war

Mostly, I hike in quiet, opening myself to sounds of birds and ancient trees – punctuated by engine roars from trucks and cars hurtling along the main roads that hem the park's edges. Occasionally, I bring an invisible companion in the form of a podcast or recorded speech. Today, I listened to Aileen Moreton-Robinson's (2015a) keynote address to a symposium exploring applications of ideas from Michel Foucault to scholarship around Indigenous Sovereignty. Though a white Frenchman caught up in western institutions of power that are problematically implicated in processes of colonization and oppression, Foucault's critiques of power have been widely embraced in the field of Indigenous Knowledges (Neale et al., 2014, p. 16). I begin my hike at the Gun Emplacement, a large clearing with a panoramic view of the city and coast. Its name is attributed to Major W. H. Edmunds, a Boer War veteran-turned-cartographer who 'could envisage the military advantage of such a site', though no actual gun emplacement was ever constructed here (Bourman et al., 2010, p. 577).

Knowing how the Gun Emplacement got its name makes me reflect on how the violences that resonate in Australia connect with those of other places. Growing up, I learned in school about apartheid in South Africa and the concentration camps of Nazi Germany. These things horrified me and my peers. Never was the thought raised that police brutalities, Indigenous deaths in custody, and refugee detention camps represent similarly horrific human rights abuses in contemporary Australia (Razum, 2022; Perera & Pugliese, 2023). *Australia is a free country, like America, a land of opportunity where anyone can make it if they just work hard enough.* That was the narrative we were fed, again and again – a curated set of partial details crafted and recited 'til the conditioning cohered into take-for-granted (un)truth.

War, Moreton-Robinson reminds me, is not only something fought on battle fields: war rages in times and places of so-called peace, too (2015a). War unfolds everyday through techniques of government as well as social interactions, both significant and banal; war injures civilian bodies, shouts brutal commands inside our minds. This different understanding of war comes from Foucault's notion of power as relational (1980, p. 39), which Moreton-Robinson (2015a) highlights among the concepts in Foucault's work that prove useful in her own work. Moreton-Robinson (2015a) is critical of Foucault's approach to sovereignty and his entanglements in the forms of Enlightenment-influenced thought that predicate themselves on the anthropocentric human subject and disconnection from the earth. But she perceives value in Foucault's ideas on how knowledge and power interrelate, mutually forming and re-forming one another.

Moreton-Robinson's emphasis on links between knowledge and power help me realize that if creative writing connects with knowledge, then it too is implicated in power. If we ignore writing-power connections, then creative writing can easily become a tool of oppression that reinstates existing systems of injustice. But if we recognize and attend to the writing-power relationship, it becomes a site at which to push for change through Truth Telling, honesty, awareness, and acknowledgement.

Compass

Chapter one posed a need for western cultures to learn from First Nations cultures about how we might revive recognition of writing-knowledge-place-relationality connections. I argued that reviving recognition of writing-knowledge connections matters for politically oriented reading and writing because it can help redress problems of extreme individualism, human exceptionalism and uprootedness. Another reason why it matters is that lost recognition of writing-knowledge connections doesn't mean they cease operating. Instead, they persist unrecognized and unchecked. As the opening vignette noted, knowledge is intricately connected with power, which connects creative writing with power too – in potentially problematic ways. Those problematics form this chapter's focus.

I begin by considering how relational power (the approach to power used throughout this book) differs from commonplace approaches to power as something people have and/or use. This entails discussion of power's mediation in discourse, of which creative writing is a part. Theories of ideology then help illustrate the ways in which creative writing may sometimes support the status quo, but at others, provide ways to contest it. Following this, I seek alternative terms for approaching things often referred to using the word power in its everyday sense. These include capital, symbolic violence, intersectional privilege, hegemony, resistance and agency. Exploring each in turn, this chapter develops a lexicon that subsequent chapters use to unravel the complexities of creative writing's involvements in systems of power, and the implications for politically oriented reading and writing.

Relational power and knowledge

Moreton-Robinson's (2015a) approach to knowledge-power connections reflects a Foucauldian notion of power as relational. Relational power differs from everyday approaches to power as something people can hold, lack, win, lose, grant, deny, exercise or expend like mined energy resources (Sugden & Tomlinson, 2013, p. 3). Rather than emphasizing *who* or *what* seemingly *has* power, a relational approach steers attention towards how power operates in dynamic interactions between individuals and groups (p. 3). In Foucault's words, 'Power in the substantive sense, *"le" pouvoir*, doesn't exist'; instead, 'power means relations, a more-or-less organized, hierarchical, co-ordinated cluster of relations' (1980, p. 198). Sara Ahmed's (2012) work on institutional racism offers an example of this approach, one that treats inequality and domination as not purely individual but 'systematic' (p. 44). Jane E. Kelley's (2008) 'critical multicultural analysis' of power in children's fairy tales explains that from a Foucauldian perspective:

> a person does not own power; rather power, to some extent, entails organized hierarchal relations that are enabled and maintained through *micro-relations* and can be provoked from the top downwards or from below to above (pp. 32–3).

Such micro-relations are observable in Moreton-Robinson's account of 'how Whiteness operates through the racialized application of disciplinary knowledges and regulatory mechanisms, which function together to preclude recognition of Indigenous sovereignty' (2015b, p. 129). This reflects power in its 'capillary form', which 'reaches into the very grain of individuals, touches their bodies and inserts itself into their actions and attitudes, their discourses, learning processes and everyday lives', thereby exercising itself *'within* the social body', rather than *from above* it' (Foucault, 1980, p. 39, original italics).

The processes of power implicate all of us in differing, dynamic ways (Sugden & Tomlinson, 2013, p. 7). Power relations may be described as relatively even and equitable, or uneven and inequitable – involving domination, exploitation, marginalization and/or other injustices against certain individuals or groups. Manifestations of power relations are shaped by situations (Ahmed, 2012, pp. 13–14). Crucial to this shaping is 'discourse' – all the texts, utterances, ideas and artefacts present in a given context, which together form a complex web wherein knowledges are formed, cohered, contested and re-formed (Foucault, 1980, p. 86). Discourse steers people's understandings of what seems to be true, which forms of knowledge matter, and what is generally taken for granted as *a priori* fact (p. 86). But these purported *truths* of discourse are cultural and contingent rather than universally true: many are later realized to be false (as in the case of new scientific discoveries that disprove older ones) (Foucault, 1980, pp. 196, 223). Some discursive truths operate to naturalize and justify uneven power relations between social groups and individuals – for instance, theories of eugenics were historically used to justify racism, sexism, ableism, and homophobia (Foucault, 1980, pp. 196, 223). Although eugenics has since been debunked, its former dominance still bears residual effects on thinking that manifest power through indirect means such as ideals of beauty and associated judgements about appearance that can aid or hinder people's chances of social acceptance, career success, and more (Jarrin, 2017, p. 8).

Discourse mediates knowledge and power relations not via any 'singular or deliberate "act,"' but instead through 'reiterative and citational practice[s]' via which it 'produces the effects that it names' (Butler, 1993, p. 2). In Moreton-Robinson's work, discourse informs the concept of 'possessive logics', which 'denote[s] a mode of rationalization ... underpinned by an excessive desire to invest in reproducing and reaffirming the nation-state's ownership, control, and domination' wherein 'white possessive logics are operationalized within discourses to circulate sets of meanings about ownership of the nation, as part of commonsense knowledge, decision making, and socially produced conventions' (2015b, p. xii). Another way discourse mediates power is by suppressing certain knowledges as 'subjugated knowledges' deemed illegitimate and illegible in comparison with the culturally-sanctioned or approved knowledges: for instance, both Indigenous Knowledges and knowledges of LGBTQIA+ being have historically been – and often still are – subjugated in these ways (Halberstam, 2011, p. 11). Additionally, discourse mediates *subjectification* – the ways in which humans become 'subjects' who are 'gradually, progressively, really and materially constituted through a multiplicity of organisms, forces, energies, materials, desires, thoughts etc.' – for discourse produces, limits and sustains 'those continuous and uninterrupted processes which subject our bodies, govern our gestures, dictate our behaviours' (Foucault, 1980, p. 97). Subjectification is particularly insidious because it encourages those born into privilege to assume their privilege as natural and normal, while discouraging those born into positions of marginalization, oppression and/or exploitation from questioning the injustices they face or wondering how things might be otherwise.

Now these critical concepts of relational power and its connections with knowledge via discourse have been relayed, the next question is how these knowledge-power connections in turn implicate creative writing in power, and what this means for politically oriented reading and writing.

Discourse and ideology

Poetry, prose, storytelling and other creative writing practices – whether written, spoken or otherwise performed – all form part of discourse, while being themselves formed *with and in* discourse. Creative writing is thereby enmeshed with discursive reproduction of knowledges that naturalize uneven power relations via processes including creation of discursive truths, encouragement of possessive logics, suppression of subjugated knowledges, and discursive subjectification. This is what I signalled when I noted that if we fail to recognize the writing-knowledge connection, then it may operate without our awareness in potentially problematic ways. Recognition of these processes, on the other hand, enables critique and intervention, opening vital possibilities for political reading and writing. Discourse is, however, via its sheer expansiveness and multiplicities, slippery to grasp. A clearer sense of how creative writing's connections with knowledge and power make it simultaneously capable of maintaining the status quo as well as facilitating struggles towards change may be realized by considering theories of ideology, particularly the idea of ideological state apparatuses as posed by Louis Althusser (1970/2006).

Althusser's and Foucault's ideas are often considered incompatible (Brady & Schirato, 2011, pp. 21–2). Yet there are numerous precedents for using the two together (Jones, 2002; Butler, 1993, p. 69; Brady & Shirato, 2011, pp. 21–2). I perceive Althusser's work on ideology as a useful steppingstone for grasping how discourse works. Kelley's (2008) Foucauldian analysis of power relations in children's literature joins theories of discourse with theories of ideology to argue that discourse conveys ideologies and coheres them as cultural norms, including norms of uneven power relations:

> Cultural norms are those ideologies that render themselves commonsensical and give the idea that this is just the way things are supposed to be. When these ideologies are not questioned, the distribution of power becomes a cultural norm. (p. 40)

'Ideology' is a 'multifaceted social process through which individual and social actors articulate their beliefs and behavior' (Malešević, 2011, p. 334). As 'a form of "thought-action"', ideology 'penetrates most of social and political practice' in ways that shape 'the distinct conjectural arrangements of a particular social order' (p. 334). Its contents are often 'for the most part, nontestable, offering a transcendent grand vista of collective authority' via constructed 'messages' that 'make potent appeal to advanced ethnical norms, superior knowledge claims, to individual or group interests, or to popular emotions to justify actual or potential social action', forming 'a complex process whereby ideas and practices come together in the course of legitimizing or contesting power relations' (p. 334). The attitudes of extreme individualism and human exceptionalism discussed in chapter one are examples of ideologies bearing current dominance in mainstream western cultures, and of the significant effects ideology can bear on human and beyond-human lives, power relations and wellbeing.

Ideology is typically both *'representational'* and *'historical'* (Wachsmuth & Angelo, 2018, p. 1042, original italics). The representational aspect entails how ideologies 'express intuitions and common sense about social reality' while the historical reflects that ideologies 'are always tied to particular historical and geographical circumstances' (p. 1042). Ideology is particularly manifest in 'institutional discourse justifying and legitimizing ... existing institutions' (Lefebvre, 1970/2003, p. 105). Althusser posed two broad kinds of institutions: official or 'state' institutions such as education, the church, and military bodies (1970/2006, p. 88) and 'ideological' ones such as the family, the media and cultural institutions including literature, the arts and sport (p. 92). Althusser conceived these as 'ideological apparatuses' via which social control is implicitly maintained, in contrast with 'repressive' apparatuses of state institutions more patently involved in policing laws, enforcing punishments, and so on (p. 92). While repressive apparatuses operate in largely 'public' ways, ideological ones bear on 'private' thought and affect (pp. 92–3).

Broaching the arts as forms of ideological state apparatus makes palpable how creative writing is involved in ideology and power. Creative writing's relationships with ideology are also emphasized by Henri Lefebvre, who described how writers including Victor Hugo, Charles Baudelaire, Gérard de Nerval and Arthur Rimbaud contributed to ideologies of 'the city' as an urban 'paradise' through works that helped form 'an image of the city tending toward a concept (that is toward an understanding)' (Lefebvre, 1970/2003, pp. 107–8). Signalling the effects of this ideology of the city on human relationships with place, space and community, Lefebvre noted that 'nature supplies certain elements of this paradise' including 'wine and drugs, fabrics and metals, carnal desire and violence' but 'reuse alters their meaning', reflecting values of capitalist extraction, nature as a resource to be plundered, and attendant lack of care for Earth (p. 108).

Importantly, discourse is not one way, but responsive to contexts and change. In a similar sense, Althusser argued that ideology is not only the 'stake' of social struggle, but a 'site' for its enactment (1970/2006, p. 94). In other words, while armies and police forces remain the tools of government control, writing and the arts are spaces in which everyday people can intervene to agitate for change. Lefebvre similarly noted creative potentials for 'criticizing, refusing, and refuting' institutional structures even while 'unfolding through them' (1970/2003, p. 105). Lefebvre's emphasis on the potentials of writing and the arts in political movements towards change was a significant influence on the Situationists, who 'argued convincingly that a commodity-based economy was irredeemable, a barrier to the project of human disalienation, individual sovereignty, and the achievement of genuine community' (Gardiner, 2000, p. 125).

While the Althusserian notion of distinct ideological institutions or apparatuses is perhaps problematic in its tendency to separate them out and imply deliberate control, Foucauldian theory gives a more nuanced sense of how discourse's multiple factors interact in complex ways that often exceed conscious intent, for via discourse, 'power is embedded in all aspects of society, including literary texts' (Kelley, 2008, p. 40). The ways it is embedded and the so-called truths it manifests are often so commonplace as to seem invisible or *a priori* – taken for granted. This means that in writing – as in other areas of life – we are liable to reflect and reinstate the ideologies and norms discourse conveys without knowing we are doing so. Awareness of this scenario opens scope for writers and readers to critically question discourse's repressive operations, resist unthinkingly replicating the established norms, and broach possibilities of intervention towards change.

Capital and symbolic violence

So far, this chapter has explored concepts of relational power, the power-knowledge connection, discourse and ideology. These explorations have shown how creative writing is entangled with discourse, knowledge and ideology in ways that render it liable to reflect and reinstate established ideologies and norms of power – even when the writer has no conscious intent of doing so and may in fact desire the opposite. At the same time, these connections with power make creative writing a site of opportunities for questioning these problematic processes of social reproduction and intervening to promote change. The remaining chapters of this book discuss varying ways in which creative writing may reinforce as well as contest power, and the implications the writing-power connection bears for politically oriented reading and writing, including practical strategies for broaching literary production and analysis. To enable those discussions, a lexicon is required for signalling those things that are often referred to using the word power as it is defined in the everyday sense (something people can hold, lack, win, lose, grant, deny, exercise or expend). From an understanding of power as relational, these things are better understood as *manifestations of power*, rather than power itself. They include capital, privilege, hegemony and agency. This section discusses capital. Subsequent sections broach the others.

Capital indicates multiple forms of 'resources accumulated within fields and partially convertible across fields' (Burawoy, 2019, p. 41). Among these, probably the most obvious is economic capital: wealth and property (Bennett, 2010, p. xviii). Of greater relevance to creative writing's links with power is cultural capital: elements of taste and disposition – for instance, a liking for and knowledge of music and literature favoured by the middle and upper classes typically lends a higher level of cultural capital than the 'popular' musical preferences of working-class people (Bourdieu, 1979/2010, p. 8). Cultural capital 'circulates within a symbolic economy of cultural value that is configured in a series of interlocking hierarchical structures' via which it is 'transmitted, acquired and accumulated' through struggles for 'legitimation negotiated through the interactions between the producers and consumers of symbolic goods' that occur 'within designated fields of cultural production' (Huggan, 2016, p. 21). For instance, the literary field may be considered as 'a space where writers operate within a constrained set of possibilities governed by certain historically determined rules' to which 'writers respond . . . based on their habitus' (Dalleo, 2016, p. 10). The 'habitus' represents the cultural capital, habits, attitudes, bodily gestures and other attributes a person acquires from the social settings in which they are raised and the differing social fields through which they circulate across their lives; their habitus continues changing as they become exposed to different fields and experiences (Bourdieu, 2010, p. 81).

Cultural capital and field-habitus dynamics normalize uneven power relations by enabling dominant groups to 'obscure their domination behind the distinction they display in the cultural sphere' by making their 'familiarity with high culture' or 'legitimate culture' appear 'a gift of the individual rather than an attribute of their class, acquired through socialization' (Burawoy, 2019, p. 24). Dominated groups may meanwhile feel 'ashamed of their inadequate appreciation of legitimate culture', not recognizing that the prestige endowed to it bears 'its basis in class-determined cultural capital', as does the devaluing of purportedly low or illegitimate culture (p. 24). Normalizing of imbalanced power relations via cultural capital is an example of symbolic power and symbolic violence – phenomena via which 'legitimate understandings of the social world are imposed by dominant groups and deeply internalized by subordinate groups in the form of practical taken-for-granted understandings' that operate 'in everyday classifications, labels, meanings, and categorizations that subtly implement a social as well as symbolic logic of inclusion and exclusion' (Swartz, 2011, p. 76). For instance, education is pitched as 'a meritocratic order' wherein hard work enables success, but mainstream educational advantages 'students endowed with cultural capital (i.e. those already equipped with the capacity to appropriate mental and abstract teaching – the symbolic goods on offer)' thereby reproducing injustice while re-perpetuating illusions about 'the possibility of upward mobility ... obscuring the class domination that it reproduces as its basis' (Burawoy, 2019, p. 24).

Another example of symbolic violence via processes of cultural capital is outlined in critiques of 'exoticism' as 'a *symbolic system*', that 'has proved over time to be a highly effective instrument of imperial power', the coerciveness of which is thickened 'by the occlusion of underlying political motives' (Huggan, 2016, p. 30, original italics). Exoticism operates by 'domesticating the foreign, the culturally different and the extraordinary' as 'a control mechanism of cultural translation which relays the other inexorably back again to the same' (p. 30). However, because full domestication of the exotic would 'neutralize its capacity to create surprises', these colonizing processes include both 'systematic assimilation of cultural difference' and 'an expanded, if inevitably distorted, comprehension of diversity which effectively limits assimilation' and keeps the exotic at a distance: 'the exoticist rhetoric of fetishized otherness and sympathetic identification masks the inequality of the power relations without which the discourse could not function' (p. 30).

The two examples of how cultural capital operates through education and exoticism to exert symbolic control also illustrate how creative writing is implicated in power. Regarding education, this occurs through the ways in which literary texts are studied in schools and other learning environments. For instance, students who have been exposed to Shakespeare in their family homes will have more familiarity with these texts and succeed more easily with studying them in school. Regarding exoticism, literature is among the key venues via which it is conveyed. For instance, Edward Said's work on 'orientalism' (exoticizing of the so-called orient from an occidental or western perspective) critiques how a '[g]eneral grandeur and passion' in orientalist novels produced 'a transcendent sense of things and little patience for actual reality', producing cultural misrepresentations 'steeped in racial and geographical platitudes' that contributed to the maintenance of imperial dominance (Said, 1979, p. 102).

In line with Althusser's treatment of literature as both a 'stake' and 'site' of struggles for change (1970/2006, p. 94), novels have also been a key venue to call out imperial violences and 'write back' against domination (Ashcroft et al., 1989). Similarly, education can operate as a space of radical pedagogy wherein to contest false divides of 'popular' versus 'elitist' cultures (Freire, 1994, p. 83). In helping to theorize these processes, Bourdieu's (1979/2010) work on the various modes of capital not only provides useful terminologies for discussing things otherwise often referred to as power, but also expands understandings of the ways creative writing interacts with power. However, capital is limited in that it does not cover all the things the word power is commonly used to express. Furthermore, Bourdieu explored cultural capital and symbolic violence primarily in connection with the maintenance of social class injustices, meaning that there remains need to consider power's operations across axes of social experience beyond class such as race, gender, sexuality, disability and more. The next section therefore considers intersectional privilege.

Intersectional privilege

While Bourdieu (1979/2010) explored cultural capital and symbolic violence primarily in connection with the maintenance of social class injustices, theorists of privilege consider injustice across a far broader range of socio-cultural axes (Collins et al., 2021). Privilege represents 'invisible . . . unearned assets' that those bearing privilege typically take for granted, not recognizing that these same privileges are denied to – and at the expenses of – those the privilege system suppresses. Privilege operates like an 'invisible weightless knapsack' full of 'passports' and tools to help those who hold it while those lacking privilege struggle along without (McIntosh, 2020, p. 17). Cultural capital and symbolic violence are among the processes via which intersecting relations of privilege are reflected and maintained. A stark example of the material – indeed life or death – consequences of the divisions privilege inscribes is provided by Collins et al. in the form of differing experiences of women in the 1980s Sudan People's Liberation Army (SPLA): 'girls drawn from the more privileged communities in the country often fought in fewer military engagements and did less of the domestic labor in SPLA camp areas' (2021, p. 714).

The benefits privilege brings 'are based on identities that are possessed not because of individual effort or virtue but because the identities are inherited' and given 'higher value' by society (Vandrick, 2015, p. 56). Much like symbolic violence, the insidious invisibility of privilege and frequent denial or non-recognition of its existence intensifies its damaging effects (McIntosh, 2020, p. 22), for privileged groups 'have long treated their partial perspectives on the social world as universal truths' (Collins et al., 2021, p. 691). As Ahmed notes, '[i]t is hard to get whiteness recognized by those whose political agency benefits from it not being recognized' (2012, p. 152). Dominant constructions of success in western cultures allow people with privilege to 'believe that they have the lives they have because of their own individual choices and actions' and 'that those with less privilege could be more successful by simply working harder' (Vandrick, 2015, p. 56). This reflects how '[i]ndividuals tend to identify with the socioeconomic order in which they hold privileged positions' (Lawrence, 1983 cited in Crenshaw, 1988, p. 1369). When confronted by 'the tension between the harsh realities of that order and their ideal images of themselves within that order', those bearing privilege often respond to resolve 'this tension between the real and the ideal' by 'legitimizing the existing structure' via 'self-mystification[s]' (p. 1369). These modes of mystification manifest discursively in 'legal arguments, judicial opinions, or theoretical discussions', among other ways that 'become part of a defense mechanism that extends beyond the individual' (p. 1369).

An illustration of how people born into privilege are culturally trained to ignore and exercise it without realizing how this contributes to the oppression of others can be offered in the context of building design. When designers fail to equip buildings with access ramps and wheelchair-friendly toilets, they may not be deliberately trying to discriminate against people with disabilities. Nonetheless, the result of this thoughtlessness is exclusion of disabled people from buildings without these features – and the events, communities and other opportunities these buildings otherwise offer. Such oversights make big differences in the lives of those who will and won't be able to work, learn, socialize or otherwise take part in benefits that able-bodied people take for granted.

Privilege is intersectional (McIntosh, 2020, p. 12): it operates across complexly connected axes of social identity including race, Indigeneity, gender, sexuality, social class, disability and more (Collins et al., 2021). The term intersectionality emerged from 1970s–1980s Black American feminism, as a response to simultaneous frustrations with white feminists who failed to perceive the significance of race, and male racial rights activists who remained dismissive of women's concerns (Cho et al., 2013). Moreton-Robinson's *Talkin' up to the White Woman* (2000) raises similar frustrations with white feminism in Australian contexts. Early modes of intersectionality, which often incorporated social class in addition to race and gender, mobilized it 'as a heuristic term to focus attention on the vexed dynamics of difference and the solidarities of sameness in the context of antidiscrimination and social movement politics', exposing 'how single-axis thinking undermines legal thinking, disciplinary knowledge production, and struggles for social justice' (Cho et al., 2013, p. 737).

In addition to axes of race, gender and social class, contemporary applications of intersectionality often also incorporate Indigeneity (which connects with but isn't the same as race), sexuality, body type (e.g. fat activism), disability, neurodiversity, age, spirituality and more (Collins et al., 2021, p. 691). For me, an intersectional approach involves attention to all these interlocking axes of human power relations, and also human relation with beyond-human being. As chapter one showed, the extreme individualism that helps maintain inequities among humans ties closely with human exceptionalism, which serves human dominance over beyond-human being. Both ideologies are also longstanding tools of colonial oppression, as colonial theft of land for mining, unsustainable agriculture, and other ecologically damaging greed driven practices has entailed subjugation of First Nations peoples and their knowledges about environmental care.

Intersectionality foregrounds 'the "interlocking nature of oppression"', indicating 'a need to change the scope of previous investigations and investigate how systems of oppression are interlinked' (Collins et al., 2021, p. 698). Theories of privilege and intersectionality are useful for recognizing the multiple axes across which injustice operates, and how their interactions shape lived experiences. Privilege theory is, however, limited in its tendency to emphasize people being either 'above' or 'below' the 'line' of privilege versus subjugation (McIntosh, 2009, p. xiii). Lived interactions are rarely so binary: across each axis of privilege, multiple positions are possible and each person's position shifts depending on contextual circumstances of change across situations and over time. To go beyond the binary above/below schema, theories of hegemony are useful and form the next section's focus.

Hegemony

In his *Prison Notebooks* (Gramsci, 1929–35/1992a, 1929–35/1992b, 1929–35/1992c), written while imprisoned under Benito Mussolini's Fascist regime, Antonio Gramsci describes hegemony in terms of ways in which hierarchical systems of social control are maintained without need for direct enforcement via military or other means. Hegemonic systems foster 'active or passive adherence to the dominant political formations' via which 'dominant groups' maintain 'consent' from those they subordinate and 'keep them under control' (Gramsci, 1929–35/2021, p. 10). As a Marxist, Gramsci was focused on questions of social class, but did recognize that groups oppressed by hegemony are often 'originally of a different race (different religion and different culture) than the dominant groups', and likewise acknowledged the 'question of the importance of women' (p. 9). Subsequent thinkers have re-applied his theories about hegemony to interlocking systems of race (Orlowski, 2011), gender (Connell, 2000), ability (Kolářová, 2016), sexuality (Kolářová, 2016) and more.

Hegemony involves a hierarchy – a tiered system of power relations wherein those at the top of the hierarchy enjoy plentiful forms of capital, privilege, and/or other benefits, while each descending tier bears fewer of these aspects, suffering increasing levels of marginalization, oppression and exploitation. The group occupying top position are described as the 'hegemonic group' (Gramsci, 1929–35/2021, p. 11). Hegemony is not the hierarchy itself but the system via which its hierarchical order is maintained. I'll clarify this point soon, but first, some elaboration on the nature of hegemonic hierarchies and terms used to describe them.

Relating hegemony to gender and patriarchy, Raewyn Connell notes that 'hegemonic masculinity' represents 'the currently accepted answer to the problem of legitimacy in patriarchy', sustaining 'the dominant position of men and the subordination of women' (1993/2000, p. 77) as well as LGBTQIA+ people (p. 162). Regarding hegemonies of race, Paul Orlowski observes that 'situating *whiteness* as the hegemonic norm in the school curriculum and corporate media' insidiously 'results in an advantage for White people' (2011, p. 8). Orlowski also notes how the hegemony of western colonizers has been supported by 'essentialist racial hierarchies' as a 'mainstream hegemonic discourse' that 'positions Europeans on top of all other racial groups', serving colonial violences including 'the theft of Aboriginal peoples' lands and the enslavement of African people, destroying much of these indigenous cultures in the process' (2011, p. 83).

Beneath the hegemonic group are various subaltern groups who are 'subject to the initiatives of the dominant groups even when they rebel and rise up' and who 'even when they seem triumphant', often remain 'in an anxious defensive state' (Gramsci, 1929–35/2021, p. 6). The subaltern groups are not singular or equal in their positions: rather than simply sitting above or below the privilege line, they bear tiered relations. For instance, Orlowski poses that in the British Empire, the British occupied the hegemonic position, with the second to top group being people from other parts of Europe, then people from various parts of Asia, and in the most oppressed positions, people of African descent alongside First Nations peoples (2011, p. 84).

Connell makes similar points regarding hegemonic masculinity, naming the group directly below the hegemonic group as the 'complicit' group, who, while they don't enjoy benefits to the same degree as those the hegemonic group bears, still enjoy certain trickle-down benefits and are aware of their position as better off than those of the groups below them (1993/2020, pp. 78–9). Connell additionally distinguishes between 'subordinated' and 'marginalized' positions within the hegemonic masculinity strata (pp. 78–80). Subordinated groups are subject to practices including 'political and cultural exclusion', 'cultural abuse', 'legal violence' (such as imprisonment), 'street violence', 'economic discrimination' and 'personal boycotts' that position subordinate groups 'at the bottom of a gender hierarchy among men' (p. 78). Marginalized groups meanwhile bear complex relationships to authority and 'authorization', which Connell illustrates via the example of how '[i]n a white-supremacist context, black masculinities play symbolic roles for white gender construction' (80). For instance, 'black sporting stars become exemplars of masculine toughness' but this 'fame and wealth of individual stars has no trickle-down effect' and 'does not yield authority to black men generally' (pp. 80–1). Ultimately, the symbol of the Black sports star is in this context still exploited by white power as a symbol to serve 'the *authorization* of the hegemonic group' (pp. 80–1). Furthermore, it is offset by simultaneous representations that vilify and demonize Black men as dangerous and suspect (p. 80). The glorific and vilifying marginalized (mis) representations ultimately play the same role – of providing a symbolic o/Other via which the hegemonic group constructs its s/Self. Like the processes of exoticism discussed earlier, both modes of marginalization are ultimately hyperbolic and superficial, saying little of the realities of the people they purport to represent. Connell adds that relationships of marginalization/authorization 'may also exist between subordinated masculinities' (p. 81) – for instance, between different groups within LGBTQIA+ communities, between feminists of different races, and so on.

Crucially, while hegemony *involves* hierarchy, it doesn't refer to the hierarchy itself: it refers to *processes via which the hierarchy is maintained*. As Connell notes, hegemony relies on 'correspondence between cultural ideal and institutional power', meaning that 'the successful claim to authority, more than direct violence' is 'the mark of hegemony' (Connell, 2020, p. 77). Orlowski (2011) signals the compatibilities of hegemony with both Althusserian and Foucauldian approaches, relaying how, via the lens of hegemonic theory:

> the state operates in a much broader framework than what is commonly thought of as the public sphere, namely, the government, political parties, and the military. The state, according to Gramsci, also includes the private sphere of civil society, including church, the media, and . . . public education. (p. 44)

Orlowski (2011) adds

> the [hegemonic] state can be seen as a social relation in much the same way that Foucault conceptualized power. Rather than thinking of the state as a distinct

institutional category, it is more profound to think of it as a form of social relations that enables capitalism and other dominant discourses to find expression. (p. 44)

Hegemony can therefore be conceived as a range of 'devices employed in the service of maintaining the status quo' (Orlowski, 2011, p. 44). It describes processes via which those who are disadvantaged by the hierarchy become convinced they should consent to it, not because they necessarily like or agree with existing conditions, but because they perceive them as inevitable or preferable to the potential alternatives. One example of how this works can be observed in the operations of the complicit groups noted earlier. They may know that their position in the hierarchy isn't the best one possible, but they're aware that it's still better than that of most others. They're worried that if they don't support the hegemonic group, they'll get bumped down the hierarchy and subject to worse treatment. Or perhaps they believe that by supporting the hegemonic group, they can ingratiate themselves and climb the hierarchy to increase their access to benefits. We can think of this in terms of a schoolyard bully and bystander relationship. The bystander witnesses the bully bullying students who occupy a subaltern position. The bystander might themselves personally not agree with the bullying, but they aid the bully – or at least, refrain from intervening – because they're scared that if they challenge the bully, they'll become subject to the bullying too, or they believe that by ingratiating themselves with the bully, they can gain access to the benefits the bully holds.

As earlier noted, combining theories of hegemony with those of privilege and intersectionality enables a complex understanding of the intricacies involved in the power relations of multiple social groups across intersecting axes of experience. Observing the forceful ways in which these interlocking systems additionally operate together with discourse, ideology, capital, symbolic violence to maintain the status quo raises two important questions. How is change possible – if it is indeed possible? And what role can creative writing play? The previous section noted that literature and the arts provide spaces wherein everyday people can contest dominant ideologies and enact struggles towards change. Orlowski raises a similar point regarding the role of 'organic intellectuals' upon 'success of the hegemonic function of the state depends' (2011, p. 44). This group comprises 'educators, journalists, and experts within various fields' (including, I venture, writers), who 'can control and further entrench certain discourses that support the dominant ideology', helping to 'manufacture consent', yet can also unsettle hegemonies through production of 'counterhegemonic discourses', which, in Orlowski's view, is 'where hope resides' (p. 44).

Producing counterhegemonic discourse is challenging because it requires overcoming the pervasive operations of discourse, ideology, privilege and other aspects of power. To address those challenges, the next section broaches questions of resistance and agency as means towards ethically oriented change.

Resistance and agency

Earlier sections in this chapter considered ideology and hegemony. A commonality between them is that both theorize processes that maintain existing systems of social control, but they differ in their accounts of how these processes operate. Ideology, as 'a form of "thought-action"' (Malešević, 2011, p. 334) works on people in ways of which we are commonly unaware. Hegemony, by contrast, fosters 'active or passive adherence to the dominant political formations' (Gramsci, 1929–35/2021, p. 10) in ways of which people are often conscious, albeit with a strong impression they lack choice. Ideology and hegemony connect with Kelley's argument that 'domination' is maintained via two forms of 'collusion' as 'internalized oppression' (2008, p. 33). According to Kelley, collusion is 'conscious when a person has knowledge of oppressive practices, and the person chooses to do nothing about it' (p. 33). For example, people 'may practice coercive power to obtain dominant power, to uphold the status quo, or merely to survive' (p. 37). Unconscious collusion, on the other hand, is 'when a person internalizes or believes the oppressive practices to be morally right, or assumes things are simply that' (p. 37).

As means beyond domination and coercion, Kelley raises possibilities of 'resistance' and 'agency'. Resistance is 'the conscious effort to challenge oppressive practices', while agency represents 'power *with* someone or something' as opposed to domination as 'power *over* someone or something' (2008, p. 33, original italics). Resistance emerges when people – including seemingly powerless ones – begin to realize that domination can be overcome (Kelley, 2008, p. 33). Resistance entails 'conscious effort' and 'questioning, which evokes challenges of oppressive practices': people 'may demonstrate resistive power for personal reasons . . . or for societal reasons'; in either case, resistance 'conscious and planned' as opposed to 'reactive' (p. 38).

Kelley contrasts resistance with agency, which involves 'conscious action for the purpose of social justice' that is 'ongoing and continuous' (2008, p. 38). While resistance 'acts against, or objects to, oppressive practices', agency is 'constructive' (p. 38), meaning it doesn't just push against existing situations but imagines creative ways to work beyond them. To take part in agency is 'to take an active role in ending oppressive practices, which includes suggesting alternative practices that are fair' (p. 38). Literature can enact agential possibilities by '[s]howing powerful new world[s] where people share power . . . making decisions that are consistent with social justice' (p. 38).

Kelley's case for agency as a more powerful means for overcoming domination than straightforward resistance reflects common understandings of agency as the 'capacity to act' (Pisa & Hruska, 2023, p. 4). While attractive for the utopian possibilities it signals, such approaches to agency can become problematic when it comes to situations where the resources required to take action are unavailable and/or external modes of control explicitly block it. In Islamic feminist Saba Mahmood's nuanced account, agency entails more than just the capacity to act: it also involves 'capacity to realize one's own interests against the weight of custom, tradition, transcendental will or other obstacles (whether individual or collective)' (2006, p. 38), which may involve decisions *not* to act via strategic 'passivity', 'docility': this kind of agency is activated 'not only in acts that resist norms but also in the multiple ways in which one inhabits norms' (p. 42). The need for such strategies reflects how possibilities for action are mediated by 'tangible (financial and material resources) and less tangible (knowledge and skills) elements' in connection with 'the enabling context . . . the institutional environment, social networks and political support' (Pisa & Hruska, 2023, p. 4).

Turning a critical eye to white feminist notion of agency that 'locate the political and moral autonomy of the subject in the face of power', Mahmood argues that 'despite the important insights it has provided, this model of agency sharply limits our ability to understand and interrogate the lives of women whose sense of self, aspirations, and projects have been shaped by nonliberal traditions' (2006, p. 33). She calls for a rethink of agency 'not as a synonym for resistance to relations of domination but as a capacity for action that historically specific relations of subordination enable and create' (p. 33). Ahmed similarly contends that '[a]gency, as we currently understand, must be challenged and updated to reflect the lived experiences of women across diverse settings', flagging how 'overemphasis on autonomous action' can 'lose sight of complex social relationships, bonds and networks women rely on to navigate power structures in tight-knit rural communities of developing countries and create better living conditions' (2020, p. 1192).

Rather than 'free will' or any innate individual quality, agency is 'interactionally achieved' via processes both enabled and constrained by 'the mediating effect of social structures', and discourse as the 'cultural resources upon which people draw when accounting for their sense-making or actions' (Warren & Ward, 2022, pp. 540–1). This makes agency 'difficult to locate' (Mahmood, 2006, p. 38) and riddled with paradoxes: courses of action that are hypothetically available may remain imperceivable and unthinkable because of conceptual limits relating to subjective standpoint, cultural conditioning and lived experiences (or inexperience). Activation of agency therefore isn't necessarily commensurate with privilege, capital, or other forms of seeming advantage.

For instance, in *Bila Yarrudhanggalangdhuray*, Wirradjuri (First Nations Australian) novelist Anita Heiss (2021) centres uneven power relations between its two central female characters: Wagadhaany, an Aboriginal woman forced into domestic servitude, and Louisa, the white woman in whose home Wagadhaany serves. Louisa is independently wealthy, educated, and socially advantaged by her cultural capital. Her potential to activate agency far exceeds Wagadhaany's. But Louisa stays faithful to an abusive husband, subjugating her needs to his for fear of social judgement. Occasionally, Louisa attempts to resist her husband by fighting back against him, but she doesn't pursue agential possibilities of leaving him to pursue a life beyond their domestic walls. By bringing theories of intersectional privilege together with those of hegemony, it is possible to observe that while Louisa occupies a privileged position in terms of her whiteness, the intersection of this with being female in a patriarchal society means that her overall position is still subordinate to the hegemonic white male group: she may be considered as representative of a complicit group within the overall hierarchy, acting in conscious collusion with the status quo, and participating in the subordination of Wagadhaany along with other servants.

Meanwhile, Wagadhaany deploys creative approaches to her given limitations. As direct resistance to her position of servitude would offer no outcomes beyond punishment, Wagadhaany activates agency through tactics often including the strategies of 'docility' discussed by Mahmood (2006). Wagadhaany develops extensive awareness of the legal rules governing her society and the position she holds within it, figuring out where there is room to move, and making use of every opportunity she finds. Wagadhanny also works collectively with others in subjugated positions – including occasional attempts to help Louisa – and her goals are collectively-oriented rather than purely personal, as she seeks to rejoin her community to support family members and play her cultural role. Over a narrative spaced across years, Wagadhaany slowly works towards escaping and rejoining her family, demonstrating levels of agency that contrast starkly with the oppressive constraints in which she finds herself. This portrayal of agency within Heiss's novel makes the novel itself viewable as a form of counterhegemonic discourse (Orlowski, 2011, p. 44) – an instance of how creative writing may form not only a stake of social struggle, but a site for its enactment.

Re-orienting

Building on chapter one's observations of the need to revive recognition of writing-knowledge connections in contemporary western cultures, this chapter explored how writing's connections with knowledge in turn connect it with power. To begin, I examined how relational power differs from commonplace uses of the word power, and how power is mediated in discourse. Exploration of ideology then helped illustrate how creative writing may provide both a stake and a site in struggles for change. This chapter subsequently explored capital, symbolic violence, intersectional privilege, hegemony, resistance and agency – key terms in the lexicon used throughout remaining chapters of this book. Chapter three extends these inquiries into writing-power connections by considering how representations of characters, settings and beyond-human actors' power can re-present social power relations in ways that may on one hand reinforce existing systems, or on the other, raise possibilities for change.

3 REPRESENTATION AS RE-PRESENTATION

Walking/writing against the code

By the big road lined with gums, the birds sing strong,
so strong they almost drown the traffic's constant hum.
How beautiful, I think, imagining these are songs of joy

but as I cross the road and wander
smaller streets, towards the reserve,
the songs grow fainter, fainter

and in the reserve itself
where I expected the most birds,
long silences stretch

like punctuation
between quiet
distanced
calls

Later, a friend tells me
birds sing for many reasons
among them being to warn of threat.

Back by the roadside, the songs chime on, strong as ever
and still beautiful, except now, that beauty squeezes
and burns my lungs, my chest,
like someone's plucking feathers from my heart

First published in *Tiger Moth Review*, under the title
'Soundtrack to Anstey Hill', 20 March 2024

The major park entrances all bear the same three-panel sign. The first panel provides general information. The second shows a map and recommended trails. The third relays the code of rules including bans on horses, fires, and littering. The code also stipulates etiquette for sharing the space with fellow 'trail users', including 'Say G'day!' The appeals to Australiana clichés in this choice of phrase make me cringe with memories of crass *Crocodile Dundee* (Faiman, 1986) films and London's problematically named Aussie 'Walkabout' pubs.

Most days I hurry past this sign. Today, I pause to spend time with it. Last night I was reading Bronwyn Fredericks's account of her research investigating Aboriginal and Torres Strait Islander women's experiences of community health providers through theoretical lenses of place, space, and belonging. Fredericks explains that place 'is made and takes on meaning through an interaction process involving mutual accommodation between people and the environment' (Memmott & Long, 2002, cited in Fredericks, 2014, p. 291). These meanings are 'politically embedded' (Fredericks, 2014, p. 291). Places are created when humans alter geographical environments and/or carry out of area-specific behaviours that become 'connected to that specific place' (p. 291). The physical location thus takes on a 'metaphysical imaginary' that operates as an ontological and epistemological 'organising principle' (p. 292). In other words, place structures being and knowing. Place is also connected with space, which represents 'a question of relations: perceptions of and actual relations between the individual, the group, institutions and architecture, with forces being perceived as restricting or enabling movement or access' (Mills, 2006, cited in Fredericks, 2014, p. 293). Beyond a mere 'arena in which social life unfolds', space forms 'a medium through which social relations are produced and reproduced' (Gregory & Urry, 1985, cited in Fredericks, 2014, p. 293) including 'power relations' (Fredericks, 2014, p. 293).

By these definitions, the park can be considered both a place and a space. Its landscape is human-altered both historically and contemporarily. Visible to me are the alterations made by mining, farming and other industries of the past, as well as current day markings of set trails and signs such as the one by which I stand. No doubt there is more I can't see, dating across time immemorial. As Crystal McKinnon (2014) notes, Aboriginal texts such as scar trees are everywhere if one knows how to read them. I am illiterate in this regard. Nonetheless, both the visible and invisible (to me) human effects on this park produce it as a place – or indeed, different places for different people – as do associations with specific behaviours including hiking, cycling, bird-watching, dog walking and wildflower-spotting (all recommended on the sign). The sign's declaration that the park 'provides a spectacular backdrop of creeks, ridgetops and view of Adelaide city' where '[f]amilies, walkers, riders, and those looking for a new fitness challenge can design their own adventure using the extensive network of shared-use trails' (Anstey Hill Recreation Park, n.d.) evokes a metaphysical imaginary that belies the realities of this harmed and hurting land. The park is also a space because its rules – explicit and implied – structure relations of those who come here. These include relations with each other, with animals and ecosystems, with history, and with institutions such as the local council and historical societies, among others involved in the park's mapping, marketing, and maintenance.

Both place and space are politically implicated in belonging – and unbelonging. Fredericks relays belonging as 'a sentiment which develops over time through the everyday activities' (2014, p. 293), for instance, 'groups of people having collective experiences . . . reinforced through feedback from ongoing experiences at such places' (Memmott & Long, 2002, cited in Fredericks, 2014, p. 293). Unfortunately, there is always also a potential 'place-based politics which is reactionary, exclusionary and blatantly supportive of dominant regimes' (p. 293). For example, Fredericks relays an interviewee's account of a Queensland-based community health complex that, when opened in 1998, positioned their services for Aboriginal and Torres Strait Islander women 'in the back room', which for the interviewee triggered memories of segregation and being 'expected to stand at the back in shops and wait to served or sit in the back of the cinema' (2014, p. 295). Fredericks additionally notes that the same health service's opening foyer walls were decorated with prints of Australian paintings by non-Indigenous Australian painter Frederick McCubbin (1855–1917) featuring 'white settlers' in vast bushscapes (p. 295). As Fredericks explains, such images 'assert an emphasis on European settler history and the claiming and clearing of Aboriginal land and erasure of Aboriginal sovereignty', acting as markers for 'centring white power within the building' (p. 295).

Fredericks's critique of how 'colonial power is inscribed and conveyed' through everyday places and spaces 'without a word even being said' prompts me to read the familiar park entry sign in new ways. It strikes me that the visual arrangement of information draws my eye towards some details faster than others. Text is structured in blocks under headings, arranged around bright-coloured pictures. The largest heading sits at the top of the general information panel, declaring, 'Welcome to Anstey Hill'. This text block is where the claim about spectacular views, family fun and fitness challenges are made. It is larger than the other blocks of text, which sit lower down. Their headings include 'Peoples of Anstey Hill', 'Shared Use Trails', 'Dog Walking', 'Flora and Fauna', 'Nature Play' and 'Relax and Unwind' (Anstey Hill Recreation Park, n.d.). The 'Peoples of Anstey Hill' heading and text is at the bottommost left of the sign. It is four paragraphs long. The first two paragraphs acknowledge the Kaurna people as the Traditional Owners of the area, noting that it was historically used 'as a winter Wardli (retreat) when food and water were plentiful' and that 'many Kaurna yerta (land) family groups continue to look after the Kaurna pangkara (country)' (Anstey Hill Recreation Park, n.d.). It's curious that they translate 'Wardli' as 'retreat' when it more accurately means 'home' (Copley, personal communication, 14 June 2024). This brings to mind the colonial lie taught to me in school that First Nations Australian peoples were 'nomadic' hunter-gatherers when in fact extensive evidence exists that for many groups '[p]ermanent housing was a feature of the pre-contact Aboriginal economy, and marked the movement towards agricultural reliance' – evidence historically suppressed to support the legal fiction of *terra nullius* (Pascoe, 2014/2018, pp. 2, 97). The sign's third paragraph explains how the name came from George Anstey, who is described as 'a South Australian pastoral and agricultural pioneer'. His involvements in attempted genocide are not mentioned. The fourth paragraph lists sites of interest including an old silver mine, a former bakery, a cottage ruin, and Newman's Nursery.

At least an acknowledgement of the Kaurna people is present, but there's no mention of the Native Title claim in place under Federal Law (Copley, personal communication, 14 June 2024). It also strikes me as odd that it is placed at the bottom rather than the top of the sign. In Australia, verbal acknowledgements of Traditional Owners are given at all public events. Cultural sensitivity guidelines advise that an acknowledgement should always be the first or near-first statement made (Pelizzon & Kennedy, 2019, p. 13). Acknowledgements are given by people not from the Country whose owners they are acknowledging (including people who are Indigenous to other regions, non-Indigenous Australians, and overseas visitors). Only a person Indigenous to the land they are standing on can give a formal 'Welcome to Country' – an official greeting and performative act that grants visitors permission to be on the land and often provides guidelines for how to treat the land with respect (p. 13). While the sign mentions Kaurna people continuing to care for Country, it says nothing of what non-Indigenous Australians and overseas visitors can do to support this caring – or at least, to avoid compromising Traditional Owners' efforts – and nothing of where to gain such knowledge.

Likewise undermining the acknowledgement's impact is that it shares a textbox with celebrations of the colonizers who stole the Kaurna people's land for mining and farming. The picture above the textbox about the 'Peoples of Anstey Hill' shows the Newman's Nursery ruins. Apart from 'Flora and Fauna', which features a cockatoo, this is the only sub-heading on its panel where the associated picture doesn't portray happy humans enjoying the park. The others depict runners, dog walkers, a young girl wondering at flowers, and a toned woman in active wear doing yoga in a large windowsill of the ruin. All the people in the pictures look white. It's the same on the other two panels, which portray middle-aged men on bicycles, a group of older people hiking with sticks, and more women in active wear, one of whom is walking a small white dog with its fur elaborately coiffed.

Re-reading the sign through Fredericks (2014), it occurs to me, I've never before questioned my right to be in and enjoy this space – though it's possible I should. I always feel welcome among the other hikers who invariably wave or smile and say hello. My appearance is not so different from that of the female hikers on the entrance sign pictures. If this were not the case, might my experience here be a different one? Though the entrance sign pitches the park as a space for everyone to share and enjoy, the all-white, middle-class images seemingly invite some to enjoy it more than others. The wordings used on the sign also reflect white western attitudes. For instance, 'trail users' as opposed to 'visitors' or 'guests' subtly re-iterates colonial assumptions of humankind's superiority and entitlement to exploit nature as a resource, as opposed to recognizing humans as part of and interdependent with natural ecosystems. Beyond the explicit bullet-pointed code of set rules and expectations, these details convey another, implicit code of white western ethnocentrism and human exceptionalism – a code most of us who come here might tend not to read in conscious ways, the impact of which is perhaps heightened by this fact and by its pervasive subconscious thrust.

As I move into and through the park, I become aware that the other morning hikers also mostly resemble the people on the signs. Apart from a few people with Indian or Asian features, the majority of us appear white – though I recognize that race and culture aren't always obvious from outward appearances, and acknowledge that discrimination takes many oft-invisible forms including but exceeding systemic, structural and symbolic ones. The general mode of dress is relatively conservative middle-class. The older hikers wear polo shirts and khaki shorts. The younger ones – who often run instead of hiking – tend towards brand label active wear. Apart from children brought here by their parents, most people are in their twenties or older. I don't spot any teenagers, though it's possible they visit at other hours.

Among Fredericks's key points is how the non-inclusive design of health care spaces discourages Aboriginal and Torres Strait Islander women from accessing medical assistance when they need it, maintaining the significantly poorer levels of health and wellbeing among Aboriginal and Torres Strait Islander peoples compared with non-Indigenous Australians (2014, p. 306). I wonder, do the signs at the entrance simply reflect the park demographic, or do they shape it? Or, as Stuart Hall (1989) might have asked, could it be that the signs *re-present* the park community in the sense of re-making what is supposedly being portrayed, and thereby influencing the material world in which the remade portrayal takes presence?

Compass

Chapter two considered how creative writing's connections with knowledge implicate it in power relations both amongst humans and of humans with beyond-human being. On one hand, creative writing may reflect and reinstate ideologies that normalize uneven power relations, helping maintain injustice. On the other, creative writing provides opportunities to question problematic ideologies and promote change. This chapter explores one way in which creative writing may operate to reinforce or destabilize existing systems of power: representation as re-presentation, specifically via portrayals of characters, settings and beyond-human actors.

The next section unpacks the concept of representation as re-presentation – in condensed terms, the idea that textual portrayals of characters, settings, and beyond-human actors affect the contexts wherein they circulate (Hall, 1997). I then consider four ways in which representation often serves to reinforce problematic power relations: normalization, negative misrepresentation, tokenism and erasure. These discussions include consideration of how politically oriented readers and writers can intervene in the problems via attention to aspects of writing including but exceeding round and flat characters, backdrop versus integral settings, and interplays of presence with absence. This chapter seeks to illustrate how representation as re-presentation, problematic as it often is, presents opportunities to call out inequity and push towards change. However, the end of this chapter notes that mainstream creative writing currently remains dominated by representations that re-present the interests of hegemonically privileged groups. In other words, creative writing bears a representative imbalance that serves the maintenance of existing uneven power relations. How and why this imbalance arose, and how to address it become guiding questions for part two.

Representation as re-presentation

As this chapter's opening vignette foregrounded, representation as re-presentation is a concept from Stuart Hall (1997). Hall was Caribbean-born, but raised in Britain, and identified as a member of a diaspora. Though diasporic experiences differ from those of colonized peoples living on their lands under invaders' rule, Hall's work has been embraced in the field of Indigenous Knowledges (Vincent et al., 2014) and is also influential across fields of race, disability, gender, sexuality and intersecting concerns (Ewart, 2010; Dutoya, 2016; Gooden & Hackett, 2020). The word representation bears two commonplace meanings. The first is 'to describe or depict', as with description of characters and settings in creative writing and visual depictions in art. The second 'to symbolize, stand for, to be a specimen of, or to substitute for' (The *Shorter Oxford Dictionary*, n.d., cited in Hall, 1997, p. 16). For example, the cross, to Christians, may simply be 'two wooden planks nailed together', but these 'stand for a wider set of meanings' about Jesus Christ and Christian faith (Hall, 1997, p. 16). Hall posed representation as 'the production of the meaning of the concepts in our minds through language' and 'the link between concepts and language which enables us to *refer to* either the 'real' world of objects, people, or events, or indeed to imaginary worlds' (p. 17). In these ways, representation is key to both how people make sense of things in our own minds, and how we communicate our perspectives with others.

Representation relies on 'concepts' that 'are arranged into different classifying systems' or 'conceptual maps' wherein '[m]eaning depends on the relationship between things in the world' such as 'people, objects and events, real and fictional' (Hall, 1997, p. 18). Representation also relies on 'signs', such as words, sounds and visual images, and even objects such as items of clothing associated with different activities and/or levels of formality (pp. 18, 37). The linking of conceptual maps with representative signs produces representative systems or 'codes' that 'make it possible for us to speak and hear intelligibly' (p. 22). Hall notes that shared representative codes are one key feature of shared culture as a framework within which people who share the same maps and signs can establish understandings. Learning the codes that govern representation is crucial to how children 'become, not simply biological individuals, but cultural subjects' who 'unconsciously internalize the codes' necessary for belonging, self-expression, and understanding other members of the same culture (p. 22). In their investigation of representations the reinstate (or interrupt) the 'cycle of bias that perpetuates disparities among Native Americans and other populations', Arianne Eason, Laura Brady and Stephanie Fryberg make a similar point when they observe that 'being human is a social project' wherein 'people are shaped by the individuals around them and the cultural context' which 'provides ideas, beliefs, and assumptions about what it means to be a person or a member of a group', offering 'a schema for understanding both oneself and others' (2018, p. 71). They use the term 'culture cycle' to indicate the ways 'ideas and representations' become 'embedded in the social fabric' (p. 71).

Hall aligned his theorizing of representation with what he termed 'constructionist' as opposed to 'reflective' or 'intentional' approaches (1997, p. 24). A 'reflective approach' locates meaning 'in the object, person, idea, or event in the real world', assuming 'language functions like a mirror, to *reflect* the true meaning as it already exists in the world' (p. 24). An 'intentional approach' conversely 'holds that it is the speaker, the author, who imposes his or her unique meaning on the world through language' and that '[w]ords mean what the author intends they should mean' (p. 25). Hall notes that there are elements of truth in each of these perspectives, but both have limits. For instance, in the case of the reflective approach, the word rose can be used to refer to real plants in a garden, but only if one knows the code that links the flower with the word (p. 25). Additionally, roses are referred to by different words in different languages, and that two people hearing the same word for rose might imagine roses of different colours or types. Some might envisage Valentine's bouquets, equating the rose symbol with romantic love. Others might start humming the 1980s ballad 'Every Rose Has Its Thorn' (Michaels et al., 1988). Others still might question the ecological implications of the floral industry, such as farming introduced species of flowers on lands that could otherwise sustain native ecosystems.

Regarding the limitations of intentional approaches to representation, Hall observes that '[w]e cannot be the sole or unique source of meanings in language, since that would mean that we could express ourselves in entirely private languages', whereas 'the essence of language is communication', which 'depends on shared linguistic conventions and shared codes' and as such 'can never be a wholly private game' (1997, p. 25). Furthermore, what a speaker intends may differ wildly from how their message is heard and interpreted. Constructionist approaches to representation recognize this by emphasizing that 'there is no absolute or final fixing of meaning . . . Even when the actual words remain stable, their connotations shift or they acquire a different nuance' because 'meaning does not inhere in things, in the world' but 'is constructed, produced' as 'the result of a signifying practice – a practice that *produces* meaning, that *makes things mean*' (Hall, 1997, p. 24). For constructionists, 'meaning is *not* in the object or person or thing, nor is it *in* the word': however 'natural and inevitable' meaning might seem, it is '*constructed by the system of representation*' and 'fixed by the *code*, which sets up the correlation and our language system' (Hall, 1997, p. 21, original italics). This is the point of representation as re-presentation: the hyphen in the latter emphasizes that it is not a straightforward portrayal of what was always there, but a complex process of re-creating and re-assigning presence to things in ways that alter them, whether subtly or dramatically. For instance, if an artist depicts a historical figure smiling happily, the viewer gains an impression of that figure as a generally happy person, even if this was seldom or never the case.

Representation as re-presentation bears pervasive effects. By Hall's account, representations 'play a part in the formation, in the constitution, of the things that they reflect' (1992, p. 14). Eason et al. pose similar points about the 'culture cycle', which encompasses '*ideas, institutions, interactions,* and *individuals*', operates to 'shape and reinforce social and cultural outcomes' via 'movies, books, and news reports' that 'reflect and reify cultural ideas' (2018, pp. 71–2, original italics). Representation as re-presentation points to the ways in which the 'world outside, "out there"' is, 'in part, constituted by how it is represented' (Hall, 1997, p. 14). Importantly, this approach does not deny the existence of 'the *material* world, where things and people exist' (p. 25, original italics). Indeed, part of Hall's point was the importance of *not* conflating material realities with 'the *symbolic* practices and processes through which representation, meaning and language operate' – that is, with the 'conceptual systems' of culture, language and other devices that 'social actors' use 'to construct meaning, to make the world meaningful and to communicate about that world meaningfully to others' (p. 25, original italics). It is *because* the two are so easily confused that those symbolic processes of representation, while distinct from and often misrepresentative of the material world, bear 'real effects' in and on it (p. 49). The point is to recognize and become critical about these processes. This chapter's remaining sections consider normalization, negative misrepresentation, tokenism and erasure as four ways in which textual representations may affect power relations both amongst humans and of humans with beyond-human being.

Normalization

One way in which textual representations and the culture cycle may bear effects on the real world is via the portrayal of 'norms that shape everyday *interactions*' as well as 'thoughts, feelings, and behaviours' (Eason et al., 2018, pp. 71–2). Portrayals of power relations in creative writing are a significant part of this. For instance, the novel *Gone with the Wind* (Mitchell, 1936), written in 1930s America when racial segregation laws were still in place, normalizes uneven power relations between the white heroine, Scarlett, and her African American maid, Ruth – who is mostly referred to by the racially-offensive term 'Mammy' – by presenting Ruth's subjugation and Scarlett's assumption of privilege as though they were natural, normal states of affairs (Yaeger, 1999). The book also encourages readers to identify with white characters who abuse servant labour and/or fear the thought that their children 'might have to go to school with "pickaninnies" [sic]', condoning racial violence, exploitation, and discrimination (p. 21).

That *Gone with the Wind* (Mitchell, 1936) reflects and reinstates (re-presents) racism is easy to recognize and critique from contemporary contexts wherein it is broadly recognized that formalized slavery and segregation were unjust (although they often persist informally via exploitative work conditions and cultural exclusion). But in the era of *Gone with the Wind*'s publication, such issues were generally ignored by readers swept up by its charismatic heroine and 'plot that moves swiftly from crisis to crisis' towards 'classic denouement', producing a normalizing effect (Yaeger, 1999, p. 21). For politically-oriented readers and writers, this exemplifies why attention to how power relations are portrayed matter. Such attention should entail mindfulness to the normalized power relations of our own geo-temporal contexts – including relations of race and Indigeneity alongside gender, sexuality, disability, neurodiversity and more. Human relations with beyond-human being – for instance, through the ways characters treat animals and the environment – likewise bear importance. Recalling chapter two's discussions, such attention should involve consideration of how these representations involve distribution of various forms of capital and privilege. Analysis should also go beyond simple above versus below the line approaches by considering hegemonic systems as well as instances where characters perhaps enact resistance and/or activate agency.

That a text portrays unbalanced power relations does not in itself necessarily mean the text condones them: in many cases, the relations may be portrayed critically to call out problems and demonstrate the need for change. Analysis therefore also needs to involve consideration of whether the portrayals of power relations justify and normalize these arrangements or critique them. For readers, the theories of intersectional privilege, capital, hegemony, resistance and agency discussed in chapter two can guide politically oriented textual interpretation. For writers, these same considerations are ones to remain aware of at all stages of writing, especially self-editing. Following this chapter is praxis module one, the first of three praxis modules in this book, each of which provides hands-on experiments in creative writing and literary analusis based on concepts from preceding chapters. In praxis module one, experiments two and three offer frameworks for readers and writers to critique intersectional privilege, capital, hegemony, resistance and agency via textual interpretation and self-editing.

Negative misrepresentation

Beyond normalizing uneven power relations, another way in which representations may reinforce injustice is via misrepresentations that proliferate negative images of certain groups, seeming to justify discrimination and other modes of abuse. Criminalization is a particularly obvious example of negative misrepresentation in action. As Hall noted, 'what we think we "know"' about crime 'has a bearing on how we regulate, control and punish criminals' (1997, p. 49). Eason et al. illustrate the ramifications this bears through their observation of how 'historic and contemporary' representations of Native American people as 'uncivilized' and 'incapable of behaving according to mainstream American norms' promote '[b]iased institutional understandings of Native people' that 'impact law enforcement officers' interactions with Native people, and ultimately, Native people's outcomes within the legal system' (2018, p. 72). Consequently, 'interactions with law enforcement are more likely to end in the use of deadly force for Native Americans than for any other racial group relative to population size' and 'even when interactions with police do not lead to violence, police often use [linguistic violence via] slurs or derogatory language' (p. 72). In courtrooms, 'Native youth are 30 percent more likely than White youth to be referred to juvenile court rather than having their charges dropped' (p. 72). As a result of these negative interactions, Native American people are often 'reluctant to turn to the legal system when they need help', which further exacerbates the 'racial disparities that undermine Native people's well-being and livelihood' (p. 72).

In the Australian context, Chris Cunneen observes how media reinforcement of 'white stereotypes' depicting 'Aboriginal people as dirty, drunk, unintelligent, lazy and ungrateful' encourage over-policing and police violence (2020, p. 83). Stereotypical representations contribute to increased rates of 'incarceration for petty offences' and alarmingly high deaths in custody rates – a problem widely observed in Canada as well as Australia (Eagan, 2020, p. 33). Police violence also affects non-Indigenous people of colour in these and other global contexts. For instance, 'portrayal of African-descended people in the Canadian media often focuses on crime and fails to highlight positive images' (Gooden & Hackett, 2020, p. 61), which contributes to 'high underemployment and unemployment . . . over policing, and higher rates of incarceration, as well as fewer opportunities for advancement in education' (p. 54). Chapters in the book *Racism, Violence and Harm: Ideology, Media and Resistance* (Bhatia et al., 2024) call out similar processes via which media representations reinforce racialized legal and systemic injustices against First Nations peoples, people of colour, immigrants, and other marginalized groups across contexts including Portugal, New Zealand, the Middle East, the USA and Europe.

These examples all illustrate how representation sustains what Hall called 'cultural racism' – 'racism as a structure of knowledge and representation' (1992, pp. 14–16). Cultural racism involves a set of processes via which '[t]he reality of race in any society' is 'media-mediated' through 'popular narratives which constantly, in the imagination of a society, construct the place, the identities, the experience, the histories of the different peoples who live within it' (p. 15). Characterized by 'racial stereotyping', 'negative imagery' and 'repetition … of a very simplified and truncated way of representing black history, life, and culture' (p. 14), such narratives reinforce 'racism as a structure of knowledge and representation' (p. 16).

In addition to racism, negative misrepresentations also commonly reflect and reinstate modes of discrimination based on gender, sexuality, disability, neurotype, body type and intersecting factors. Historically, women in literature have predominantly been portrayed by male authors as either submissive 'angels' or dangerous 'monsters', the real world effects of which are notable in the ways 'many real women have for so long expressed loathing of (or at least anxiety about) their own, inexorably female bodies', particularly 'concern with odours and aging, with hair which is invariably too curly or too lank, with bodies too thin or too thick' as examples of 'efforts women have expended not just trying to be angels but trying *not* to become female monsters' (Gilbert & Gubar, 2020, p. 34). This 'misogynistic and homophobic male literary tradition in which women who act outside of the patriarchal order embody a threat which must be repressed and ignored at all costs' bears particularly on same sex attracted women, who have historically been either portrayed as monstrous figures or omitted altogether (Carlin, 2012, p. 348).

Same sex attracted men have also commonly been portrayed as either weak, pitiable figures or dangerous predators via 'representations of effeminacy, female-identification, and pathology' (Carlin, 2012, p. 346). By associating male femininity with weakness and/or pathology, such representations re-present not only homophobia, but also transphobia. Representations of disabled people meanwhile often re-present 'medical model notions of disability' that perpetuate 'the misunderstanding that disabled people are seeking to be "cured" and are unhappy with their impaired bodies' (Houston, 2020, p. 50) while neurodivergent people confront social misunderstandings generated by their frequent representation as either 'idiots' and/or 'savants' – for instance, in films like *What's Eating Gilbert Grape?* (Hallström, 1994) and *Rain Man* (Levinson, 1989), and the television series *The Big Bang Theory* (Lore & Prady, 2007–18) (see discussion in Murray, 2008,

p. 65). Equally problematic are fatphobic representations, particularly in young adult novels that 'routinely describe characters' bodies' in ways that figure 'the thin ones as desirable and the fat ones as disgusting or flawed' (Nolfi, 2011, p. 55). As Kathryn L. Nolfi notes, this compounds feelings of low self-esteem for young people who turn to books because they are socially outcast only to find 'not support and validation … but instead exhortations to diet and obsess about their appearance' (p. 55)

In addition to social discrimination amongst humans, negative misrepresentations denigrate beyond-human being via portrayals of setting and beyond-human actors that evoke 'ecophobia' (Normandin, 2018, p. 51). Ecophobia is 'a pathological aversion towards nature, an aggravated form of anthropocentrism expressed variously as fear of, hatred of, or hostility toward nature at least in part motivated by a sense of nature's imagined unpredictably' (Estok in Normandin, 2018, p. 52). It 'induces an ideology according to which "everything outside of the human … exists as an object to a desperately insecure humanity"' (Normandin, 2018, p. 52). Ecophobia reflects and reinstates a version of human exceptionalism that not only emphasizes a human / beyond-human split, but purports to justify violence against beyond-human being via claims it is dangerous and requires taming.

As Jack Halberstam observes, ecophobic portrayals of 'wildness' in literature commonly reinforce divisions between 'the domestic world' of human civilization and 'the wild world of lost and lonely creatures', which is associated with 'exclusion' and 'exile' because it presents 'a challenge to an assumed order of things … simultaneously a chaotic force of nature, the outside of categorization, unrestrained forms of embodiment, the refusal to submit to social regulation, loss of control, the unpredictable' (2020, p. 3). This 'suggests a romantic wild, a space of potential, an undoing that beckons and seduces', but 'has also served to name the orders of being that colonial authority comes to tame: the others to a disastrous discourse of civilization, the racialized orientation to order, the reifying operations of racial discourse (wild "things")' (pp. 3–4). As examples of texts that portray wildness as dangerous and/or needing taming, Halberstam cites works by T. S. Eliot, W. B. Yeats and Joseph Conrad, among others (Halberstam, 2020, pp. 23–4). Additional examples include Walt Whitman's 'Pioneers! O pioneers!', which celebrates colonization of the American west through lines like 'We primeval forests felling / We the rivers stemming, vexing we and piercing deep the mines within / We the surface broad surveying, we the virgin soil upheaving' (1891/2024), and Dorothea Mackellar's 'My Country', wherein colonial Australia is presented as 'a sunburnt country, / A land of sweeping plains, / Of ragged mountain ranges, / Of droughts and flooding rains' where 'beauty' juxtaposes with 'terror' reflected in the 'pitiless blue sky' of 'A wilful, lavish land' (1908/2024).

Like the normalization of uneven power relations, negative misrepresentations form a site requiring careful attention and critique from politically readers and writers – in the case of readers, via critique of works by other writers, and in that of writers, as something to avoid and/or edit out through our revision processes. In both instances, this attention should entail consideration of broad stroke factors, which for characters includes defining qualities and actions, and for settings includes general implications about whether a setting is desirable or undesirable, beautiful or ugly, safe or dangerous, and so on. Critical attention to negative misrepresentations should also entail of finer details such as the language of description. Jeanine Leane's (2010) use of Critical Discourse Analysis (CDA) (Fairclough, 1995/2013) to critique representations of Aboriginality by non-Aboriginal authors illustrates how linguistic choices can subtly steer readers' responses. CDA makes implicit cultural ideologies and assumptions explicit by showing how 'the language spoken by a particular cultural group is permeated by common-sense assumptions that are known and accepted by the collective' and '[n]o choice of words that go together to construct representation of the "other" is neutral . . . no choice of words used to construct any text is neutral' (Leane, 2010, p. 34).

To illustrate, Leane cites a scene from the 1976 novel *A Fringe of Leaves* by Patrick White wherein a white woman attends the burial ceremony of an Aboriginal child:

> They allowed her to accompany the funeral procession, *traipsing* into the forest until they found a hollow log in which to *shove* the body. At once their grief *evaporated*, except in the mother's case, who was prepared to keep up her snivels, but only a while for they were returning to the fish feast.
>
> **WHITE**, 1976, cited in **LEANE**, 2010, p. 35, italics added

The problems with this scene are multiform. As Leane notes, choices of verbs including 'aimless "traipsing"', 'the irreverent "shove"' and 'the apparently superficial grief that "evaporates" when food takes over', the combination of which 'positions Aboriginality on a lower rung of the human ladder' (2010, p. 35). Harriet Gaffney (2017) similarly critiques verb choices in an 1836 report by Joseph Tice Gellibrand, the former Attorney General of Van Diemen's Land (Australia), of an Aboriginal woman who had been violently raped. In one part of the report, Gellibrand wrote, ' . . . this woman was proceeding towards the Settlement to see her mother and *fell in* with one of the Shepherds' (Gellibrand, 1836, cited in Gaffney, 2017, p. 4, italics added). As Gaffney notes, 'Gellibrand's choice of the phrase "fell in" immediately renders the woman complicit – and even today maintains the idea of acquiescence and poor judgment' (2017, p. 4)

Leane connects these subtle implications of word choices with the concept of register: 'a subconscious trigger that occurs in the minds of readers triggered by association and familiarity' (2010, p. 35). Leane explains, register 'relates to the ideational function of language . . . the ideology that has given rise to the choice of words on a page and the types of responses they will elicit from a particular cultural group' (p. 35). Register plays a key role in discourse as 'a way in which people make sense of the world around them collectively, how they make sense of themselves in the world *and* how they make sense of "others"' (p. 35). As Leane observes, 'anthropological', 'romantic' and 'racist' discourses on Aboriginality 'all seek to represent Aboriginality in terms of "otherness" and they all claim some authority to represent based on Aboriginal deficiency' (p. 35). The same processes can also operate via small language choices used to negatively misrepresent (and re-present) other social groups including women, LGBTQIA+ people, people with disabilities, neurodivergent people, and fat people, among other groups commonly subject to discrimination.

Alongside broad stroke aspects in the portrayal of characters, settings and beyond-human actors, fine details of language therefore form an important site of attention for politically oriented readers and writers, with verb choices and register being among the linguistic features worthy of explicit care (though certainly not the only ones).

Tokenism

The previous section focused on misrepresentations of explicitly negative varieties. These are relatively easy for readers and writers to identify and address in our own writings and those of others. Tokenistic misrepresentation is trickier, for it often manifests in works by writers who bear no ill intentions – or indeed imagine they are positively contributing to representative inclusivity. Tokenism refers to scenarios wherein writers include people from marginalized groups as minor characters, seemingly to promote inclusivity, but without effort to flesh these characters out as complex and interesting people who genuinely matter (Chandler & Munday, 2020, p. 742). Tokenistic misrepresentations often present as 'close approximations' that 'reflect only vague contours of the identities and lived experiences', whether these be of major or minor characters (Enriquez, 2021, p. 104). Misrepresentations via close approximation are a frequent problem in texts produced by writers who don't bear lived experiences of the perspectives they seek to portray, and don't address this via consultation with the communities they problematically seek to speak for (p. 104).

Where characters are concerned, a way in which readers and writers can identify tokenistic misrepresentations is via attention to the differing levels of complexity with which various figures are presented, and how these seem to relate to intersecting axes of social power relations in the context where the text was written. E. M. Forster's (1927) notion of round versus flat characters is a useful tool for framing complexity. Forster defined round characters as those who bear internal complexities and are 'capable of surprising in a convincing way' (p. 118).

Flat characters, on the other hand, are 'constructed around a single idea or quality' (pp. 103–4) and are typically 'not changed by circumstances' (p. 106). Forster remarked that 'If it never surprises, it is flat. If it does not convince, it is a flat pretending to be round' (p. 118).

By Forster's (1927) account, flat characters often frustrate readers, as their over-simplicities can seem an insult to the complexities of real life. Nonetheless, flat characters are sometimes useful in fiction because they are easily recognized and remembered (p. 105). Forster posed that 'a novel that is at all complex requires flat characters as well as round' because flat characters help to set the scene and move the story along without distracting the reader from the main characters or overwhelming them with more information than required (p. 108). Nonetheless, he saw them as ultimately 'not in themselves as big achievements', noting that '[i]t is only round people who are fit to perform tragically for any length of time and can move us to any feelings except humor and appropriateness' (pp. 111–12).

Flat characters are in themselves not necessarily a problem. However, if most or all the round characters represent social groups bearing privilege across a certain axis or axes of social identity while most or all the flat characters represent social groups subject to subjugation across those same axes, then the implications regarding the importance of these groups and individuals in society become problematic. For instance, Nolfi critiques the ways in which young adult fiction authors often include fat characters 'only to further the agency of the main (read thin) characters, to provide instruction about bullying, or as a vehicle for character development through the magic of weight loss' (2011, p. 55). While '[t]he fat girl never gets to be the main character' and 'never gets to talk, really talk, about her life and her feelings and her dreams', often becoming 'the sidekick, sexless and hungry or desperately oversexed', '[t]he fat boy is sloppy, grotesque and lonely', or else, 'the funny man', but in either case, acutely 'pathologized' (p. 55). Similar observations can be made about flat and round characters across most intersecting axes of identity.

Beyond characters and human power relations, I pose that the idea of flat and round characters bears parallels with representations of settings and beyond-human actors in terms of what Jerry Watson calls backdrop and integral settings. As Watson relays, a backdrop setting is one that 'has little influence on the characters, plot, or theme' and is frequently 'universal regarding its place and time' – scantness of detail makes it possible to imagine the same story occurring unchanged across multiple geo-temporal and cultural contexts (1991, p. 638). An integral setting, on the other hand, is richly described and exerts 'a great deal of influence on the values, speech, and actions of characters, the movement of plot, and the presentation of theme and mood': characters move 'through' integral settings rather than 'over' them, and the setting may also 'serve as a symbol' for key ideas (p. 638).

If settings and beyond-human actors seem to function as mere backdrop and window dressing for the human characters and their actions, then the text can be seen to re-present ideologies of human exceptionalism. On the other hand, if the settings and beyond-human actors themselves play integral roles in the story – or indeed, seem characters in their own right – then the text can be seen to unsettle human exceptionalism and promote more equitable relations between humans and beyond-human being. An example of a beyond-human actor that bears an agential role is the river in Tony Birch's short story 'The Ghost River' (2013). The story's first-person protagonist is an Aboriginal young man who likes going to hear stories from older men who camp beside a river near the town where he lives. Early in the story, one of the older men, named Moses, explains that the river is a 'ghost river', which means:

> You believe in her, she's there to take care of you. If you're no believer that girl will take you down and teach you a rock-hard lesson. Don't expect her be spitting you back neither. You fuck up on her, you never be coming back.
>
> BIRCH, 2013, para. 23

Towards the end of the story, the protagonist jumps into the river – something he has done many times before, but this time, for inexplicable reasons, he finds himself close to drowning:

> As I fell through the air I'd suddenly be gripped by the craziness that I would never find the river and would fall through the sky forever.
>
> But I did hit the water. But not like I always had. Soon as I went in and plunged beneath the surface a shock of cold clawed at my lungs. I knew there was something wrong. I couldn't breathe, in or out. I was sinking into darkness and swallowing poison water. I was afraid and knew I didn't want to be with the river boys and I didn't want to be an outlaw. But I couldn't help myself. My body was stiff with cold. And then I heard him, Moses, clicking his tongue, stamping his foot and calling to the Ghost River, not to take me but set me free.
>
> BIRCH, 2013, paras 67–8

The protagonist lives, but knows it is time for him to leave the river town and focus on developing learning so he can return and contribute more strongly to his community. This is an example of a non-human actor that features in the story as both a part of the setting and a character that influences the other characters, outcomes and meanings of the text. Re-presenting the river in this way resists dominant western human exceptionalist conceptions of human-nature power relations based in ideologies of nature as a passive backdrop for human action, or a wild force to be tamed and harnessed, but in either case, designed to be subservient (Rose, 2017, p. 55). Instead, Birch's river is powerful beyond human understanding – dangerous if treated poorly, but ultimately caring, supportive of life, and deserving of respect.

For politically-oriented readers and writers seeking to critique and/or avoid tokenism, round versus flat characters and backdrop versus integral settings provide helpful ways to identify and redress issues. Praxis module one experiments two and three include activities to support such critique.

Erasure

Previous sections on normalization, negative misrepresentation and tokenism have shown the significant material effects representation can bear through what it actively portrays. Equally significant are the effects of what it omits. As Hall noted, there persists a 'complex inter-play between *presence* (what you see, the visible) and *absence* (what you can't see, what has displaced it within the frame) (1997, p. 59, original italics). Representation works 'as much through what is not shown, as through what is' (p. 59). This is consistent with Wachsmuth and Angelo's (2018) observation that ideological representations of social reality and its complexities tend to emphasize 'some aspects of this complexity more than others', which sustains 'unequal power relations' by 'reproducing those relations' (p. 1042). In the case of racism, representation maintains injustices by expressing itself:

> through displacement, through denial, through the capacity to say two contradictory things at the same time, the surface imagery speaking of an unspeakable content, the repressed content of a culture.
>
> **HALL**, 1992, p. 15

This makes it essential to consider 'the people who appear to have no content at all—who are just pure form, just pure, invisible form' (Hall, 1992, p. 15).

African American scholar and educator Rudine Sims Bishop's (1990) case for 'mirrors', 'windows' and 'sliding glass doors' in children's literature raises a similar point about the problems of representative absences, as does the significant body of literature Bishop's work has since inspired (see discussion in McNair & Edwards, 2021). Mirrors in literature include characters, cultures and situations similar to the reader's own life. Windows are characters, cultures and situations that differ from the reader's. In some cases, the windows can become sliding glass doors that promote feelings of connection and empathy with people who might otherwise seem unfamiliar (Bishop, 1990, cited in McNair & Edwards, 2021, p. 207). A key problem is that literature is dominated by white western representations, meaning that white western readers have greatest access to mirrors that affirm self-identity, and fewer prompts towards empathy with people beyond the white western subject position. Conversely, people of colour and people from non-western cultures constantly encounter books wherein they must connect and empathize with white western protagonists but find far fewer representations to affirm their own cultural identities and senses of self.

For instance, Grace Enriquez relays her school education experience of being 'one of a handful of Asian students attending my school' where the only texts with Asian protagonists on the curriculum were 'fables and legends from Ancient China' (2021, p. 104). In high school, Enriquez discovered *The Babysitters Club* series (Martin, 1986–2000), which she 'devoured . . . relishing any mention of Claudia Kishi, a second-generation Japanese-American girl who behaved nothing like I did, dressed nothing like I did, and had different interests than I did' because she felt 'desperate to find any mirror to help me make sense of my life experiences (Enriquez, 2021, p. 104). This bears similarities to the experiences of the character August in *The Yield* by Wirradjuri (First Nations Australian) novelist Tara June Winch (2019). As a young First Nations girl growing up in rural Australia, August relishes reading books from a mobile library that visits her town. However, 'in every mobile-library book, she could never find herself or her sister', which contributes to her feelings of loneliness and compounds experiences of bullying from white classmates (p. 62).

Examples of representational erasure's damaging effects on human wellbeing are evident through intergenerational patterns in Black American women's experiences of 'medical erasure' that compromises health and healing (Winfield et al., 2024, p. 1). In the USA, there is 'lack of culturally competent healthcare providers' for Black American women, as well as serious issues of 'medical racism' because of which Black American women endure 'prolonged pain, delayed care, and sometimes, untimely deaths' (p. 1). These injustices are among 'the very real impacts of culture, identity, and power on Black women's health' (p. 1) wrought by the 'spiral of silence', which describes

> how public opinion, society's idea of right and wrong, and individual's willingness to voice their own opinions have affected the way that Black women have historically not expressed their wants, desires, hurts, and traumas for fear of being alone.
>
> **WINFIELD** et al., 2024, p. 2

The spiral of silence is one part of how Black people in America generally are 'often silenced and made invisible' by the 'historical, dominant, hegemonic, patriarchal systems that have controlled healthcare in the U.S. since its inception' (Winfield et al., 2024, p. 2).

The life-or-death effects of medical erasure on Black American women's health bear similarities with those Fredericks (2014) raises regarding Indigenous women's experiences of community health providers in Australia. As this chapter's opening vignette relayed, among the factors that discouraged Indigenous women in Fredericks's study from accessing medical services when they needed them was the lack of Indigenous representation in the art displayed on foyer walls in community health organizations. I earlier mentioned the McCubbin paintings, which feature colonial-era 'white settlers' in vast bushscapes (Fredericks, 2014, p. 295). I now note that the implied emptiness of the Australian bush in these settings – the non-representation of the people who were living on the land at the time of the British invasion and had been since time immemorial – can be viewed as an evocation of '*terra nullius*' ('"land belonging to no one"') (Vincent et al., 2014, p. 19), a legal myth initiated by Captain James Cook,

> who stated that the Indigenous people of Australia had no form of land tenure because they were uncivilized, which meant the land belonged to no one and was available for possession.
>
> **MORETON-ROBINSON**, 2004, p. 76

The conjuring and use of *terra nullius* in Australia bears parallels with that of *terra incognita* in America (Hall, 1989, p. 74). Similar devices of representational erasure in law and ideology have also been mobilized in other contexts including the Andaman Islands (Sen, 2017), India (Kapila, 2022) and Ethiopia (Makki, 2014). In the Australian context, strategic evocation of *terra nullius* as a 'legal falsehood' was key to how invaders 'legitimated the British Crown's assertion of sovereignty in 1788' (Vincent et al., 2014, p. 19). Its official force persisted until 1992, when it was overturned by the *Mabo* decision, which recognized the land claim of the Meriam people of the Murray Islands, becoming the first formal recognition of Traditional Ownership in Australia (p. 19). Nonetheless, the ongoing ideological and material impacts of *terra nullius* remain persistent, as 'the nation's legitimacy and territorial unity' form keystones of Australian identity, which is 'premised on the displacement of Indigenous societies and their knowledges, language, economies, geographies and sovereignty within the national culture' (p. 19).

Evocations of *terra nullius* are evident in poems by non-Indigenous Australian writers such as Banjo Paterson, who celebrated 'those explorers of the bush – the brave old pioneers' who 'rode the trackless bush in heat and storm and drought' and 'forced their way ahead / By tangled scrub and forests grim towards the unknown west' in 'rough unsettled years' becoming 'The founders of our nation's life, the brave old pioneers' (1917/2018). In a poem about the Australian Eureka mining stockade of 1854, Henry Lawson made a similar move in depicting 'the men ... who saw our nation born' as including English, Irish, Scottish, and American immigrants, whom Lawson claimed were together representative of 'all the nations in the New World and the Old / All side by side, like brethren here ... diving after gold' (1889/2015). The poem makes no mention of First Nations peoples or their potential objections to mining – nor to other races and cultures present at mining sites and surrounding areas at the time, including Chinese Australians and Arab Australians.

Beyond the Australian context, Nilanjara Chatterjee and Anindita Chatterjee critique literature's role in framing the Arab world for European people. Although *terra nullius* was 'not legally applied on the land and its people, it was ideologically perpetuated via 'nineteenth- and twentieth-century European texts . . . injected with the idea' (2024, p. 1). As one example, they cite representations of the Arab world in the Belgian *Tintin* comics (Hergé, 1946–93), the hero of which is a young white explorer, and the narratives of which typically other and exoticize the cultures with which Tintin interacts in ways that normalized colonial mentalities of white western ethnocentrism (Chatterjee & Chatterjee, 2024, p. 1). *Tintin* representations of the Congo have been similarly critiqued as 'ostensibly and naively permeated with primitivistic and colonialist stereotypes' (Met, 1996, p. 131).

Beyond race and Indigeneity, representational imbalances of visibility/invisibility and their material effects are also observable with sexuality and disability, among other axes of intersecting hegemonies. For instance, Virginie Dutoya observes how the 'invisiblization' of LGBTQIA+ people in mainstream Indian literature contributes to social exclusion (2016, p. 254). Regarding disability, Chris Ewart raises the problems of how 'hegemonic, normative ideology—shaped by the collective efforts of European and North American eugenics programs under the guise of the modern era' erases most 'histories of disability' except for 'those of experimentation and erasure' (2010, p. 150).

Erasure of beyond-human being is equally problematic. For instance, lack of representation or minimal representation of animals in creative writing helps normalize the ways in which 'animals have been erased in many people's lives . . . encountered only as meat, pets, [or] pests' in ways that belie 'the relation of humans to other animals' as 'a matter of pressing environmental, social, economic and philosophical concern' (Cook, 2015, p. 587). I venture that the same applies for other modes of beyond-human being including but exceeding trees, landforms, waterways, fungi, bacteria and the complex ecosystems in and through which they interrelate. If these things do not feature in texts, or if they feature only as backdrop without attention to how humans are also implicated in and part of those same ecosystems, then texts can be seen to subtly reinforce human exceptionalist assumptions that humans are distinct from the natural world and exempt from responsibilities to beyond-human kin – assumptions that in turn promote normalization of human disregard for and exploitation of beyond-human being.

Redressing erasure of beyond-human being is a difficult objective, for we cannot consult with animals or other forms of beyond-human being, which makes misrepresentation virtually unavoidable. My poem at the start of this chapter is an example of how easy it is to fall into traps of misrepresenting beyond-human being, even when we write from the best of intentions. At the start of the poem, my speaker assumes the birds' songs to be songs of joy – imposing anthropocentric understandings of singing, without contemplating the possibility birds might think differently. This is also a kind of erasure – one that the poem calls out via the later realization that the birds might be singing to warn each other of the dangers posed by myself and other humans. Yet the speaker's self-critique still depends on information from another human, and the poem remains flawed in that it cannot offer more than comparisons between different human interpretations of animal behaviour.

Ecopoets find a powerful solution for this problem via the use of visual layouts featuring typeless spaces to signify things beyond human communication and/or comprehension (Walker, 2022, p. 191). Space becomes a way of 'holding absence present' (pp. 192–4). I have deployed this technique in the poem of this chapter's opening vignette via the use of diminishing line lengths across the first four stanzas, and the larger gap between the fourth and fifth stanzas. These devices are intended to call attention to the limits of human comprehension, and thus, pay respect to wisdoms beyond those limits. In prose, similar gestures towards limits are possible by posing unanswered questions and/or foregrounding the unknowable aspects of beyond-human being – with respect and wonder for these unknowns rather than ecophobic demonization. Birch's *The Ghost River* (2013) illustrates how this can work via the respectful awe the human characters pay the river, which has existed since '[b]ack in the old time, before the humans', and will by suggestion remain long after they are gone (Birch, 2013, para. 17).

Like normalization, misrepresentation and tokenism, erasure forms an important site of attention for politically oriented readers and writers. For readers, this attention involves noting who is present and who is not, and considering what these presences and absences have to do with power relation in the textual production context. For writers, it is trickier. As I have noted in relation to portrayals of beyond-human being, attempting to portray experiences and perspectives that are not ours often entails risks of imposing our assumptions and falling into traps of misrepresentation. With representations of human characters, similar points apply via problems of ethnocentrism and/or speaking for people who can better articulate their perspectives first-hand. With representation of beyond-human being, I have posed that the most viable option might be to make limitations visible by 'holding absence present' (Walker, 2022, p. 192), posing questions, and expressing respectful awe for the unknown. These approaches may sometimes also be appropriate for human representations. Or writers can also seek advice from people with lived expertise via accessing professional cultural consultation services. It is important that consultants be paid for their time and expertise. Otherwise, their invisible labour becomes another mode of exploitation. Another means for avoiding erasure and/or problematic misrepresentations is co-authoring, a strong example of which is *False tales of colonial thieves* by Yamaji (First Nations Australian) poet Charmaine Papertalk Green and non-Indigenous 'Australian' poet John Kinsella (Green & Kinsella, 2018).

Re-orienting

This chapter explored representation as re-presentation of characters, settings and beyond-human actors as one example of how creative writing is involved with power. I began with an overview of representation theory, then explored how representation manifests problematic effects via normalization, misrepresentation, tokenism, and erasure. Each of these requires careful attention from politically oriented readers and writers. Although I have devoted more discussion to negative effects that we should seek to critique and/or avoid re-perpetuating, my point in every case has been to signal ways in which creative writing can become both a 'site' and a 'stake' in struggles towards positive change (Althusser, 1970/2006). Therefore, I have also gestured towards ways in which politically-oriented readers and writers can use representation to promote increased social equity amongst humans, and human kinship with beyond-human being. Praxis module one extends this point by providing experiments to structure textual analysis (for readers) and self-editing (for writers).

Ultimately, the take home should be that representation provides rich opportunities for those of us engaged in political writing and/or reading. However, the sober reality remains that mainstream writing and publishing historically have long been dominated by privileged social groups who (knowingly or otherwise) re-present themselves and o/Other in ways that help maintain the status quo. Efforts are being made to change this situation, with some degrees of success (WNDB, 2024), but overall, representative imbalance persists, indicating that such efforts must remain ongoing (Thomson, 2023). To inform this objective, part two focuses on how representative imbalances historically have been – and remain – mediated by the western literary canon, the publishing industry, cultural notions of literary merit, and the various social institutions with and in which these things are implicated.

PRAXIS MODULE ONE: RETHINKING REPRESENTATIONS

Overview

The experiments in this module can be used in formal group learning or independent practice. They offer ways to consolidate key ideas from part one via activities of textual analysis and/or creative writing. Those ideas include the following, with critical concepts in **bold**:

1   The role creative writing plays in shaping collective knowledges steeped in relations with places and communities – in other words, **the writing-knowledge connection**, recognition of which has been largely lost in western cultures, and needs reviving.

2   The ways these writing-knowledge connections in turn manifest **writing-power connections** – specifically, through writing as a part of **discourse** implicated in the maintenance or renegotiation of **power relations** between individual humans and social groups, as well as those between humans and beyond-human being.

3   Concepts of **ideology**, **capital**, **intersectionality**, **privilege**, **hegemony**, **resistance**, and **agency**.

4   **Representation as re-presentation**: on one hand, how dominant stories and texts tend to reflect and reinstate the interests of dominant social groups while suppressing those of o/Other groups as subjugated knowledges, but on the other hand, the scope for intervening in this scenario to promote change.

5   How techniques for portraying **character**, **setting** and **beyond-human actors** may contribute to re-presentation of the status quo – or equally, to

its subversion via calling out injustices and signalling scope for change. Questions about **flat versus round characters**, and **background versus integral settings** bear relevance here.

Experiment one relates primarily to points one and two, while experiments two and three focus on points three, four and five – experiment two with focus on portrayals of human characters, and experiment three with focus on settings and beyond-human actors. However, all five points are relevant to all three experiments, and vice versa.

Experiment one: decoding the signs

Visit a park or other site bearing historic signage (e.g. of buildings and/or landmarks deemed significant). If physically visiting a location is not possible for you, work from a historic text or tourist brochure, but choose somewhere you have been to, ideally somewhere you know well. Analyse the sign or other text in relation to the following questions:

- Which/whose histories are being told?
- Which/whose histories are being erased?
- What sorts of power relations does this reflect?
- What is your personal relationship to these told and untold histories, and to this place?
- How do the told and untold histories relate to your experience of the place? In considering your experience, draw on as many senses as possible: sights, sounds, smells, tastes, tactile sensations and bodily responses may call attention to things you otherwise might not notice.

Craft a personal essay based on your answers to the above questions. You can use the vignettes from chapters one and three as text models.

Experiment two: power relations between characters

Choose a short story or other creative writing text. Or as a variation, use one of your own writing drafts, in which case this activity can form part of your redrafting processes. You can also swap with a fellow writer to offer one another feedback.

Select two or more characters from your chosen text. Produce a privilege map for each character using table 1. The first row has been filled out as an example.

Now compare the characters you have mapped. Consider the following questions:

- Do the power relations between the characters seem even or uneven? Consider not only how the characters relate to each other in the text, but how they are portrayed. Take note of misrepresentation, tokenism, and round versus flat characters.

- Are these power relations potentially influenced by the characters' intersecting relationships with axes of privilege?

- Are there complexities at play? For instance, there could be complexities in the power relations between two characters who are each simultaneously privileged by one axis of identity but disadvantaged by another, such as a racially privileged woman interacting with a man subject to racial discrimination.

TABLE 3.1 *Privilege mapping characters*

Axis of privilege	Normative power relations in the story setting and/ or the context of writing	Character's relationship to these power relations	Examples from the text
Race	White privilege is normalized in the story's setting, which reflects the writing context	Character is white and benefits from privilege	In one scene, the character waits for a taxi. A character of darker appearance is also waiting. The taxi driver takes the white passenger, even though the other customer has been waiting longer.
Indigeneity			
Gender			
Sexuality			
Disability			
Neurodiversity			
Age			
Spirituality			
Language			
Add more as you see fit			

- Are there hegemonic systems at play? For instance, there might be two characters who are both disadvantaged by the dominant system of privilege, but one character may participate in the oppression of the other – thus colluding with their own oppression – because they belong to a complicit group and perceive themselves as better off than they might otherwise be due to trickle-down benefits from the hegemonic group.

- What forms of resistance and agency seem available to each character? To what degrees to they activate these opportunities – or fail to do so?

- How do these operations of power relations within the text relate to those of the writing context?

Use your note to respond to the story in one or both of the following ways:

- Critical response: produce an essay analysing power relations in the story. Include reflections on how these re-present those of the context where it was written (which could mean maintaining the status quo, or subverting it, or elements of both).

- Creative response: craft a fanfiction that reimagines the characters' power relations otherwise. Or if you are working with your own draft, rewrite it to address any problematic re-presentations you have identified through these processes.

Experiment three: settings and beyond-human actors

Choose a story, poem, or other text (as for experiment two, you can use your own draft, or swap drafts with a fellow writer as a feedback process). Using three highlighter pens of different colours, highlight all the parts of the story that depict setting (in one colour), all those that depict beyond-human actors (another colour), and those depicting humans (the third colour). Some sections may include more than one, in which case you can highlight in one colour and underline in the other/s. Then answer the following questions:

- What is the setting (or settings if more than one)? Note time, place, and cultural norms.

- From what narratorial perspective or perspectives is the text portrayed (e.g. first person from a human point of view, third person omniscient or limited omniscient, etc.)?

- What percentage breakdown is given to setting, beyond-human actors, and human characters?

- What do these percentages suggest about power relations between humans and the beyond-human?

- Would you describe the setting as universal or specific? If the setting is universal, how universal is it really, and what worldviews or assumptions might it nonetheless portray?

- Would you describe the setting as background or integral?

- Do the beyond-human actors feature as mere backdrop, or do they play an active role in the story?

- What normative attitudes to human characters display towards animals, the environment, and other aspects of beyond-human being?

Drawing on the above reflections, respond to the story in one or both of the following ways:

- Critical response: produce an essay analysing how the text portrays power relations between humans and beyond-human being. Include reflections on how these re-present those of the context where it was written (which could mean maintaining the status quo, or subverting it, or elements of both).

- Creative response: craft a fanfiction that alters the story's portrayals of power relations between humans, settings, and beyond-human actors. Or if you are working with your own draft, rewrite it to address any problematic re-presentations you have identified through these processes. Among other possibilities, this could involve turning a background setting into an integral one, shifting the story into an alternative setting, and/or telling the story from a different perspective.

PART TWO

CANONS, PUBLISHING, AND THE MYTH OF LITERARY MERIT

4 REPRESENTATIVE IMBALANCES IN THE WESTERN LITERARY CANON AND PUBLISHING

Walking/writing off the map

In chapter one, I mentioned the teenager-shaped holes in the fence that divides the park from the old Highbury mine. Well, I'm the same height at forty as I was at fourteen. I fit through those holes. Though actually, there's no need: around the other side of the mine, the main gate lies bent and broken off its hinges, and has for as long as I've known this place. It appears someone drove a robust vehicle towards it at high speed. On the fence beside the fallen gate, a large worksite protocols placard has been sprayed over with a fat black anarchy symbol.

Inside, there are no maps, no signs except a few faded, sometimes fallen old Give Way and speed limit markers on broken up bitumen down which mining trucks once roared. There's also warning markers of unstable mounds prone to caving in, and areas that look like firm flat plains but are actually sandy lakes hungry to swallow anything they catch. These signs I heed with care, sticking mostly to the former roads. None have names and they branch frequently. Many of the intersections look the same. Deciding which turn to take is a mix of instinct, memory, and close attention to fine detail landmarks. I never come here on workday mornings, only weekends and holidays when there's time to lose and find myself if needs be.

Without bush care teams to monitor weeds and nurture native seedlings, the local and feral plants negotiate a new hybrid ecology. The scent of aniseed mingles with pine and eucalyptus mingles with metallic mineral sands. And trash. So much trash. The local councils set narrow limits on free waste collections, and the fees for extra disposals at proper dump sites are high. With unemployment widespread and rents ever climbing, it's unsurprising that many people have made this their solution. The former carpark near the entrance is strewn with dented whitegoods, busted furniture, bald tyres and children's toys. A former bed mattress lies with rusted springs exposed like ribs in a headless carcass: time has eaten it near-clean but for a few last clinging strips of sodden foam. Then there's all the soiled clothes, partnerless shoes and nappies spilling from plastic bags split open, surrounded by broken glass from smashed mirrors and television screens.

Rubbish is but one indication I'm not alone in coming here. In a former parking area, car and motorbike prints loop and arc in dizzy patterns round stacks of old tyres marking what I figure to be a race track. The glittering blue mounds of dolomite that surround it are also tyre marked – bike jumps? It'd make a good set for a dystopian film. Further into the site are the remnants of old buildings – mostly just concrete slabs, with the odd wall still standing, most of them covered in aerosol art. I guess these were offices or tea rooms for staff. Some were multi-level, cutting into hillsides where old concrete staircases still lead between open platforms framed by bricks holding back the earth, pressing otherwise undulating slopes dead vertical. Some of the ruins create amphitheatres where I can easily imagine people giving performances or rap battling. Strewn beer cans and junk food packets prompt me to imagine lively party scenes.

I think again about place, space and belonging, about how I never see teenagers in the main park. Here I do sometimes encounter them – lanky figures slinking round beneath baseball caps and low-slung backpacks. Recalling my own punk misfit years, it makes sense they'd feel more at home here, in this anti-Eden, this wounded wonderland. If we have to pass each other, we do so at distances, without eye contact or g'days. Though nowhere displayed, there's a code of etiquette, as in the main park. It's just a different one. Courteous acknowledgement takes the form of non-acknowledgement: if I don't see you, then you don't see me, which means none of us were ever truly here.

Following ventures into the old mine, I see the real park in new ways. Indeed, I ask myself what I think I mean by that word – real. Is the official park more authentic because care has been taken to restore its landscapes closer to what they would have been like before the British invasion began in 1788? Or does its rigorously maintained beauty breed false comforts, belying bald truths of colonial ruin that the mine's unapologetic brokenness reveals? Despite fences, the two are ultimately the same earth, like masks of comedy and tragedy or Janus profiles of the one face: presentable Jekyll and Hyde the shadow self. But in truth, the park/not-park border is far blurrier than this – an amorphous transition no fence could ever truly mark. Beyond and within the approved zone's edges are multiple paths that don't have names and appear nowhere on the map of recommended routes hierarchically colour-coded by levels of fitness and experience required. Even when I wander without intention to follow set trails, and though I can always turn any way I want at any moment, subtle details of design pull me towards certain sites, away from others. For instance, better trail surfaces often make the mapped routes more inviting, as do signs promising lookouts or historic sites. These are things I rarely notice until I actively consider the curation at play.

I get thinking about a friend who is nuts for comics. They're always going on about what's canon and what's not – canon being the books serials and films the fan communities recognize as properly belonging within the world and storyline of a given hero or series, and non-canon being everything else (Romagnoli & Pagnucci, 2013, pp. 188–9). The notion of a comic canon came from the western literary canon, which in turn came from Christianity's practices of distinguishing approved scriptures from heretical ones (the Gospels of Matthew, Mark, Luke and John versus Mary Magdalene's, for instance) (Turner, 2010, p. 14). The western literary canon represents a broadly agreed-upon (by western cultural authorities) set of books and authors deemed worthy of regard, which has majorly steered the set text lists of school curricula and undergraduate literature courses (Nicol, 2008, p. 22). The mapping of park trails seems a kind of canonizing too – or perhaps canonizing might be considered a map-making activity. Either way, both canons and maps are devices of attention: they say, focus on this, not that; heed these voices and perspectives; forget those ones.

In the early twentieth century, Simone Weil deemed attention 'the rarest and purest form of generosity': an act of deep noticing that takes the first step towards empathy and care – towards *attending* to another's needs (Weil, 1942/1976, p. 462). Today, attention is economized, bid for and exploited as a resource (Odell, 2019). To reap the attention of others is to assume certain relations of power. For instance, social media influencers may earn money by attracting likes or use their status to promote political agendas (Tomasena, 2019, p. 4). As attention devices, literary canons are caught up in power (Nicol, 2008, p. 23): they mediate who can most easily speak through creative writing, and on what terms, sustaining the representative imbalances chapter four discussed. The chapter ahead explores how the western literary canon arose in connection with social institutions including religion, education, colonization and the publishing industry, all of which framed the canon's implications in ideologies of race, gender, capitalist economics and social class inequity. I also consider resistance to the canon from literary critics, educators and creative writers.

Compass

Part one raised a need for contemporary western cultures to learn from First Nations writers and thinkers about connections between writing, knowledge, place and relationality, particularly the implications writing-knowledge connections bear for power. This sparked exploration of representation as re-presentation as one example of how creative writing affects real world power relations, both among humans and of humans with beyond-human being. Representation can on the one hand serve the maintenance of existing inequities, or on the other, provide ways to challenge them and promote change. However, creative writing and publishing historically has been – and remains – representatively imbalanced towards the benefit of hegemonic groups and white western ideologies. Part two illustrates these imbalances via discussion of the western literary canon and publishing. This chapter begins by defining the canon and its problems. I then inquire into the historic, institutional, and material factors that formed the canon, particularly connections with institutions of religion, education, imperialism and publishing. Publishing is considered across two broad historical eras: the 1400s–1700s, when moveable type first came to Europe, and the 1800s, when publishing was transformed by steam technologies and social changes. Overall, this chapter maps historic circumstances that shaped the representative imbalances evident today and raises a new question for chapters five and six: how to redress these imbalances in both the canon and publishing.

The western literary canon

The western literary canon arose in the 1700s and gained dominance in the 1800s (Nicol, 2008). Until the mid-1900s, literary critics, educators and other white-western cultural authorities declared the canon to represent 'those texts that are traditionally, perhaps even universally, recognized as being worthy of veneration and academic study' (p. 22). The canon also refers to the authors whose writings are canonized, some of whom include William Wordsworth, Walt Whitman, William Blake, Robert Browning and Samuel Taylor Coleridge (Nicol, 2008, p. 23). Those who championed the canon pitched it as an important preserver of cultural tradition and intellectual integrity, and some still argue 'that the canon should remain important because of its aesthetic superiority and self-evident excellence of having been written by genius authors' (Aston, 2017, p. 39). Among the most vocal advocates of the canon in the late twentieth century was American literary critic Harold Bloom. For Bloom (1994), 'canonical excellence' equated to universal timelessness and formal superiority of texts wherein

> the flames of invention burn away all context and grant us the possibility of what could be called primal aesthetic value, free of history and ideology and available to whoever can be educated to read and view it. (p. 65)

Despite these grandiose claims to tradition and timelessness, even Bloom acknowledged that the concept of a western literary canon – or at least, the use of the word canon to hierarchize literary texts – '[did] not actually begin until the middle of the eighteenth century, during the literary period of Sensibility,

Sentimentality, and the Sublime', making it a relatively recent invention in the historical longview (1994, p. 20). Previously, the term canon was primarily used in Christian religious contexts, where it from the 1400s onwards evoked 'the Scriptures, the books of the Bible accepted by the Christian church' and more generally, any church 'decree', 'rule or principle', or 'standard of judging' religious morals and codes of behaviour (Harper, 2024). Transference of the word canon to literature maintained religious implications via arguments for education about canonical texts to provide a 'set of values and standards' and counter 'the loss of religion as a moral centre to society' (Turner, 2010, p. 14) by promoting 'a moral ideology for the modern age' (Eagleton, 1983, cited in Turner, 2010, p. 14). This stance is reflected in the words of George Gordon, an early Professor of English Literature at Oxford, who declared, 'England is sick, and English literature must save it' (Gordon, 1922, cited in Turner, 2010, p. 14).

In addition to religion and education, Turner associates the rise of the western literary canon in the eighteenth and nineteenth centuries with British nationalist efforts to cohere 'the emerging nation-state' of British imperialism, as part of which 'a desire to standardize English' played a significant role (2010, p. 17). The canon is also historically connected with colonization, for as Frantz Fanon noted, imposition of the colonizing culture's language on colonized people was a key means via which Britain and other imperial nations asserted dominance and control (1986, p. 18). By valorising approved ways of using English over purportedly incorrect or inferior ones, the canon enabled British colonizers to mobilize their proficiency as first-language English speakers as cultural capital via which to naturalize symbolic – and actual – violence against colonized people for whom English was an additional language.

The canon's connections with English standardization additionally reinforced patriarchal dominance and social class, for women and members of non-privileged social classes also bore fewer opportunities to pursue formal education about using English in the approved ways. This appears to have been among contributing factors to the canon's historic privileging of 'dead white men' from the middle to upper-classes (Nicol, 2008, p. 23) – a situation that became self-perpetuating, as observations that the canon featured only texts by authors from this select social group became fuel for asserting that white men were naturally more capable of writing texts bearing superior literary merit. This discouraged many women and people from non-privileged social classes from attempting to write. Those who did faced greater challenges. To achieve publication, many women used male pseudonyms and/or adopted themes and styles reflecting those of successful male writers (Joseph, 2019, pp. 59–60). Some women did make individual achievements via these strategies, but in ways that still reified the canon's patriarchally-oriented homogeneity. As late as the 1970s, Frank Kermode curated a 'Modern Masters' book series featuring almost exclusively male authors – a move Kermode presumed to justify in his preface by remarking, '[t]here is no male or female viewpoint; there is only the human viewpoint, which happens always to have been male', playing into universalist notions of a singular human viewpoint relevant to all times and places while dismissing the possibility that people of differing genders, cultures, classes and other backgrounds of experience might bear many varying viewpoints, each worthy of hearing (Kermode, 1979, cited in Turner, 2010, p. 29).

The western literary canon is no longer explicitly championed with the vigour it once was. Nonetheless, educational research shows that texts either drawn from the traditional canon or featuring the sorts of themes and styles it favoured continue to dominate school and university reading lists today (McLean Davies et al., 2021, p. 821). This in turn influences publishing and general tastes, for school purchases represent a significant market, and following school, many students will throughout their adult lives gravitate towards texts resembling those they studied at young ages (Aston, 2017, p. 46). The canon seems to maintain a strong implicit influence, reflecting Raymond Williams's (1977) notion of dominant, residual and emergent ideologies. Dominant ideologies are those currently in mainstream favour, residual those that have lost their previous dominance but still bear force, and emerging those currently rising towards dominance (pp. 121–5). Though the western literary canon is no longer revered to the degrees it once was, its residual force remains significant, making it a site still worthy of attention to understand representational imbalances in creative writing today.

Canonical inequities

Since the mid-twentieth century, the literary canon has been critiqued for intersecting inequities it reflects and reinforces (Nicol, 2008, p. 23). Various alternative canons have been proposed to represent the literatures of broader cultures and contexts (Krupat, 1983; Gates, 1991; Mulford, 2007; Somerville, 2021). For instance, in a 1983 study of the canon's exclusion of First Nations American authors Arnold Krupat emphasized:

> the canon, like all cultural production, is never an innocent selection of the best that has been thought and said; rather, it is the institutionalization of those particular verbal artifacts that appear best to convey and sustain the dominant social order. (p. 146)

Also writing in the late twentieth century, African American literary critic Henry Louis Gates (1991) equated the dominant canon with

> the 'antebellum aesthetic position,' when men were men, and men were white, when scholar-critics were white men, and when women and persons of color were voiceless, faceless servants and laborers, pouring tea and filling brandy snifters in the boardrooms of old boys' clubs. (p. 29)

Gates added that 'None of us is naive enough to believe that "the canonical" is self-evident, absolute, or neutral' (1991, p. 29). This aligns with Nick Turner's (2010) observation that the system of value judgements via which texts of the western literary canon have been historically presented as bearing greater literary merit than others is arbitrary, subjective, and representative of socio-cultural inequalities rather than anything intrinsic to the works themselves:

> works of art have no value in themselves, and only acquire meaning when placed in a social context (thus, obviously, any object can be deemed a work of art should a cultural institution deem it one). (p. 17)

As noted earlier, the canon is no longer as explicitly dominant as it once was, but maintains a powerful residual influence on education, publishing and general tastes. This influence is evident in the account given by Māori writer and academic Alice Te Punga Somerville, who remarks that '[c]anons steal the limelight from everyone else, implying they are not as deserving of attention and/or they simply do not exist' (2021, para. 11). Somerville relays some of the 'real-world effects' the western literary canon still bears as follows:

> When I first talked about teaching Māori literature in an English department in New Zealand, a number of people questioned whether there would be enough writing to justify a whole course, let alone a whole job. This assumption is not accidental – it grows out of a colonial view that Indigenous cultures are non-literate (evidence of our inferiority), as well as a colonial presumption to know everything about Indigenous people ('if there were any other good Māori writers out there I would know about them, so I will assume they don't exist'), and is nourished by the overwhelming whiteness of New Zealand literary culture, publishing, cultural infrastructure and book prizes. (para. 12)

Contemporary Mandandanji (First Nations Australian) researcher and educator Amy Thomson similarly observes 'a saturation of privilege in these texts and the social hierarchies created by upholding the definition of "canonical literature"', noting that 'historically, privileged sociocultural groups, including homogenized presentations of religion, nationality, sexuality, gender, race, and class, are at the forefront of what defines "canonicity"' in ways that serve 'maintenance of Eurocentric social power and agency' (2023, p. 2). Thomson's (2023) and Somerville's (2023) accounts align with evidence that despite 'ongoing attempts to unsettle the literary canon', school curricula 'continues to foreground works written by cis-hetero-white (British) men and reproduce predominately cis-hetero-white (British) narratives' (McLean Davies et al., 2021, p. 821). By continuing to influence education, the canon also continues to influence publishing and reading tastes on a broader scale, for it is shown that educational reading lists bear significant impact on book sales, and thus, the markets publishers cater for (Aston, 2017, p. 46). This is not only because of direct sales of books to educational libraries and students, but because what students are exposed to in school tends to shape their reading tastes beyond the classroom too (p. 46).

The canon's historic dominance and ongoing influence provides a context for the representative imbalances chapter three observed. However, questions remain as to how and why the canon became so imbalanced in the first place. This section has provided partial explanation in the form of the canon's connections with social institutions including religion, education, and British nationalism. The canon's connections with the publishing industry are also worth considering, for as Marissa Joseph notes, the canon's popularization across the 1800s coincided with a period of 'dynamic change' in British publishing spurred by the industrial revolution (2019, p. 20). Indeed, Joseph identifies the 1800s as the era in which 'the publishing industry developed as an industry' (p. 24). Yet publishing in the forms of printing, book selling and related practices date back far earlier (p. 23). The next section considers publishing from the 1400s (the beginnings of moveable-type printing technologies in Europe, though *not* the first developments of such technologies in worldwide terms) through to the 1700s. These discussions will contextualize subsequent exploration of how 1800s changes to the publishing industry were connected with the western literary canon's rise to dominance in ways that shaped the intersecting modes of social inequity it continues to reflect and reinforce.

Publishing in the 1400s to 1700s

Invention of the printing press is commonly dated to the 1450s and attributed to the German inventor Johannes Gutenberg (Rose, 2009). However, Gutenberg's press may more accurately be identified as the first invention of its kind to be widely taken up in European countries: as early as 1377, moveable type printing was already realized in Korea, where Buddhist monk Baekun Hwasang used it to produce a book of Zen teachings called *Jikji* (Rose, 2009). Furthermore, overemphasis of Gutenberg's role even within the European context overshadows the 'multiple determinations within the cultural economy' involved in 'the introduction of print' (Kuskin, 2008, p. 8). As print historian William Kuskin (2008) notes:

> In forgetting the complexity of the process, literary and print historians misrecognize its nature and treat one particular technological innovation as a mode of production in its entirety, one launched – like Athena – from Gutenberg's genius and superimposed upon a pre-existing culture as the prime mover of change. (p. 9)

Working counter to such approaches, Kuskin emphasizes how print was complexly 'intertwined with and born from the fifteenth century's imagination' through 'an uneven marriage of forms involving manuscript production techniques, mercantile financial and distribution expertise, and a number of individual craftsmen and partnerships interested in refining Gutenberg's initial invention' (2008, p. 9).

The first book printed in the English language using moveable type technology is reputed to have been *Recuyell of the Histories of Troye* in 1475 by William Caxton, who is commonly recognized as the first English printer (Kuskin, 2008, p. 13). Publishing dates back far earlier than this, with practices including hand-scribed books, scrolls, parchments and slate tablets. The major shift enabled by printing innovations in the 1400s was volume: whereas Caxton's predecessors relied on patronage in the form of one-on-one transactions with wealthy book purchases to whom they made 'the necessarily personalized offering of a single manuscript', Caxton produced 'printed books in editions that usually numbered somewhere between three hundred and six hundred copies' (Rutter, 1987, p. 443). Indeed, Kuskin names volume as 'print production's guiding principle of innovation and its rule for survival' because 'a working print shop can only be financially viable if it maintains a high enough output to pay off its initial investment' (2008, p. 17).

Observing how volume dramatically increased the need for printers to generate capital, Kuskin argues that 'capitalism is a part of English printing from the start, not as the dominant mode of production of English society but as one element within its system of representations, practices, and conflicts' (2008, p. 18). Jeremiah E. Dittmar similarly observes how changes to printing in the 1400s drove 'innovations in bookkeeping and accounting' as well as transformations to 'business practices and social groups' that 'drove the rise of European capitalism' (2011, pp. 1134–5), while Raul del Pont considers publishing as 'one of the first industries to make a consistent and successful effort to rationalize and standardize mass production from its origin' (2024, p. 2). Examples of proto-capitalist practices in the early print industry include Caxton's strategic use of marketing to create audiences for the books he published (Kuskin, 2008, p. 17); early practices of buying and trading shares in publications wherein publishers who found success tended to be those who 'were active in buying shares that were rising in value from other publishers and getting rid of those that were poorly performing' (Joseph, 2019, p. 121); and shifts in models of labour and production (del Pont, 2024, p. 2). As del Pont notes, publishing was 'one of the first [industries] to incorporate hourly labor as part of its processes', becoming 'an archetype for the systematic erosion of labor modelled under the predominance of the benefactor State that has given way to the precarious work of globalizing neoliberalism' – although publishing also sparked 'some of the earliest trade unions' (p. 2).

Under the pre-1400s patronage models of publishing, books were commissioned by wealthy patrons – typically members of the nobility – and catered to their tastes, which included religion, British history and stories of the British monarchy and the nobility themselves (Rutter, 1987, p. 456). While Caxton broke away from material dependence on noble patrons, he remained influenced by their tastes, operating 'through a logic of reproduction that assembles its mode of production by combining pre-existing practices' (Kuskin, 2008, p. 10). The cultural capital associated with topics the nobility valued were an appealing marketing tool for his broader pool of buyers (20). Although books had become more accessible than previously, the primary book-buyers were still 'the wealthy—those who had enough income to spend frequently on luxury leather-bound titles' (Joseph, 2019, p. 126). Caxton also came from a background of relative privilege, having previously undertaken 'substantial judicial and diplomatic responsibilities' in his role as a governor with the English Merchant Adventurers (Kuskin, 2008, p. 14). He bore strong personal friendships with many members of the nobility (p. 14). Similar observations apply later figures of influence on publishing like Charles Mudie, Richard Taylor and George Routledge: to enter the industry and succeed required economic capital to purchase copyrights, print books, market and distribute; symbolic capital in the form of social connections and a respected family name; and cultural capital to navigate social interactions of the publishing business (Joseph, 2021, pp. 125, 156).

Caxton's exploitation of 'the overlap between the noble and non-noble in English society' was 'attractive to the nobility because it reinforces a symbolic connection between literary production and social authority, in which the literary product appears an extension of that authority' and equally 'attractive to the classes beneath the nobility because it facilitates the appropriation of that authority as property' (Kuskin, 2008, p. 20). Kuskin characterizes books as 'symbolic machines of social reproduction' (p. 2):

> Print reproduction contains a double action: it appropriates authority from the past and consolidates it into a new object, the printed book, which is in turn geared for subsequent reproduction in the wholesale and retail market. (p. 17)

As part of this argument, Kuskin poses that, although the word canon was not then used in relation to literature, Caxton's 1400s practices of strategically selecting and grouping books into a 'material and intellectual consolidation of English culture … invested with literary authority' may be seen as an early instance of implicit canon-making that laid foundations for explicit canonization of literature in the 1700s and 1800s (2008, p. 17).

Publishing in the 1800s to 1900s

The canon's popularization across the 1800s coincided with a period of 'dynamic change' in the British publishing industry – by Joseph's account, the inception of the industry itself in the form we know it today (Joseph, 2019, p. 20). These changes included new technologies such as steam-powered papermaking and steam-driven printing presses, which 'provided opportunities for printed materials to be supplied in large quantities', meaning that publishers could print books in higher volumes for lower costs, making reading available to a wider audience for whom prices had previously been prohibitive (p. 20). Better railway links additionally increased ease of distribution across more geographically dispersed areas (p. 132). Train travel also created a market for the 'railway novel': 'cheaply produced paperback novels' that were 'designed to be read on the train and then discarded' (p. 135). The same era saw 'changes in societal attitudes in which "competition and entrepreneurship" were more openly accepted, allowing new roles to enter the field, one of which was the literary agent' (p. 20).

The previous section noted Kuskin's (2008) account of how existing judgements of cultural capital were reproduced in the 1400s: although moveable type enabled production for books for readers beyond the nobility, the range of books published still tended to reflect the same standards of taste the nobility had already established. Similar patterns characterize the 1800s when even greater volumes and distribution became possible via steam technologies (printing and trains), low-cost paperbacks (as opposed to afford the leather-bound hardback books marketed to wealthy buyers), and circulating libraries where members could rent books at affordable costs (Joseph, 2021, pp. 20, 126, 132). These innovations made reading more accessible for lower-middle and working-class people (p. 126). However, once again, the tastes of the privileged classes continued to sway publishing lists, for the common strategy of publishers was 'to issue a title in hardback in order to test its reception in the market', following which, 'if [a book] proved popular publishers would then reprint the title in paperback to attract a wider readership' (p. 126).

Circulating libraries make a particularly strong illustration of how representative imbalances were maintained even via practices that superficially appeared to further equity. Circulating libraries began in the 1600s but remained relatively small and uncommon until the 1800s when Charles Edward Mudie developed a business model that would 'propel [the library's] power into the industry with such vigour that he would guide the tastes of the reading public and influence how publishers commissioned their lists' (Joseph, 2021, p. 127). Like Caxton and other influential figures in publishing, Mudie was born into privilege in the form of economic capital, social connections and a habitus that easily suited him for building social and professional networks of influence (Joseph, 2021, p. 127). Mudie was a shrewd businessman who 'created a dominant position for himself by convincing publishers to keep the price of the three-volume novel high', which kept book purchasing inaccessible to most readers, increasing the demand to rent books from his libraries while maintaining the interests of publishers who 'could profit from sales either from the bookshop or the library' (Joseph, 2021, p. 130).

This led to talk of 'Mudie's monopoly' (p. 128) and suggestions 'that he and those who worked closely with him operated as a cartel, which protected their common interests' (p. 130). Mudie used his power 'to push his reading tastes to the public, publishing only what he would want to read, dictating the taste of the market' as 'publishers clamoured to supply him with titles' while 'the public were left with little choice as to where they could borrow' (Joseph, 2021, p. 128). The influence of Mudie's purchasing habits extended to 'how publishers commissioned new works', and even what authors wrote: many became 'disgruntled as they felt as though they were only to write according to Mudie's personal preferences' (Joseph, 2021, p. 128).

The roles that Caxton, Mudie and other major figures of the publishing industry's development meant that when critics and educators began forming a western literary canon across the 1700s and 1800s, their selections were limited by what had and had not been published and promoted well. This selection pool was in turn shaped by the tastes of those who possessed wealth, including the publishers themselves, the privileged classes to whom they marketed books and, via residual influence, pre-printing-era book requests of the nobility, which had already long-established modes of symbolic and cultural capital reproduced in and through books across the centuries. There are thus extensive historic, material, economic, technological and cultural reasons for why the canon came to privilege the interests of middle- and upper-class readers and writers, who in Britain at the time were also predominantly white.

Additionally, because British women could not own property until 1870, they were less able to become publishers and formed a less significant market of readers for those selling books. The earliest example I have been able to find of a female publisher in Britain was Emily Faithfull, who together with other women's rights activists established the Victoria Press, which championed 'women's rights to work' alongside other key 'political and economic rights' (Frawley, 1998, pp. 88–9). Yet Faithfull, too, is problematic in that she specifically championed the rights of middle-class women (Frawley, 1998, p. 89), showed allegiance to the monarchy via publicization of 'the endorsement she received from Queen Victoria, who made her "Printer and Publisher in Ordinary to her Majesty"' (p. 83), and refuted alignment with the suffragette cause (p. 88). Furthermore, it was in the 1800s still 'more difficult for women to reach the higher strata of literary fame' not only due to discriminatory attitudes of the time that assumed women to be intellectually and otherwise inferior to men but because '[m]iddle- and upper-class women were expected to be at home' and so to avoid being 'defined by this cultural stigma', those who did write and publish 'contributed to periodicals in some cases anonymously or under male pseudonyms' (Joseph, 2008, pp. 59–60).

Kuskin argues that attention to 'the premodern past' is a way to 'recognize the symbolic complexity inherent in the introduction of printing', and thus, to 'understand the way cultural, financial, and technological instruments intersect in

a process of symbolic reproduction that occurred in the past and still occurs today'
(2008, p. 3). By making such a return, this section has illustrated the factors of
capitalist economics, social class, race and gender that shaped the publishing
industry before and at the time of the western literary canon's emergence. The
canon's formation was at the time influenced by material constraints of publishing
that advantaged white males from privileged classes. Following its emergence, the
canon in turn influenced publishing, the two forming a feedback loop that
ongoingly naturalized and re-perpetuated the representative imbalances that
persist today.

However, in observing that representative imbalances persist today, I
simultaneously note that since the twentieth century at least, there have been
significant changes to both the canon and publishing. These changes – which
remain ongoing – have involved publication and canonization of books by women,
people from backgrounds of racial oppression and openly queer writers, among
many o/Other groups previously excluded from the canonical mainstream. These
changes raise both hope and questions of how to best approach ongoing efforts
towards even greater representative equity – questions that steer the next two
chapters.

Re-orienting

This chapter mapped the historic, cultural, institutional and material forces that
shaped the representative imbalances of mainstream creative writing observed in
part one. As publishing has historically been largely run by and most easily
accessible to white men from the middle-to-upper-classes, it is unsurprising that
this group has long been – and remains – overrepresented in the western literary
canon and mainstream publishing compared with women, people of colour, the
working classes and o/Other groups similarly disadvantaged by the intersecting
axes of privilege that characterize contemporary western societies. Despite all this,
both the canon and the publishing industry have across the twentieth century
undergone significant changes – and continue changing – towards improved
representation of groups mainstream literature previously excluded, albeit with a
long way still to go. To inform ongoing efforts, the next two chapters examine these
changes – and their limitations. Chapter six focuses primarily on the literary canon,
and chapter seven on publishing as well as the vexed question of literary merit.

5 THE CANON AS A SITE OF CONTESTATION

Small moments walking/writing

hillside sunrise:
brown summer grass
wet with autumn rain

      a park sign notes, the trees here are native
      to lands miles east of here

            flocking to spy a koala,
            a crowd tramples greenhood orchids

      in the distance, a white pipeline
      climbs the round hill, then dives in
      like cabling on a cyborg's shoulder

at the park's edge, a barbed wire fence
beyond it, the former quarry's toxic lakes

First published in Unusual Work no. 36,
19 November 2023 under the title 'Moments at Anstey Hill'

Compass

Chapter four mapped the historic forces that shaped the representative imbalances still evident in creative writing today. As noted, the canon and publishing have long reflected and reinstated uneven power relations across intersecting axes of identity. Since the twentieth century at least, efforts from literary critics, educators and writers have helped push both the canon and publishing towards greater inclusivity – albeit with far yet to go. To inform ongoing movements to improve representative equity, this chapter considers the canon as a site of contestation. Sites of contestation are 'places where differences are aired, negotiated, struggled over, per-formed, remembered, survived, and exposed' (Rimstead & Beneventi, 2019, p. 5). They simultaneously 'imply disagreement, debate, dissent, and non-concurrence', while forming sites 'where differences are aired, negotiated, struggled over, performed, remembered, survived, and exposed' towards 'the hope that knowing conflict is a viable way of living conflict more progressively' (p. 5).

I begin by discussing canon critiques by literary critics and educators around three focal areas: race and colonization; social class, gender and/or sexuality; and disability and/or neurodiversity. I then consider creative writing counter-narratives through practices of life writing and poetry; textual re-placing; and speculative fiction. These all demonstrate ways the western literary canon may become a site of contestation to pursue change. However, the end of this chapter notes finds canonical critiques and counter-narratives ultimately limited because canons remain tied to the publishing industry, which is in turn tied with capitalist reproduction and white western ideologies. Efforts to change publishing therefore set a starting point for chapter six.

Critiques foregrounding race and colonization

Critiques of the western literary canon focusing on race and colonization include those of postcolonial, decolonial and anticolonial theory. As Sara Ahmed notes, postcolonial theory in its ideal form, offers 'a space in which those who experienced colonialism could challenge that legacy' (2014, p. 17). In *The Empire Writes Back*, Bill Ashcroft, Gareth Griffins and Helen Tiffin insist the 'post' should not be misread as suggesting colonization to be over or in the past (1989, p. 2). Rather, they state their usage intends to cover 'all the culture affected by the imperial process from the moment of colonization to the present day' with emphasis on 'a continuity of preoccupations throughout the historical process initiated by European imperial aggression' (p. 2). Postcolonialism by their account remains concerned 'with the world as it exists during and after the period of European imperial domination and the effects of this on contemporary literatures' (p. 2). Ahmed similarly reflects, '*post* doesn't necessarily mean "after"; it can also mean an ambivalent relationship to the colonial as an unfinished history – colonialism as a structuring of the present' (2014, p. 17, original italics).

However, Ahmed (2014) also relays her initial reaction to postcolonialism as one of disenfranchisement:

Postcolonialism was not a word I ever really strongly identified with, I think partly because I first encountered that word as a literature student in Australia.

It was taught within the context of Australian literature, and *postcolonial* was used to index the relation between Australia as a nation and 'the mother country.' The way it was taught to me gave me the impression that the postcolonial was about white Australia (I have learned since that, if this whiteness was not remarked on, then *that* is the mark of whiteness). Postcolonial theory in this rendering did not have much to do with indigenous people or Asian Australians. (p. 17)

Ahmed's concerns about postcolonialism and preferences for decolonial theory align with Indigenous scholars' critiques of postcolonial theory as a space often ironically dominated by writers and critics from colonizing cultures. For instance, Wiradjuri (First Nations Australian) writer Jeanine Leane observes postcolonial theories as 'embedded in intellectual movements such as philosophy, literature, political science and film by the representation and analysis of the historical experiences and subjectivities of "victims" of colonial power' (2010, p. 35). This, Leane adds, 'casts us as "victims" and thus powerless in the colonial scheme' because '[w]ithin postcolonial discourse, Aboriginal people are spoken about in terms of "closing gaps" … or "Aboriginal Australians harnessing the mainstream"' – descriptors 'embedded in deficiency theories' that 'reinforce the superiority of the white mainstream as "the norm" … to which cultural minorities should aspire to achieve' (p. 35). Another problem with postcolonialism is its tendencies to emphasize primarily twentieth century works of literature, ignoring how 'Aboriginal people have used literature, music, letter writing and poetry well before this era', including 'in early colonial encounters' (McKinnon, 2014, p. 374). As Crystal McKinnon remarks, 'the often used catch-cry of postcolonial studies that "the empire writes back" would more accurately read: "the empire has already written back"' (p. 375).

Decoloniality is frequently pitched as an alternative to postcoloniality that works sometimes with, sometimes against, and ideally beyond postcolonial frameworks (Colpania et al., 2022). Writing in a Latin American context, Olimpia E. Rosenthal identifies the decolonial approach as having arisen in response to dissatisfaction with postcolonialism among scholars who distrusted its 'over-generalizing and transhistorical approach', noting how it ignored previous work by intellectuals from colonized cultures, and likening 'the dissemination of postcolonial frameworks' to 'a form of 'internal (cultural) colonialism' (2022, p. 17). Gianmaria Colpania, Jamila M. H. Mascataand and Katrine Smiet similarly observe how decoloniality aims 'to expose and challenge "the philosophical and ideological blind spots of postcolonial theories"' and even 'to "decolonize" postcolonial theory itself' via critique of 'the Anglophone legacy of postcolonial theory and its origins in the context of the former British Empire' (2022, p. 3).

Yet decoloniality is in turn critiqued by anticolonial critics for its 'expansive moves', particularly the ways 'decolonial critics tend to recode *anti*colonialism as decoloniality' (Von Eschen, 1997, p. 4, original italics). Anticolonialism emerges from 'a creative, political project among an international group of activist intellectuals' in the 1940s and onwards, wherein

> activists who came from radically different regional political economies and lived within different national boundaries engaged in a lively debate about the nature of their bonds and the political strategies best suited to their common liberation.
>
> VON ESCHEN, 1997, p. 5

As Lydia Ayame Hiraide observes, the prefix 'anti' evokes 'an explicit posture of overt resistance' that, although associated with 'historical social movements of opposition to direct rule (as well as cultural domination)' is 'also relevant to the practices and political postures of a number of communities in continued resistance today', particularly 'indigenous communities who live in contemporary settler colonies, such as Canada, the US, Australia, and Aotearoa (. . . New Zealand)' because it 'emphasises a radical critical force of opposition, which struggles against a colonialism that persists' (2021, p. 13). While emphasizing the importance of recognizing differences between postcolonial, decolonial and anticolonial approaches, Hiraide argues for 'a position that regards these terms as part of a wider common picture, in which they can be understood and practised in tandem rather than in competition' (2021, p. 14). Hiraide's position guides the one I adopt in subsequent parts of this book: I draw across the literatures of all three movements, but do so carefully, with a critical eye to issues raised by critiques such as those of Leane (2010) and Colpania et al. (2022).

Critiques foregrounding social class, gender and sexuality

Marxian, feminist and queer critics have also troubled the canon, respectively signalling issues of social class, gender, sexuality and more. The examples cited in this section largely recognize these issues as intersectional, which is why I am discussing the three together. Marxian critiques of the canon challenge the canon's privileging of middle- and upper-class literature at the expense of working-class voices. John Guillory's *Cultural Capital: The Problem of Literary Canon Formation* (1993) approaches this using Bourdieu's (1979/2010) theory of cultural capital. Turner similarly notes ways in which canonical texts 'are invested with value such that other works of art acknowledge their influence and status', suggesting '[c]ultural capital is thus, loosely speaking, a more thorough, socially based definition of canonicity' (2010, p. 17). Turner's approach articulates class inequalities with those of gender and race, avoiding the problems of the single-axis approach for which social class theories are sometimes criticized (Crenshaw, 1988).

Another Marxian approach to critique of the western literary canon involves engagement of dialectical theory. Writing in the South African context, Hayley G. Toth and Brendon Nicholls pose a '"polythetic" dialectic' approach to canon formation based on Marxian and Hegeleian dialectical strategies re-read via Steve Biko's theories of Black Consciousness (Toth & Nicholls, 2020, p. 42). Their model of canon-making 'does not emerge from a settled consensus, but instead re-coalesces on every occasion that it is submitted to contestation or is approached via conflicts in the social' (p. 42). This raises scope for the canon to 'negate institutionally-privileged texts while still making them momentarily visible via the "popular" cultural forms and traditions of struggle that contest institutional privilege' while also submitting those '"popular" cultural forms and traditions of struggle' themselves to 'gender critique, LGBTQI+ critique, environmentalist critique, among others' (p. 42). Such an approach, they pose, can help 'manage the complexities of contestation and reaction via which the canon emerges and is (endlessly) revised' (p. 42). Again, Toth and Nicholls incorporate race and gender alongside social class, reflecting a multi- rather than single-axis approach to the complexities of social inequality.

Feminist and queer critiques of the western literary canon have unsettled canonical re-presentations of power relations involving gender and sexuality. Feminists have focused on 'interrogating "great" male literature, both in terms of its content and how the canon sets the boundaries of "greatness"' (Riley, 2015, p. 384). Queer theorists have promoted 'dissident reading' practices of revealing queer themes in canonical texts previously presumed to be heteronormative (Sinfield, 1994, p. 1). Both groups have also sought to revive texts and voices from earlier times – for instance, Carla Mulford attests to the power of archival work 'using early women's writings to create a new way of writing history by writing women into history' (2007, p. 113), while Natalie Marena Nobitz attends to 'a glaring gap in the canonized recollection of an allegedly homogeneous and heteronormative war [the Second World War]' (2018, p. 13) via re-readings of queer themes in twentieth century and early twenty-first century texts. As with Marxism, feminist and queer approaches are sometimes criticized for a lack of attention to intersecting axes of experience, particularly those of race (Moreton-Robinson, 2000). In the cases of Sinfield (1994), Mulford (2007) and Nobitz (2018), however, attention is given to race among other modes of social injustice, reflecting intersectional rather than single-axis approaches.

Critiques foregrounding disability and neurodiversity

For critics studying disability and/or neurodiversity, the canon presents different challenges than the issues of erasure and silencing primarily considered in the previous two sections, for 'disability, far from being peripheral to the literary canon, has in fact suffused it' (Sanchez, 2020, p. 193). Examples of disabled authors whose works have risen to majorly influential if not canonical status include Lord Byron, who had a club foot (Hirschmann, 2020), Emily Dickinson, who was blind (Mullaney, 2019), James Joyce, who was also blind (Morse, 2018), Virginia Woolf, who lived with chronic mental and physical illness (Fenton-Hathaway, 2022), and Marcel Proust, who also lived with chronic illness (Douglas, 2016). Disability has also long been explicitly represented in canonical literature, including works by the writers just mentioned as well as non-disabled writers' works. For instance, Mary Shelley's *Frankenstein* (1818/1993) has been a particular site of interest for disability theorists who have explored and critiqued its central questions of 'grief, innovation, community, prejudice, and responsibility' (Fenton-Hathaway, 2022, p. 236).

Tracing histories of neurodiversity in canonical writing is somewhat more problematic, because current understandings of neurodiversities such as autism and ADHD are a relatively recent historical development, meaning people in the past who potentially lived with neurodiversity were unlikely to identify as such. Posthumous diagnoses of individuals who can no longer speak for themselves by affirming or denying the suggestion are in my view ethically troublesome. Julia M. Rodas (2018) demonstrates a more viable approach, using linguistic analysis of canonized authors' works to argue mainstream literature has long celebrated the literary merits of autistic language patterns that medical discourses frequently pathologize (without diagnostic implications about the authors themselves). Wes Folkerth (2020) similarly attests to a long history of neurodiverse representations in canonical literature via critical re-reading of characters from Shakespeare's dramas (again, with no posthumous diagnosis implied, but rather suggesting neurodiverse people existed in Shakespeare's circles and provided inspiration at times).

While it is therefore possible to argue that disability and neurodiversity have long been represented in mainstream and canonical literature, these representations have frequently involved problematic misrepresentation, tokenism and normalization of ableist discrimination. Kristen Harmon describes portrayals of deaf characters in canonical literature as 'highly symbolic, stylized, idealized, or dehumanizing', noting that 'when juxtaposed with hearing and speaking protagonists and characters, deaf and signing people often are shown to be deficient, or lacking, in comparison' (2020, p. 46). Folkerth's re-reading of neurodiversity in Shakespearean drama reveals similar issues: characters reflecting neurodiverse traits are typically cast as clowns and fools (2020, p. 141). Even authors who lived with disabilities have at times been critiqued for producing representations reflecting their internalizations of ableist values dominant in their socio-historic contexts. For instance, Chloe Leung problematizes the 'blatant eugenicist attitude' borne in Virginia Woolf's 'negative representations of disability/

disfigurement' (Leung, 2023, p. 41). To counter this, advocates have sought to establish canons privileging self-representations of disability (Johnston, 2020, p. 254) and neurodiversity (Rozema, 2019) including specific canons of specific disabilities or intersections of experience including the 'canon of Deaf literature' (Harmon 2020: 44) and the 'Indigenous disability literature canon' (Senier, 2020, p. 10). Disability theorists have also turned to language and aesthetics. Rebecca Sanchez (2020) poses:

> Analyzing the relationship between deafness and modernism, then, needs to not only be about the recovery of work by deaf authors and analysis of deaf characters or language explicitly pertaining to deafness, but also a project of analyzing the ways in which deaf history, culture, and language use are always relevant to experimental modernist praxis, even and especially when no literal deafness is present in a text. (p. 194)

Anthony Mellors in his work on 'disabled poetry' similarly poses a need to consider 'traits in both the working practices and forms of contemporary writing' that 'radically oppose the humanist presuppositions of canon-formation' (2014, p. 385). Mellors advocates for texts that 'make a virtue of being prosthetic, broken, voiceless, and club-footed', arguing these 'should not be seen as aberrations in the history of form and taste' but rather celebrated for how 'they evince the non-identical basis of artistic practice in general' (p. 385).

Creative counter-narratives: life writing

The previous three sections considered ways in which literary critics and educators have critiqued the western literary canon's representative imbalances and argued for representative equity. This chapter's remaining sections consider critiques of the canon from creative writers via counter-narratives. Counter-narratives enact 'relational resistance' to 'master narratives' as a means via which people whose voices dominant discourse suppresses can 'challenge hierarchies and reposition themselves within imagined and lived space as a way of understanding but also acting on the world' (Rimstead & Beneviti, 2019, pp. 14–15). The poem with which I opened this chapter projects a subtle counter-narrative to the national park's marked tourist attractions by paying attention to overlooked details such as the greenhood orchids – a delicate native flower, the sight of which is to me rare and more exciting than a koala, but which most international tourists would neither recognize nor think to look for, because it has not been iconized as koalas have. This section focuses on practices of counter-narrative through life writing.

Life writing encompasses forms and genres including but exceeding 'literary autobiography, personal essays, testimony, letters, diaries, lyric poems, blogs, and a wide variety of popular memoir genres . . . ranging from cookbooks to performance art' (Grubgeld, 2020, p. 4). Occupying 'a place between fiction and non-fiction . . . between literature and history', life writing centres 'embodied experience', 'underlying emotion' and 'testimony' (pp. 4–5). Though life writing has conventionally been associated with narratives of individual human lives, recent developments in posthuman life writing show the capacities life writing bears for sharing collective histories and centring beyond-human foci without necessarily deploying narrative as conventionally understood (Batzke et al., 2021, p. 3). Posthuman life writing texts 'do the work of making non-discursive space legible' by drawing 'the material, nonhuman background into the foreground' in ways that bring legibility to 'experiences of both human and more-than-human life that are illegible in narratives dominated by oppressive, patriarchal epistemologies' (Fairfield 2022, p. 1191).

Life writing has figured strongly in historic and ongoing political movements as a mode of 'resistance to dominant cultural narratives' (Grubgeld, 2020, pp. 4–5). African American writers have used personal stories to challenge oppression since the 1700s at least (Gould, 2011, p. 39), particularly via 'autobiography to bear witness against slavery' (Carretta, 2011, p. 57). In Australia, Aboriginal and Torres Strait Islander life writing has contested British invasion since the first fleets arrived in 1788 (Brady, 2014, p. 115). As Anita Heiss and Peter Minter observe, following invasion 'Aboriginal people were unable to live traditionally and were prevented from speaking their native languages' which made use of English 'a necessity within the broader struggle to survive colonisation' and writing 'a tool of negotiation in which Aboriginal voices could be heard in a form recognisable to British authority' (2014a, p. 2). First Nations Australian life writing powerfully contests dominant non-Indigenous Australian versions of history that 'reinforce an unspoken or unacknowledged position of power in terms of control over truth' (Brady, 2014, p. 115). Life writing bears similarly long histories of significance in First Nations peoples' struggles against colonial domination in Canada (Rymhs, 2019; Dagenais, 2019), the USA (Jansen, 2021) and New Zealand (Makereti, 2015). In India, life writing has been important in both struggles for Independence and asserting Dalit rights – the rights of people historically and ongoingly subject to caste-based discrimination (Nayar, 2011).

Life writing has also featured in women's rights movements since the 1600s at least (Dowd & Eckerle, 2007, p. 1), combatting patriarchalism by raising 'the identity of a woman in a male-defined world' (p. 8). In Ireland, early women's life writing commonly confronted these issues of gender in connection with those of culture and identity in the face of English colonization and hegemonic domination (Eckerle & McAreavey, 2019, p. 6). Queer writing, too, bears long traditions – although these are harder to trace because queer people have historically been erased, and writers have frequently used oblique strategies of symbolism and allusion to evade legal and/or personal consequences (Streitmatter, 1995).

Examples include Oscar Wilde, A. E. Housman and Countee Cullen (see discussion in Gargaillo, 2022). Oblique references appear to have been particularly necessary in cases where queerness intersected with other axes of oppression – for instance, nineteenth century 'working-class and African American women' whose worker-run periodicals used 'alternative codes and tropes' to 'represent same-sex attachments and queer possibilities' (Coccia, 2020, p. 19). The memoir of intersex writer Herculine Barbin (Barbin & Foucault, 1980) both demonstrates and defies pre-twentieth century LGBTQIA+ erasure: written as a journal in the 1800s, the book was first published in 1978, after Michel Foucault found the manuscript in the French Department of Public Hygiene archives. Similar modes of erasure and oblique reference apply for pre-twentieth century political life writings on disability and neurodiversity, in line with issues noted in the previous section. Nonetheless, for those who understood the codes at play, life writing played a strong role in affirming identity and solidarity despite erasure's violences (Coccia, 2020, p. 19).

Much early life writing appeared in epistolary forms such as those of personal letters, journals and official correspondence. First Nations Australian writers commonly deployed 'genres that are common to political discourse: letters by individuals to local authorities and newspapers, petitions by communities in fear of further forms of dispossession or incarceration, and the chronicles of those dispossessed' (Heiss & Minter, 2014a, p. 2). Early samples of feminist life writing similarly range 'from the more explicitly autobiographical – such as diaries, letters, and memoirs – to less obvious choices like religious treatises, fictional romances, and even cookbooks' (Dowd & Eckerle, 2007, p. 1) as well as 'autobiography-inflected poetry, correspondence, depositions, petitions … nuns' chronicles, spiritual testimonies, and conversion narratives' (Eckerley & McAreavey, 2019, p. 4). The letters and petitions of Palawa (First Nations Tasmanian) woman Mary Ann Arthur (1819–71) exemplify the importance epistolary writings bore. Along with her husband Walter George Arthur, Mary 'demanded improved conditions for their people' via open letters in the *Flinders Island Chronicle,* of which Walter was co-editor, and a petition to the Queen of England describing the abuses their people faced (Heiss & Minter, 2014b, pp. 11–12). In a later letter to the Colonial Secretary, Mary Arthur raised fears about backlash to their petition from white superintendent Henry Jeanneret:

Dr. Jeanneret does not like us for we do not like to be his slaves nor wish our poor Country to be treated badly or made slaves of. I hope the Govr will not let Dr. Jeanneret put us into Jail as he likes for nothing at all as he used he says he will do it & frightens us much with his big talk about our writing to the Queen he calls us all liars but we told him & the Coxswain who Dr. Jeanneret made ask us that it was all true what we write about him.

ARTHUR, 1846, cited in **HEISS & MINTER**, 2014b, p. 12

Through the twentieth century and into the twenty-first, more politically oriented life writers have employed explicitly literary modes of autobiographical and biographical stories and poetry. Earlier legacies often remain evident in these works via epistolary techniques (using imagined letters and/or diary entries to tell stories). For instance, Alice Walker's *The Color Purple* (1982) uses letters to tell a story inspired by her grandparents' earlier lives, including the racism they experienced as Africa-American people in early 1900s America (Beauchamp, 2016). Janet Frame's *Owls Do Cry* (1957) incorporates diary entries into a story confronting the realities of poverty, social class discrimination, gender inequity and sanism (discrimination against people deemed mentally ill) in 1930s New Zealand. Yamaji (First Nations Australian) poet Charmaine Papertalk Green's *Nganajungu Yagu [My Mother]* (2019) is based on Papertalk Green's correspondences with her mother while living at an Aboriginal girls' hostel as a teenager in the late 1970s. As some of their letters were lost, the book combines direct quotes from saved ones with poems that re-create the emotions Green (2019) experienced as a teenager far from home and loved ones, interspersed with present-day reflections on the deep significance the saved letters and memories bear:

> These are not just letters on paper
> these are mother's letters to me
> her daughter, blood, her hopes
>
> . . .
>
> a long line of forever flowing blood
> of Yamaji women bound together
> from a continuous womb of love (p. 8)

In such works, epistolary techniques provide a means for 'disregarding Eurocentric ways of teaching and writing composition' to pursue a more 'innovative, freer, easier and more authentic way of expressing emotions' (Oettli, 2011, p. 102).

Twentieth and twenty-first century life writing has also seen the emergence of more works explicitly relaying lived experiences of people who were previously erased through discrimination or forced to tell their stories in oblique, coded ways. Examples include queer poetry by writers such as Frank O'Hara (Pritchard, 2022), Cyril Wong (Centre for Stories, 2024), Adrienne Rich (Clements et al., 2013) and Audre Lorde (Clements et al., 2013). There has also been a rise in transgender memoirs such as those of McKenzie Wark (2023), Kate Bornstein (2012) and Quinn Eades (2015). As Juliet Jacques notes, transgender writers 'first used memoir to counter sensationalistic mass media coverage', then later 'deconstructed the conventions and clichés that the transition memoir genre had developed' (2017, p. 357), seeking to:

> document gender-variant lives beyond a generalized desire for public acceptance and in response to social concerns: the policies of the gender

identity clinics, who decided who could access medical services, and on what terms, especially the demand that patients 'pass' in their acquired genders and hide their histories; and the exclusion of trans people from feminist spaces, and gay/lesbian politics. (p. 357)

Intersex writers such as Thea Hillman (2008), Aaron Apps (2015) and Michael Noble (2010) have also used memoir to push back against both medical discourses and public misunderstandings. Intersex activists' concerns differ significantly from those of transgender activists, but they share a common quest for bodily autonomy – while transgender people often seek more equitable access to surgery and hormone therapy, intersex activists often seek the right to refuse these treatments and prevent medical intervention upon the bodies of infants and children unable to give informed consent (see discussion in Walker et al., 2017). Figuring bodies in texts makes an important contribution to these agendas as a means via which to 'inhabit the "scene of writing," to tell stories, to speak . . . to enact a form of narrative and civil disobedience: an unerasing of the corporeal from text' (Eades, 2015, p. 25).

Disabled writers such as Keah Brown (2019) and Melissa Blake (2024) also commonly foreground 'conditions of the body' to 'produce new kinds of stories, offering variations on given cultural scripts' to 'reevaluate circumscribed identities' (Grubgeld, 2020, p. 7). As Thomas Couser notes, '[f]or many people with disabilities, culture inscribes narratives *on* their bodies, willy-nilly', which makes autobiography 'particularly important' because it is 'written from inside the experience' and 'involves self-representation by definition', which specially suits it 'for revaluation of that condition' (2005, p. 605). From a post-Cartesian perspective that overcomes binary body/mind divisions to recognize thought as an embodied phenomenon, similar observations can be made about neurodivergent memoirs such as those of Paige Layle (2024) and Jory Fleming (2021), who foreground neurodiverse thinking and contest neurotypicality's hegemonic dominance.

Another common feature of twentieth and twenty-first century political life writing is 'witnessing': 'auto/biographical work that seeks to make visible and/or remedy inequity' (Gilmore & Marshall, 2019, p. 6). This particularly includes texts bearing witness to experiences of trauma commonly 'hidden in plain sight, permitted by social norms of violence' (p. 6). For instance, the autobiography *Karobran: The Story of an Aboriginal Girl* by First Nations Australian writer-activist Monica Clare (1978) relays Clare's childhood and teenage experiences as a ward of the state, while Sally Morgan's *My Place* (1987) is based on Morgan's experiences of growing up believing she was of Indian descent, then learning her family had hidden their Aboriginality. First Nations Australian poets such as Paul Collis (2021) and Ali Cobby Eckerman (2023) similarly deploy personal lived experience to convey collective experiences of racial injustice and environmental destruction. Acts of witnessing are also common throughout the twentieth and twenty-first century African American, queer, disabled and neurodiverse life writing texts cited across previous paragraphs. Witnessing trauma brings visibility not only to injustices, but also commonly emphasizes strength and survival, building solidarity among survivors. For instance, *Through My Eyes* (1978) by Biripi woman Ella Simon tells of her experiences growing up on a mission, then participating throughout her life in movements for Aboriginal rights and becoming the first female Aboriginal Justice of the Peace in NSW. In such texts, 'new forms of witness and knowledge become visible through traumatized histories retold as stories of resilience' (Gilmore & Marshall, 2019, p. 9), demonstrating 'how knowledge and even hope can arise through self-representation' as 'a way to push back against the abuse' (p. 10).

The works noted in this section comprise but a few among the many historic and contemporary examples of life writing's capacities to raise issues of injustice and promote change. Limited though this survey has been, I hope it has helped illustrate how life writing counter-narratives can help redress the western literary canon's representative imbalances. The next section considers another counter-narrative practice: textual re-placing.

Textual re-placing

Textual re-placing or 're-placing the text' is a strategy drawn from postcolonial theory (Ashcroft et al., 1989, p. 77). While retaining critical awareness of the problems previously noted in relation to postcolonial theory, textual re-placing remains worth considering for the ways in which it tackles canonical narrative head-on via practices of re-writing canonical texts in subversive ways. As Ashcroft et al. (1989) observe,

> Writers such as J. M. Coetzee, Wilson Harris, V. S. Naipaul, George Lamming, Patrick White, Chinua Achebe, Margaret Atwood, and Jean Rhys have all rewritten particular works from the English 'canon' with a view to restructuring European 'realities' in postcolonial terms, not simply by reversing the hierarchical order, but by interrogating the philosophical assumptions on which that order was based (p. 32).

To illustrate, Ashcroft et al. (1989, p. 32) cite *Wide Sargasso Sea* by Jean Rhys (1966), which re-centres the canonical novel *Jane Eyre* by Charlotte Brontë (1847/2022). In *Wide Sargasso Sea*, the new centre of the text is a character called Bertha, who in the original never appears in the story itself but is discussed in hushed tones by other characters as the so-called mad first wife of the romantic hero, Rochester. In addition to discrimination against her mental illness, Bertha is racially oppressed and marginalized for being from a lower social class, as well as a woman in a society of patriarchal privilege. By centring her story above those of characters privileged by ableism, whiteness, social class, gender and sanism, *Wide Sargasso Sea* calls out the intersectional injustices inherent in the original, exercising textual agency by working with the constraints of the western canonical tradition to indicate perspectives and issues beyond those the traditional western canon has historically privileged. A more recent example of similar strategies is Bunjalung (First Nations Australian) poet Evelyn Araluen's *Drop Bear* (2021), poems in which critique erasure of First Nations peoples in dominant non-Indigenous Australian works of children's literature. By calling out the effects these stories of erasure bore on her as a child, Araluen celebrates her ability in adulthood to resist erasure by critically re-reading and writing back to them.

As Harmon notes, 'Deaf writers are also "re-writing" canonical works, and in doing so, are "talking back" to the ideological constructs that frame or exclude differences of various kinds' (2020, p. 54). As an example, Harmon cites playwright Gilbert Eastman's reimagining of George Bernard Shaw's *Pygmalion* (1913/2021). Shaw's original tells 'the story of two upper-crust bachelor linguists who decide to take on a penniless young woman who speaks with what they see as a "dreadful" Cockney accent' and 'train her in proper speech and manners' so 'after some time, she is able to "pass" for upper class' (Harmon, 2020, p. 54). Eastman's *Sign Me Alice* (1973) calls out the 'brutality of such an exercise' via depiction of a protagonist who is fluent in American Sign Language, then becomes forced to train in '"U.S.E." or "Using Signed English," a satirical riff on Signing Exact English' (Harmon, 2020, p. 54). The play's 'pivotal moment' is when the protagonist realizes:

In my heart, Sign real mine . . . Yes, I sign English to you, but I feel more comfortable with my Sign. Nothing can change me . . . U.S.E. has nothing to do with being a lady. A lady can use sign.

EASTMAN, 1973, cited in HARMON, 2020, p. 54

Re-writing texts has also been a frequent strategy of feminist and queer writers. A particular focus for feminists has been the re-writing of fairy tales to critique their patriarchal overtones and/or invest female characters with greater agency (Walker & Bodnaruk, 1997). Rewriting fairy tales has likewise proven a popular approach among queer writers (Baker, 2010). Ronan Ludot-Vlasak also notes intertextuality as another vital way in which queer writers have subverted the canon's dominance, pointing out how the use of quotations from canonical literature in queer television shows serves 'to question and regenerate the literary canon by inviting us to revisit it and look at it from a different angle' (2012, p. 266).

Textual re-placing doesn't always necessarily entail working with a specific text. Some writers instead work with tropes and features of canonical genres. For instance, Amita Murray's *Unladylike Lessons in Love* (2023) re-invents the regency novel genre via the story of Lila Marley, the daughter of an Indian woman and an English earl in nineteenth century London. Murray's depiction of Marley raging against snobbery and constraints contests canonical literature's erasure of Indian people living in Britain during the 1800s, while also providing a strong feminist antidote to gender stereotypes, both historic and contemporary. The book also features a queer character. In New Zealand, and the USA, Māori and First Nations American writers deploy similar strategies of re-placing genre via 'Native Noir' and other subversive approaches to crime fiction, a historically white-dominated genre (see discussion in Bennett, 2024).

Textual re-placing can also involve subversion of English itself as the canonized *lingua franca*. Ashcroft et al. term this 're-placing language': strategies engaging '[t]he crucial function of language as a medium of power' by 'seizing the language of the centre and re-placing it in a discourse fully adapted to the colonized place' (1989, p. 37). They pose 'two distinct processes' by which re-placing language operates: 'abrogation or denial of the privilege of "English"', which 'involves a rejection of the metropolitan power over the means of communication', and 'appropriation and reconstitution of the language of the centre', which is a 'process of capturing and remoulding the language to new usages' to mark 'separation from the site of colonial privilege' (p. 37).

Ashcroft et al. pose abrogation and appropriation as most effective when used together (1989, pp. 37–8). While abrogation enacts powerful refusal of 'the categories of the imperial culture, its aesthetic, its illusory standard of normative or 'correct' usage, and its assumption of a traditional and fixed meaning "inscribed" in the words', constituting 'a vital moment in the de-colonizing of the language and the writing of "english"', if engaged separately from the process of appropriation 'abrogation may not extend beyond a reversal of the assumptions of privilege, the "normal", and correct inscription, all of which can be simply taken over and maintained by the new usage' (pp. 37–8). In plain terms, re-placing language means playing with words, grammar and spelling to reinvent the colonizer language in resistive ways. An example may be observed in the poetry of John Agard, who pitches 'mugging de Queen's English' as a dangerous, subversive act. He writes:

> I don't need no axe
> to split/ up yu syntax
> I don't need no hammer
> to mash/ up yu grammar
>
> . . .
>
> I'm not violent man Mr. Oxford don
> I only armed wit mih human breath
> but human breath
> is a dangerous weapon (1967/2006)

Agard writes in the tradition of dialect poetry and dialect writing more broadly, in which writers deliberately play with spelling and grammar in ways that would be deemed 'incorrect' by the rules of dominant standardized English (Leonard, 2011). By foregrounding breath while working within the form of oral performance poetry, Agard also privileges oral over written literary practices, inverting white western assumptions about stories in books bearing greater esteem than those shared aloud. He thereby brings attention to how the very idea of correct and incorrect ways of writing has historically been mobilized to re-produce inequality by advantaging those who grew up with English as their first language and cultural mother-tongue. Additional examples of subversive linguistic play can be observed in the novels of Scottish writers who incorporate Scots dialect (Rodriguez Gonzalez, 2016), and First Nations Australian authors who incorporate First Nations languages into their books (Brewster & Scott, 2012).

Instances of writing back via linguistic play are also observable in feminist writing through practices of *écriture feminine*, a French theory of 'writing the feminine' attributed to Hélène Cixous, who argued ideologies of patriarchalism are embedded in the normative language patterns of French, English and other dominant white-western languages, and who argued for women writers to remake language in subversive ways via experimentation with words, grammar, form, and syntax (Cixous & O'Grady, 2014). Queer writing practices often take this same argument further still to expose and overcome linguistic ideologies of heteronormativity, cisnormativity and binary thought as a dominant fallback in many western cultures (Baker, 2010).

Speculative fiction

Another powerful counter-narrative practice is speculative fiction, which, though it doesn't always necessarily engage with canonical literature, can be seen to enact similar modes of re-placement on dominant contemporary and/or historicized versions of reality. Speculative fiction in its broadest sense refers to literature that speculates about how the world could be otherwise, which is frequently enacted via genres including but exceeding science fiction, fantasy, horror, alternative history, utopian writing, dystopian writing, the imagining of future worlds, and hybrids of these and other possibilities (Doubinsky & Kkona, 2024). Speculative fiction's definition is, however, contested. While some treat it as an 'umbrella term' encompassing all of the genres just mentioned, others call for finer distinctions between science fiction as 'literature dealing with impossible things' and speculative fiction as exploring 'things that could really happen but just hadn't completely happened when the author wrote the books' (Burger, 2020: 1). Yet this treatment sits at odds with others still who distinguish between science fiction as 'literature dealing with possibilities' versus fantasy as 'literature dealing with impossibilities' (p. 1). Novelist Margaret Atwood observes, '[w]hen it comes to genres, the borders are increasingly undefended, and things slip back and forth across them with insouciance' (Attwood, 2011, cited in Burger, 2020, p. 1). I am here less interested in debating the bounds of what speculative fiction is and is not, and more interested in the political possibilities of the variously named writing practices that push us to think about how life could be otherwise.

Sébastien Doubinsky and Christina Kkona identify speculative fiction as a genre 'haunted by the other: aliens, ghosts, cyborgs, monsters, and other hybrid and supernatural creatures populate its different universes' (2024, p. 5). They locate its origins with works such as Mary Shelley's *Frankenstein* (1818/1993) and Charlotte Perkins Gilman's *The Yellow Wallpaper* (1892/2021), noting how these 'legacies seem to have influenced many invisible women writers and publishers' and how later figures such as Ursula K. Le Guin, Joanna Russ and James Tiptree Jr 'demonstrated the importance of feminist thought since the 1960s and paved the way for the feminist science fiction of the 70s', which 'immersed itself in questioning social inequality, rethinking power relations, and challenging gender stereotypes through imagining alternative settings', tackling not only gender stereotypes but also 'questions of sexuality, race, class, and species' (Doubinsky & Kkona, 2024, pp. 4–5).

Sherryl Vint also argues for the political potentials of speculative fiction, arguing that in a contemporary world where 'capitalist realism is our dominant ethos, prompting us to accept the world-as-seen-by-capital as given, rather than one alternative among many' (2021, p. 8). Vint considers speculative fiction a 'form of inquiry':

a way to shape our affective investments in the new, to orient how we think about technologies and the new social arrangements they entail toward greater social justice rather than greater capitalist accumulation (p. 8).

Sami Schalk (2018) likewise emphasizes:

how politically astute speculative fiction can be, how it can comment on our world and make us imagine alternative possibilities: the good, the bad, the ambivalent, and the downright terrifying. (p. 1)

For Schalk, this is particularly notable through resistance to normative constraints around disability, race and gender in black women's speculative fiction. Bibi Burger similarly draws attention to critiques of colonialism and heteronormativity in queer African speculative fiction, which Burger poses 'should be taken to include not only science fiction (with which the term is often conflated), but also tales of wonder: folktales and legends of a speculative nature' wherein 'great possibility' resides 'for investigating the queer potential of folktales from our continent that concern gender, sexuality, and outsiders' (2020, p. 2). Citing Nigerian-American author Nnedi Okorafor's novel *Lagoon* (2014), which features a 'plurivocal narrative technique enmeshed with Nigerian folktales and myths' (Burger, 2020, p. 2), Burger poses that 'these folktales and myths can themselves be considered examples of speculative fiction', meaning 'Okorafor is therefore not only appropriating traditionally Western forms of speculative fiction, but also engaging with older speculative literary forms' (p. 2).

Similar strategies are notable in *This All Come Back Now: An anthology of First Nations Speculative Fiction* (Saunders, 2022), works in which sometimes 'summon ancestral spirits from the past', and at others 'look straight down the barrel of potential futures, which always end up curving back around to hold us from behind' (UQP, 2022, para. 2). Claire G. Coleman's novels *The Old Lie* (2019) and *Terra Nullius* (2017) likewise blur the boundaries of historical fiction, alternative history and science fiction by imagining future dystopias plagued by violences strongly resembling those of Australia's 1788 invasion by the British. In a review of *That Old Lie*, Iva Polak remarks on the ingenuity with which Coleman 'evokes the blemished chapters of Australia's history as the basis of a dystopian futuristic Earth . . . using the metaphor of a secular apocalypse . . . in the form of a space opera' (Polak, 2020):

> [Coleman] interrogates historical colonialism on a much larger scale to bring to the fore the distinctive Indigenous experience of Australia's *terra nullius* and its horrific offshoots: the Stolen Generations, nuclear tests on Aboriginal land and the treatment of Indigenous war veteran, but this time experienced by the people of the futuristic Earth. (p. 1)

Along with life writing and textual re-placing, speculative fiction exemplifies counter-narrative strategies via which creative writers challenge canonical dominance and representative inequity. Together with literary and educational theorists' critiques, these creative counter-narratives make the canon a site of contestation via which to challenge injustices and advocate change.

Re-orienting

This chapter considered the canon as a site of contestation at which literary critics, educators and creative writers have found ways to call out representative imbalances and advocate change. Literary critics' and educators' efforts to expand the canon have included critiques relating to race and colonization; social class, gender and sexuality; and disability and neurodiversity. Creative writing counter-narrative practices include life writing and poetry; textual re-placing; and speculative fiction.

The operations of contemporary publishing remain in need of attention, for although expanding the canon does to some degrees affect publishing, critics and educators who push this cause still rely on the publishing industry to produce books to argue for as worthy of canonization. Similarly, writers who produce canonical counter-narratives rely on publishing to reach readers and create impact. Indeed, with the canon's influence becoming more residual than dominant, attention to publishing seems ever more important. It therefore provides the starting point for chapter six.

6 PUBLISHING PARADOXES AND THE MYTH OF LITERARY MERIT

Walking/writing the yellowcake road

Today I cannot walk my normal paths. I am far from home, on Whadjuk Noongar Country, otherwise known as Perth, Western Australia, where I have travelled for work. Instead, I take a morning walk in Kings Park, a 400 hectare stretch of gardens on a hill plateau overlooking the Swan River and Perth inner city. Based on botanical gardens I have visited back home and in other cities – and given the place's naming after British monarch Edward VII – I expected a prissy English affair full of roses and other things ill-suited to the dry Australian climate. It's a pleasant surprise to discover I'm wrong: the park is mostly native plant life: gum trees, banksias, Balga grass trees, velvety red and yellow tufts of kangaroo paw – even an ancient boab.

Entering the main gate, I turn left and follow a path along the plateau's edge. A sturdy fence sections off the steep drop to where a busy road skirts the riverbank. At a lookout, I pause and gaze at ferries cutting their way across the blue, soft and unhurried as tiny pale clouds. Further afield, the urban skyline shimmers bottle-green, reminding me of *The Wizard of Oz* (Fleming, 1939) – the moment when Dorothy first spies the Emerald City from afar. I am awed, but also unnerved by this glistening Mecca. The skyscrapers appear mostly built within the past five-to-ten years. That would make sense, given Western Australia's relatively recent economic boom. The tallest ones are made of glass contoured into smooth curves and oblique angles, all eking the same theme in different variations, parading distinct feats of engineering prowess. A majority bear the names and logos of mining companies. The rest were likely also built with mining dollars – hotels for fly-in-fly-out workers, massive malls and nightlife spots for big earners to blow their cash. I recall my first visit to this city in my late teens, more than two decades ago. It was such a different place. An unexpected shiver seizes me. I keep walking.

Although the plant life seems relatively faithful to what would've been here before British invasion in 1788, these gardens are nonetheless undoubtedly a heavily controlled and curated space – even more so than the park back home. There are countless statues – a massive King Edward, among other British monarchs and military memorials. The largest is a walk-in World War One shrine, the inner walls of which list names of soldiers who never returned. Nearby, a flame of remembrance burns in their honour, mounted on a vast granite plinth in a concrete area that doubles as fire safety and emphasis. Later, I discover another memorial specifically to Aboriginal and Torres Strait Islander soldiers – 'in all wars and actions involving Australian armed forces and services since the Boer War' (Kings Park and Botanic Garden, n.d.). It's far smaller and less grandiose than the World War One memorial – just a rock with a plaque, barely taller than me. It's not mapped or signposted: I find it only by accident, in a section of the park less busy than others. The individual wars aren't listed, let alone individual servicepeople. I wonder how many of them made it onto the walk-in memorial's inner walls.

The trail signage also pays heed to Traditional Owners. The richness of culture and life here before British invasion is much better represented than in the park back home. I learn that in Whadjuk Noongar culture there are six seasons, and the grass plants can be used to make medicine and glue. First Nations aesthetics also feature in the two large 'nature play' areas constructed for children and families. It unnerves me, though, to see nearly all signs branded with mining company sponsorship. These are the same companies who elsewhere destroy sacred First Nations sites through fracking, uranium mining and radioactive waste dumping. One exception is a walkway sponsored by the lotteries foundation. (Is the gambling industry not also a kind of mining – a drilling into human dreams to extract others' earnings?)

I'm reminded of a time early in my writing career when I was offered and accepted a lucrative contract with a community arts program travelling to schools in rural and remote areas. I was in my twenties, very raw. On arrival, I was presented with two T-shirts bearing the same bold corporate logo – a uniform I was to wear the whole time while on the job. Only then did I realize, the project had been funded by a mining firm wanting to salvage its image following bad press about brain damage to children due to airborne lead from its smelters. I was one of eight artists on the team. The others included painters, theatre-makers, a rapper and a clown. We were partnered up and shipped to various schools. My partner was the clown. I felt like one too – ludicrously dressed up with a garish smile to mask the forced-back tears. The students loved the workshops, and parents gratefully exclaimed what a rare and wonderful thing it was to receive such opportunities so far out from the urban centres. I was glad for the chance to do that work but wracked with guilt over how, by doing it, I was condoning the ongoing damage the company was wreaking. A couple weeks' salary for a handful of artists was small change compared with the massive profits those smelters were pulling from the town. Likewise, Kings Park's Noongar-themed walkways and playgrounds of this park would be a fraction of a per cent of what the sponsoring companies make through continuing desecration of sacred sites. I think of Christianity's old days, when the rich could just buy atonement and keep on sinning. For every Emerald City there's a place where the magic has been sucked dry – mountains hollowed, rivers poisoned, skies dyed necrotic grey.

The more I walk, the more these gardens seem a natural museum displaying colonial hypocrisies and white-western misappropriations of First Nations cultures into white-western agendas (see discussion in Kovach, 2009). Henri Lefebvre theorized something similar in the form of 'recuperation' – when capitalist culture absorbs and transforms that which threatens its dominance back into the status quo (2014, pp. 849–55). The transformation of torn jeans from a DIY punk statement against social class into an expensive fashion product is one example of recuperation in action. The mainstreaming of jazz, rap and hip hop are others.

The thought of recuperation prompts me to reflect on the canon critiques and counter-narrative strategies discussed in chapter five. While I don't wish to downplay any of these strategies – and still attest their ongoing importance – it now strikes me, they all target the canon's representative imbalances in isolation from the publishing industry. Yet as chapter four showed, the publishing industry majorly shaped the canon's early emergence, and the two remain profoundly interconnected. Attempts to expand or write back to the canon thus remain implicated in publishing, alongside other social institutions that also helped shape the canon, such as education and religion. This in turn implicates such attempts in mainstream western culture and capitalist economics. It therefore seems to me, any subversion or reworking of the canon remains vulnerable to recuperation back into the maintenance of the status quo – at least, if the contemporary publishing industry is not also subjected to scrutiny.

Compass

Chapter five discussed how literary critics, educators and creative writers have made the western literary canon a site of contestation via critiques and counter-narratives promoting change. These practices have brought some success, efforts that directly target the publishing industry are equally if not more important. This chapter considers, first, the efforts of twentieth century and contemporary independent publishers to promote writers the mainstream industry overlooks. Then I discuss ongoing social media movements such as *We Need Diverse Books* (WNDB, 2024), which pressures mainstream publishers to increase their ranges, with some degrees of success. However, the intricate entanglements of both publishing and social media in capitalist economics renders online activism susceptible to recuperation back into the economic, cultural, material and symbolic modes of reproduction that have characterized mainstream publishing since the 1400s at least (Kuskin, 2008). This is one of at least two factors limiting scope for long term change via demands for diverse books alone.

The second limiting factor is that such actions have to date typically foregrounded *whose* books are being published, without considering the influences editors and other publishing industry intermediaries bear on content and style. Such interventions date at least to the 1700s, when publishing of works by African American and First Nations authors was commonly mediated by religious institutions and/or colonial ethnographers. Today, editorial interventions still affect writers across many intersecting axes of identity. Interventions are frequently couched in notions of 'aesthetic superiority' or so-called literary merit and sustained in part via dominant education practices (Aston, 2017, p. 39). Creative writing education in the Philippines illustrates just how culturally domineering so-called literary merit can be (Cruz, 2017). This raises the need to consider how representation as re-presentation operates not only through what texts explicitly portray (as in chapter three), but also via textual aesthetics – the focus for Part Three.

Independent publishers

Chapter four emphasized publishing's links with religion, education, colonization and capitalist economics – and thus, publishing's involvement in reproducing hegemonies of social class, race, gender and more. However, like the western literary canon, publishing can also provide a site of contestation. Alongside the big money-making presses are independent ones who subvert dominant ideas about what is and is not worthy of publication. These publishers prioritize books that matter over churning profits, promoting works by writers the mainstream presses dismiss. Such publications sometimes prove big sellers, and independent presses thereby influence larger ones to rethink their assumptions, shifting the industry's dynamics (see discussion in Henningsgaard, 2019, p. 119). This section considers three independent press examples: Sheba Feminist Press, which in early 1980s Britain published books by authors including Audre Lorde and Barbara Burford (Withers, 2021, p. 364); Honno, the Welsh Women's Press, which was established in 1986 to publish feminist writing in both Welsh and English to help preserve and celebrate Welsh language and cultural identity both within Wales and to overseas readers (p. 357); and Magabala Books, an Australian press founded in 1987 by the Kimberley Law and Cultural Centre 'expressly to publish Indigenous writing by and for Indigenous readers' (Freeman, 2010, p. 3).

The contrasting trajectories of Sheba and Honno starkly illustrate the vulnerabilities such publishing ventures bear to economic and other circumstances beyond the publishers' control. While Honno, which has received consistent support from Welsh government funding grants, remains the longest-running women's press of their scale in the world, Sheba suffered the 'catastrophic impact' of funding was suddenly withdrawn under the Thatcher government in the late 1980s (Withers, 2021, p. 364). Sheba subsequently 'struggled to sustain their activities in an environment that called upon the not-for-profit workers' co-operate to sharpen its "business wits"' – a tough objective to meet given Sheba lost not only its own funding, but also partnerships that previously provided distribution and promotion networks, and thus sales income (p. 364). This was because countless organizations previously crucial to their 'cultural ecology' of 'cultural and social services delivered by and for minority groups' (particularly 'gay, lesbian, Black and Asian, women and disabled' people) also relied on the same funding and lost it at the same time (p. 364). In contrast, much of Honno's capacity to survive relates to its 'alternative value criteria' in the eyes of the Welsh government, particularly its capacities for 'promoting the idea of "Welsh distinctiveness"' via their Welsh language publications and 'project[ing] "a new image of Wales across the world"' to boost tourism and pride in national identity (pp. 366–7). The 'Our partners' page of Magabala's website (Magabala, 2024) reflects a similar situation:

> Our partnerships are vital to ensuring the diversity and dynamism of our publishing program and social impact projects is realised. We couldn't do all that we do without the incredible support of our major government, corporate, community and philanthropic partners. (para. 1)

Though currently successful, both Honno and Magabala thus rely, as Sheba did, on cultural ecologies in turn dependent on 'interconnections across value chains' and 'embeddedness in regional and national economies' (Withers, 2021, p. 368). The same applies for many funding-reliant presses and literary magazines in other parts of the world, which, like Sheba and Britain's cultural industries in the 1980s, could be 'dramatically disrupted if changes to its structures were introduced too quickly, without attentiveness to how its parts relate to the whole' (p. 368). Exceptions to the rule include privately-funded presses run by people with the capacity to spend their own funds on publishing as a passion project, or supported by non-government philanthropists. While many of these presses do indeed present excitingly radical catalogues, the costs in setting up one's own press are unfeasible for most people from marginalized backgrounds, which effectively reproduces a situation not unlike literary patronage wherein marginalized writers depend on the good will of those better off. Also of note is that there are many parts of the world where government and/or philanthropic support is not available. Indeed, some publishers not only need to self-fund, but contend with additional challenges of government censorship and/or legal consequences (Fernandez-Moya & Puig, 2021, p. 1282). Paradoxically, capitalist economics sometimes proves advantageous in such cases: otherwise, draconian governments exhibit flexibility around censorship if a publishing business is seen to offer significant benefits to the country's economy (p. 1277). But this relies on commercial appeal to global market demands shaped by white western tastes.

As long as capitalism persists, then, independent publishers in most cases must still attend to what Magabala Books editor Rachel Bin Salleh's remarks on as 'the commercial imperative of publishing' (Bin Salleh & Vaarwerk, 2022, p. 147). This is challenging in many cases, as the target audiences for books by and about people marginalized by dominant culture will typically have less disposable cash for buying books, regardless of how keen they are to read them. These readers will strategize by using libraries, buying second-hand or sharing copies among friends. This means lower sales comparable with books marketed to target audiences who can buy books without a thought, place them on shelves unread and forget them. Sales statistics do not reliably indicate how much a book is loved or the impact it creates. Furthermore, even when independent presses' target readerships *do* bear capacity to purchase, such presses typically have smaller budgets for marketing than their mainstream counterparts, making it harder to spread awareness about new titles. But small presses and marginalized authors have allies on this front in the form of reviewers and cultural influencers who offer recommendations of their books and/or seek to change mainstream ideas about what is and isn't a good read. For instance, chapter five already noted how educators have helped create markets for books outside the mainstream via their work to expand the western literary canon and/or set reading lists. More recently, social media influencers have come to play a major role, too. The next section examines their impact – and constraints.

Social media activism

In the same sense, authors write not books but words the publishing process transforms into books and physical commodities (Joseph, 2019, p. 23), the publishing industry is but one among many 'producers of the meaning and value of the work … agents whose combined efforts produce consumers capable of knowing and recognizing the work of art as such' (Bourdieu, 1993, cited in Tomasena, 2019, p. 2). It is important to consider how 'editors, academic critics, common readers, and mass media reviewers' take part in 'shaping textual forms, literary reputations, and literary tastes' (Graham & Ward, 2011, p. 2). Especially notable across recent years have been the changes stirred by readers acting as reviewers and cultural influencers – and the changing demographics of those undertaking these roles. Literary criticism and cultural commentary were in the past often limited to those from backgrounds of privilege who could publish articles and reviews in literary, academic and mainstream journals, magazines and newspapers. Such figures might also have been invited to share opinions on public panels, radio or television. Since the late twentieth century, technological changes have opened such practices to far more people. Reviewers and cultural influencers now reflect a much broader range of people including young readers, people from socio-economic backgrounds and/or personal circumstances of struggle, people with disabilities or neurodivergences that previously hindered participation, and those whose participation was hindered by other intersecting factors of social power. These figures are speaking up to tell publishers what they want to read, demanding more books about characters beyond the white and privileged ones who have hitherto dominated literary representation (WNDB, 2024).

Examples of online platforms on which everyday readers air their reaction to books and publishing include but are not limited to Goodreads, reviews on bookseller websites, podcasting, and vlogging (video-blogging) as a mode of social media influencing (Tomasena, 2019, p. 1). A key example of social media activism to change publishing is the #WeNeedDiverseBooks movement (#WNDB). #WNDB originated via a Twitter exchange between authors Ellen Oh and Malinda Lo expressing 'their frustration with the lack of diversity in kidlit . . . in response to the all-white, all-male panel of children's authors assembled for BookCon's May 31 reader event' (WNDB, 2024). This piqued the interest of 'other authors, bloggers, and industry folks' who 'piped up saying they would like to be involved as well' and led to 'a three-day event . . . to raise awareness, brainstorm solutions, and take action (Diversify Your Shelves)' with the first use of the #WeNeedDiverseBooks / #WNDB hashtag being made by Aisha Saeed on 24 April, soon after which it 'started taking off, officially trending for the first time on April 29' (WNDB, 2024).

The rapid rise of the #WNDB hashtag is demonstrative of the significant cultural force social media activism bears. WeNeedDiverseBooks has since grown into a not-for-profit organization focused on the vision of a 'world where everyone can find themselves in the pages of a book' (WNDB, 2024). Alongside related social media movements, #WNDB has helped generate 'sustained interest in the issue [of inclusion] among readers, booksellers, librarians, bookbloggers, and industry professionals' (Booth & Narayan, 2018, p. 196). The publishing industry has been forced to sit up, take note and publish more titles catering to these tastes (p. 196). Some book bloggers even become celebrities in their own rights, with significant capacity to sway the purchases of those who visit and subscribe to their channels, acquiring 'social capital and a sense of what their audience wants that is highly valuable for publishers' (Tomasena, 2019, p. 2). They represent 'key players' for a publishing industry undergoing 'deep transformation regarding how books are marketed, distributed, and sold' (p. 1).

There are at least two reasons for caution around overestimating the successes social media activism has won and stands to produce in the longer term. The first can be demonstrated via the #OwnVoices movement. #OwnVoices originated on social media through a Twitter hashtag created in 2015 by young adult literature author Corinne Duyvis for 'kidlit about diverse characters written by authors from that same diverse group' (Duyvis, 2015, cited in Crisp et al., 2020, p. 5). Through #OwnVoices, Duyvis issued 'a call to privilege the voices of those who have been traditionally marginalized in publishing' through the raising of questions regarding 'questions of multiculturalism; the complexities of identities; the roles, functions, and responsibilities of youth literature; and who has the "right" to tell which stories' (cited in Crisp et al., 2021, pp. 5–6). The hashtag was subsequently 'adopted by the YA [young adult] fiction bookblogger community, and diversity advocacy groups more broadly', which initially included WeNeedDiverseBooks (Booth & Narayan, 2018, p. 197). But in 2021, #WNDB issued a blog post explaining they would no longer be using the #OwnVoices hashtag and were removing it from previously published online materials, instead opting to 'use specific descriptions that authors use for themselves and their characters whenever possible (for example, "Korean American author," or "autistic protagonist")' (Lavoie, 2021, para. 1). #WNDB explained how the hashtag, originally 'intended as a shorthand book recommendation tool in a Twitter thread, for readers to recommend books by authors who openly shared the diverse identity of their main characters' had 'expanded in its use to become a "catch all" marketing term by the publishing industry', stirring issues of 'the vagueness of the term' and its capacity 'to place diverse creators in uncomfortable and potentially unsafe situations' (Lavoie, 2021, para 2). I personally also find using 'diverse' to indicate everyone o/Other to the hegemonic norm uncomfortable, which is why I signal 'so-called diverse voices' in subsequent discussions of this movement.

That the publishing industry so quickly turned #OwnVoices into a marketing tool reflects Henri Lefebvre's notion of 'recuperation' – dominant culture's tendency to absorb resistance back into the status quo (Lefebvre, 2014, pp. 849–55). It is also a reminder of social media's deep embeddedness in capitalist economics. This embeddedness is, paradoxically, part of how and why social media activism has made an impact – by striking publishers where it hurts (Tomasena, 2019). But it also renders blook vloggers and other social media influences caught in economic, cultural and symbolic processes of capital, and thereby in modes of reproduction perhaps not so different from those Kuskin (2008) raises in relation to Caxton and the early print industry. To gain the subscribers who bring them influence, social media critics need to impress their audiences – or in other words, 'use their accumulated social capital . . . to establish themselves as key players' (Tomasena, 2019, p. 4). One way to do this is by playing to existing trends. Another is demonstrating connectedness in elite literary circles via interviews with important authors, attending exclusive literary events, and/or getting access to new releases before they hit the shelves for general readers.

Aware of the dynamics driving social media popularity, publishers court influencers into relationships of 'collaboration' – deals that 'are not necessarily monetary, but constitute the core of the symbolic and material exchanges with which they participate in the literary field' (Tomasena, 2019, p. 6). For instance, '[p]ublishers invite them to special events, like movie premieres or meetups with their authors', and provide 'free books in exchange for reviews', including advance copies (pp. 6–7). Major commercial publishers bear greater capacity to offer such rewards than smaller ethically driven ones do. As a result, influencers often 'compromise their autonomy', becoming part of the industry and less able to critique it (p. 9). Mainstream publishing thus retains its 'power to confer cultural legitimacy, even when authors have a much wider audience in digital platforms', and can continue 'reinforcing the values and logic of mainstream publication' while 'leaving unnoticed . . . the eccentric, marginal, and revolutionary books' (p. 10).

The second reason for caution around over-estimating the change-making capacities of social media movements to sway mainstream publishing is that these movements tend to focus so heavily whose voices gain airtime, they ignore the role played by editors and other intermediaries.

Publishing interventions into textual content

African American literature from the 1700s and 1800s provides a strong illustration of the ways in which the publishing industry may even through promoting so-called diverse voices still massage content towards ideologies of the status quo. Although writing and publishing offered powerful platforms for activism against the transatlantic slave trade (Gould, 2011, p. 40), their radicality remained constrained by the fact most early works were 'as-told-to narratives . . . recorded by white amanuenses' (Carretta, 2011, p. 52). As Philip Gould observes, 'the very act of entering the "public sphere"' for African American writers involved negotiation of 'fragile dynamics between black subjects and white authorities – editors, patrons, and/or publishers' (2011, p. 40). The amanuenses who transcribed the narratives and the publishers who produced them as books were mostly Protestant Christian missionaries (Carretta, 2011, p. 54). It thus seems unsurprising most African American literary works printed at the time endorsed the Protestant faith, particularly through conversion narratives and poems about Christian spirituality (p. 55). Even where amanuenses weren't required, African American authors who didn't believe – and weren't willing to feign belief – in Protestantism lacked access to the same publishing avenues, and those who could gain access were seemingly encouraged to tell stories supporting their publishers' agendas (p. 55).

For instance, Phillis Wheatley, whose poems 'frequently combined Christian piety and Classical allusions' was in the late 1700s among the first African American poets to attract a wide audience beyond American shores among British poetry readers (Carretta, 2011, p. 58). Wheatley endorsed not only Christianity, but also the British monarchy via the dedication of a poetry book to the Countess of Huntingdon (who graciously 'allowed' Wheatley to do so) (Carretta, 2011, p. 59). It is hard to know how many of Wheatley's pro-religious and pro-monarchy statements reflected her own genuine sentiments versus to what degree Wheatley perhaps strategically deployed these tropes as a means towards literary and personal empowerment via Protestant Christianity as an institution that 'gave blacks the authority and opportunity to guide others through speech and print' conditional upon an 'expectation that Christians bear witness to their faith' (Carretta, 2011, p. 55). As Vincent Carretta (2011) observes:

> Undoubtedly underlying the emphasis on religion in most of the writings by eighteenth-century black authors was the long-standing belief that conversation to Christianity merited emancipation from slavery. (p. 55)

Indeed, Wheatley's international success did lead to her freedom being granted. Following emancipation '[h]er antislavery stance became more overt than in her poems published while she had been enslaved' (Carretta, 2011, pp. 60–1), perhaps reflecting previous need for caution about expressing activist views too explicitly. Beyond religion, African American writers also found stronger chances of publication if they played to white tastes by telling 'tales that combine elements of adventure, conversion, crime, and travel' (Carretta, 2011, p. 54) or via recourse to white-western ideologies (Gould, 2011, p. 40).

In pre- and early twentieth century Australia, the church's role in mediating publication of First Nations literature is perhaps even more problematic. Traditional stories were frequently co-opted into 'the production of nationalist myth-making' – 'the appropriation and re-making of Indigeneity' to serve colonial agendas (Nettelbeck, 2008, p. 9). Religious missionaries and ethnographers frequently transcribed stories and song cycles not intended for public sharing, publishing these works under their own names rather than those of the people who shared their knowledge, and reshaping them in ways that reinscribed First Nations Australian spiritual practices as '"religion," or primitive forms of Christian practice' (Rademaker, 2020, p. 1). The first Aboriginal writer to be recognized as such in the non-Indigenous Australian mainstream was David Unaipon, a mission-educated lay preacher and pamphleteer who wrote, lectured and preached widely on 'strong parallels' between Aboriginal spirituality and Christian beliefs (Leane, 2015, p. 28). Yet even Unaipon's major work (Unaipon, 1930/2006), was initially published under the name of non-Indigenous Australian anthropologist W. Ramsey Smith, who seemingly took the manuscript under the pretence of helping Unaipon publish it, then claimed the work (and profits) as his own (Leane, 2015, p. 29). Unaipon's authorship was posthumously asserted in 2001 by scholars Adam Shoemaker and Stephen Muecke, who with the help of Unaipon's descendants, the Kropinyeri family, retrieved the original manuscript from the State Library of New South Wales to prove it was Unaipon, not Ramsey Smith, who had written it (Leane, 2015, p. 29).

First Nations Australian memoirs also frequently seem to have been selected by publishers for content capable of 'tapping white middle-class interest' (Thomas, 1988, p. 755). For instance, Morgan's *My Place* (1987) has been critiqued for appeals to 'liberal racial attitudes based on a sense of common humanity' (Thomas, 1988, p. 761). Playing into such attitudes may be seen to undo the book's radical force because they are also 'used to support assimilationist and integrationist racial policies' favoured by 'white, middle-class swinging voters' equally enthralled with 'right-wing policies and economic pragmatism' (p. 761).

Similar issues pertain to gay and lesbian writing in the 1970s – which I refer to as such because cis men and women's writings of same sex attraction developed as 'separate and gendered canons' from which bisexual, transgender and intersex experiences were excluded (Carlin, 2012). The gay and lesbian literary genres were themselves defined by cissexist notions of 'sex as biologically determined' that govern 'the social/political world through (en)gendered systems of power' (Carlin, 2012, p. 344). Only certain kinds of queer stories were deemed publishable, on criteria supporting ongoing subjugation of o/Other LGBTQIA+ lives by 'a homophobic publishing industry and an often stridently antagonistic literary reviewing establishment [that] shaped what novels made it into print and the reception they received if fortunate enough to be published' (p. 346).

Despite improvements since the 1970s, queer young adult publishing remains dominated by stories about 'coming out' (publicly revealing one's sexuality or gender), which, while an important step for many LGBTQIA+ people, is not common to all members of the community, and reflects but one among many LGBTQIA+ concerns (Bowden, 2021, p. 67). Also problematic is the 'limited cultural and geographic perspective of queer gender' such narratives tend to provide of primarily 'white and middle-class . . . American' protagonists (p. 75). Likewise with disability and neurodiversity, publishers seem to prefer narratives falling into 'one of two camps: a portrayal of how awful it is to be disabled, or a character striving to overcome their disability to prove to themselves and the world that they've triumphed over tragedy' (Batchelor, 2023, para. 2).

Even when superficially promoting so-called diverse voices, mainstream publishing thus heavily curates these voices' articulations. Its ways of doing so often reify ideologies of the hegemonic status quo counter to the broader interests of marginalized communities. This section has considered how the publishing industry mediates textual content. The next considers style.

Publishing interventions into style and the myth of literary merit

For so-called diverse voices in the publishing industry, demands to satisfy mainstream tastes involve not only textual content, but also style. African American literature from the 1700s and 1800s again provides strong illustration of how mediation of style has historically manifested, and why it is of political concern. As Keith Leonard (2011) and Mark A. Sanders (2011) separately note, African American poetry published in the late 1800s and early 1900s typically reflected one of two broad tendencies – Romanticist lyrics in Standard English styled after figures like Tennyson and Keats (Leonard, 2011, p. 209) and dialect poetry that 'used phonetics to replicate a version of African American speech' (p. 206). Both involved complex negotiation of agential constraints and compromises. African American writers who produced lyric poetry effectively capitulated to the dominant white culture's privileging of literary devices from British and European and its erasure of the equally complex devices characteristic to African people's own rich long-standing history of literary creation – for instance, the varied forms and sub-forms of 'Signification' ('direct attention to the way in which language is used') discussed by Henry Louis Gates Jr (1988, p. 21). In Frantz Fanon's terms, taking on the syntax and morphology of a given language 'means above all to assume a culture, to support the weight of a civilization' and someone 'who has a language consequently possesses the world expressed and implied by that language' (1986, pp. 17–18). To write in the lyric form was thus to take on white values and ways of thinking. This was a strategic and agential compromise on the parts of many writers who used lyric poetry for activism, but nonetheless reflects the oppressive frameworks they were forced to navigate.

African American writers who opted for the dialect style also took on a white-created genre – one with particularly fraught connections to slavery and white dominance. For although dialect poetry is often initiated by speakers of the dialect themselves who mobilize it as defiance against the status quo (see chapter five), in the case of African American dialect poetry, the genre was one 'white Southern writers had created for such stereotypical characters as happy darkies, picaninnies, sambos, coons, and mammies [sic]' who 'often expressed their own and their creators' nostalgia for the days of slavery' (Leonard, 2011, p. 206). Sanders likens early dialect poetry to racist 'blackface' performance, noting how the 'awkward pronunciation (often signaled through misspelled words), grammatical errors, and malapropisms' of the genre 'announced the comic feebleness of black speech and thus black being' (2011, p. 221). However, dialect poetry's existing popularity among white audiences made it a genre African American writers could lever via textual re-placing to subvert the stereotypes by turning flat stock characters into round people deserving empathy, and by providing more authentic accounts of African American experience. One poet who achieved success via this strategy was Lawrence Dunbar, who with the support of white patron and dialect poetry writer James Whitcomb Riley 'travelled the country sharing with his mostly white audiences his versions of the wit and charm and humor associated with these stereotypical characters' (Leonard, 2011, p. 206).

The inner conflict Dunbar experienced about working in the dialect poetry genre is evidence in his metaphor 'the mask that grins and lies' to signify 'how

African Americans, whether poets or not, had at times to adapt versions of these popular images [racist stereotypes] in their daily interactions with whites in order to survive' (Leonard, 2011, p. 207). By Leonard's analysis 'the mask was burden, protection, and motive for public self-definition' (p. 207). Dunbar also wrote poems in the romanticist lyric style, often publishing his two styles of work alongside each other as a gesture to remind readers he was knowingly deploying a 'broken tongue' style in his dialect poems not because he was ignorant of grammar but to meet generic conventions. His lyric poems meanwhile demonstrated his expert command of Standard English and traditional white western literary aesthetics. By showing his mastery of the two forms' distinct conventions, he engaged a 'multiple paradox that conservative racial uplift, black folk culture, and Eurocentric poetic conventions and ideals could serve together as the foundation of progressive ethnic affirmation' (Leonard, 2011, p. 208), thereby 'rework[ing] the mask to reveal the difficulty of articulating a black self fully in the language of Reconstruction-era culture' (p. 210). Leonard (2011) attests:

> Dunbar was not, as some critics have suggested, writing his dialect for black audiences and the Standard English for the white, nor was he simply speaking in a double voice, forking its tongue for both audiences at once. Rather he was affirming what he saw to be common values in different cultural forms, a practice that revealed both that which prevented blacks from seeming to achieve those values and the cultural source by which they did achieve it. (p. 210)

In these ways, Dunbar managed to negotiate white readers', editors' and publishers' expectations in radical ways, activating strong creative agency in the face of tight constraints. Nonetheless, his need to do so is again reflective of the extensive modes of oppression at play. I wonder, how might he have styled his poems if not bound to these frameworks?

Constraints on literary style resembling those enforced on eighteenth and nineteenth century African American writers are observable across multiple intersecting axes of social identity, through the twentieth century and beyond. For instance, the Australian First Nations writers Oodgeroo Noonuccal, Margaret Tucker and Monica Clare all represent Aboriginal rights activists as well as writers who in the 1970s became some of the first Aboriginal Australian women to be published by mainstream publishers and achieve dominant literary success (Butler, 2009, p. 147). As literary historian Jennifer Jones shows in *Black Writers, White Editors* (2009), all had troubled dealings with editors who amended their original manuscripts to fit notions of literary merit the editors believed would make the books more saleable with white readers. In this way, 'the distinctive, political vision of their narratives was altered to conform to the expectations of a white reading public' (Butler, 2009, p. 147).

Per Henningsgaard (2019) raises similar issues regarding Alexis Wright's *Carpentaria* (2006), which was first published by Giramondo Press. In a public interview, Giramondo editor Ivor Indyk relayed how on receiving the manuscript he found the language 'ungrammatical but expressive' and 'really wanted to work on it' (Indyk, 2006, cited in Henningsgaard, 2019, p. 119). When the book was first released, reviewers routinely remarked not only on Wright's literary talent but Indyk's editorial prowess, attributing him 'a creative influence that is rarely credited to a publisher of white-signed texts' while patronisingly implying Wright's success to be reliant on his input (Ravenscroft, 2012, cited in Henningsgaard, 2019, p. 119). Likewise notable are Tyson Yunkaporta's remarks about the need he feels to reconfigure traditional modes of Indigenous storytelling and craft narratives western readers can comprehend in line with different understandings of temporality and what a story / Story ought to be (2023, p. 15).

Regarding writing about gender and sexuality, feminist and queer writers have critiqued the 'phallogocentrism' of dominant language and literary conventions favoured by mainstream publishers. 'Phallogocentrism' indicates 'masculinism of Western European knowledge systems and discourse, based on privileging the male signifier and identifying this with the hegemonic *Logos*' as a set of 'rationalized representational powers attributed to speech and language, and thus to the masculine persona in science and philosophy' (Sandywell, 2011, p. 461). To counter phallogocentrism, feminist and queer writers have mobilized techniques of 'écriture feminine' (writing the feminine) and queer writing figuring 'nonlinear and fragmented' modes of language and textual structure designed to represent feminine experiences and queer lives in more authentic ways (Shihab, 2019, p. 69). Disabled writers raise similar critiques regarding dominant 'expectations' of illness stories including both 'the events and the narrative of those events, the way they are told' (Wasson, 2023, p. 284). For instance, in the case of chronic pain, '[c]ultural contexts and expectations of illness story influence what can be heard in pain, what can be known about it, and who is respected as knowing' (p. 284). Strategies of 'unsettling certain conventions of writing or illness expression' though experimental writing techniques thus become 'matters of epistemic justice' (p. 284).

Yet these experimental writing practices remain largely marginal practices, for mainstream publishers tend to favour more conventional styles they claim bear greater literary merit. Literary merit in these contexts appears euphemistic for alignment with the formal and stylistic conventions developed in and favoured by traditional western canonical literature by dead white middle class males (Nicol, 2008, p. 23). The notion of literary merit – I dare say, the *myth* thereof – thereby becomes a gatekeeping device for justifying ongoing representative imbalances in favour of privileged groups or admitting so-called diverse voices only on the condition that they sing in the dominant key by appeasing hegemonically defined tastes.

The hegemonic force the myth of literary merit wield is evident in the Filipino context, where it has served imposition of white western ideas onto local people – in other words, cultural colonization. As Conchitina Cruz (2017) explains, Filipino literature is dominated by aesthetic ideals promoted by the Silliman Workshop, a creative writing education program founded in the 1960s by Filipino husband and wife Edilberto K. Tiempo and Edith Tiempo (Cruz, 2017, p. 5). Both had in the 1950s studied creative writing at the Iowa Writers' Workshop in the United States of America through an American government scholarships program (p. 5). These scholarships were part of a post-World War Two 'cultural diplomacy' program via which America sought to 'create a "foundation of trust" with other peoples, which policy makers can build on to reach political, economic, and military agreements' (Engle, 1967, cited in Cruz, 2017, p. 12). The scholarship program was part of a broader strategy in America's cultural colonization of the Philippines wherein 'education was, first and foremost, a military strategy' that 'taught Filipinos to idolize American heroes and to view Filipino resistance leaders as '"brigands and outlaws"'' (Cruz, 2017, p. 8). Cruz characterizes Eldiberto Tiempo as 'a clear-cut embodiment of the colonial subject shaped by both militarization and education' (p. 9).

At the time the Tiempos attended it, the Iowa Workshop was dominated by New Criticism, which emphasized 'art for art's sake', depoliticizing literature through its 'teachable mechanics for analyzing the autonomous artwork that was disentangled from the web of authorship, history, and material and sociopolitical realities' (Cruz, 2017, p. 16). New Criticism's tenets set those of the Tiempos' Silliman Workshop, which in turn became the model for other creative writing education programs in the Philippines. In line with New Critical emphases on a 'universalism and timelessness' (Cruz, 2017, p. 17), the Silliman Workshop also insists on monolingual literary production in 'accent-less' English, implying its linguistic and cultural superiority to the Filipino language (pp. 7, 17). Fanon's points regarding language as a colonizing strategy bearing 'the weight of a civilization' again seem relevant here (1986, p. 21).

Although New Criticism has since fallen out of favour in America and most other countries where it once held prominence, it remains central to the pedagogies of the Filipino Silliman Workshop, which 'dominates the tradition of Philippine literature' (Cruz, 2017, p. 5). For aspiring Filipino writers, attending the Silliman Workshop is a pathway to success and 'cultural capital through connections' (p. 15) with an 'all-too-welcoming band of sisters and brothers happy to pass on and share their global networking experiences' (Yuson, 2015, cited in Cruz, 2017, p. 15). Those who don't attend the workshop and/or subscribe to its New Critical aesthetics face a tougher path. The Silliman Workshop acts as 'literary gatekeeper many times over' against writers who try to operate outside its terms, 'as evident in the degree-granting programs, award giving bodies, university and mainstream presses, and creative writing classrooms that privilege and replicate the aesthetics and politics it systematized' (Cruz, 2017, p. 26).

The Filipino situation, coupled with the other examples this section has noted of how publishing companies massage so-called diverse voices into the dominant key illustrate why current activism foregrounding whose books are published can only go so far – as can efforts of canon critique. To affect more significant change, these movements need to incorporate critique of the systems via which literary merit is judged. As part three demonstrates, form and structure are not mere window dressing: they actively shape what texts can and cannot articulate, which drives a need for politically oriented readers and writers to carefully consider what chapter seven calls *aesthetics as content*.

Re-orienting

This chapter has explored publishing's role in shaping representative imbalances. I first considered independent publishers, which bear important impact by promoting writers the mainstream industry overlooks, but remain constrained by challenges of economic survival within capitalist frameworks. I then considered book marketing, particularly social media activism, which has made gains in pushing mainstream presses to promote so-called diverse voices. However, publishers may mobilize these voices in ways that reify mainstream ideologies via mediation of content and style. The myth of literary merit serves to obscure the cultural domination enacted via demands on writers to edit their style towards hegemonically defined tastes. Need exists to consider how representation as re-presentation operates not only through what texts explicitly portray, but also via implicit features of textual aesthetics. Part Three therefore explores the operations of *aesthetics as content*.

Notwithstanding the limitations just outlined, strategies of canon critique, counter-narrative, independent publishing and social media activism remain valuable. Their limitations merely signal the need to combine them with the considerations part three explores. Praxis module two's experiments prepare for those explorations via activities to consolidate and extend concepts from this chapter and the previous two.

PRAXIS MODULE TWO: CONTESTING CANONS AND PUBLISHING

Overview of experiments:

This module's experiments extend key points from part two. As with module one's experiments, they are adaptable for group learning in formal education, as well as independent practice. The key points include:

1 The role of **canons** and **publishing** in maintaining existing imbalances of representation as re-presentation that in turn help maintain intersecting hegemonies of social inequity.

2 The possibilities canons and publishing present as **sites of contestation** at which to call out inequities and promote change.

3 **Canon critiques** by literary theorists and educators (including postcolonial, decolonial, anticolonial, Marxian, feminist, queer, disabled and/or neurodiverse approaches)

4 The creative strategies writers engage to generate **counter-narratives** (including through life writing, poetry, textual re-placing, and speculative fiction).

Experiments one and two both relate primarily to points one and two. Experiment three relates primarily to points three and four. However, once again, all points are relevant to all experiments and vice versa.

Experiment one: contemplating canonical encounters

Think back to your previous education experiences. List ten texts you recall studying, which could include novels, plays, poems, short stories, films, or works of creative non-fiction. These are in effect the canon to which you were / are exposed. For each text, note the following things:

- The main setting/s and cultural norms associated with the setting.

- The main protagonists and their relationships with intersecting axes of identity (you may like to use the privilege mapping tool from praxis module one, exercise one).

- The main antagonists and their relationships with intersecting axes of identity (see bracketed note above).

- The minor characters and their relationships with intersecting axes of identity (see same note again).

- Do any characters appear to be stereotypes, flat characters, tokenistic representations, and/or problematic misrepresentations (e.g. criminalization of particular social groups)?

- What normative attitudes and values do characters express regarding axes of privilege such as gender, race, and social class?

- What normative attitudes and values do characters express regarding human relations with beyond-human being?

Based on your collated answers for all ten texts, reflect on the following points:

- Which social groups and/or culture/s does this canon primarily represent as main character protagonists and/or seem to align with via the cultural attitudes it portrays as normative?

- Which other social groups and/or cultures does this canon represent, and how does it represent them (e.g. as antagonists, tokenistically, etc.)?

- Which social groups are altogether absent?

- What attitudes do these texts generally normalize regarding human relationships with place, the environment and/or beyond-human actors? (If these relationships seem absent, or lacking significance, then it is possible the text normalizes detachment, indifference, and perhaps uprootedness.)

- What sorts of readers would be most likely to relate to the main characters and other aspects of the texts in this canon?

- What sorts of readers might feel alienated from these texts or struggle to connect with the dominant sorts of characters and themes?

Using your notes from both previous stages of this process, respond in one or both of the following ways:

- Critical response: produce a personal essay about your experiences studying this canon of texts. Include contemplation of which texts you liked and/or disliked. How do these reactions relate to the ways in which the texts do or do not represent experiences relevant to your own cultural background and intersectional identity? If possible, also consider how peers or other readers responded to the same texts in similar or different ways, and how those responses relate to intersecting axes of power relations. Work towards expressing a perspective on how this canon use contributed to the maintenance or unsettling of established power relations in the context where you studied it (e.g. did it reflect and reinstate existing norms, or had the educator who selected the texts perhaps done so with a conscious aim of challenging the status quo and signalling alternative possibilities?)

- Creative response: instead of an essay – or in addition to one – express the same ideas creatively via a story or poem in which the characters are students and educators studying the same canon of ten texts. You may like to extend the story forward five, ten, or more years into the future to ponder the effects these texts had (or failed to have) on each reader. Or you could apply a speculative fiction approach, for instance by imagining how people in a futuristic setting might respond to those same texts in a context where norms of language and culture have changed

Experiment two: canon (re)making

Create your own canon featuring ten texts you believe would be engaging and important for young people in your own time, place, and context (attempting to create a universal canon from such a small number of texts would be unfeasible, but playing to the needs of a particular time, place, and situation is slightly more feasible, albeit still very challenging). Aim to include a balanced mix of windows and mirrors for readers across as many intersections of identity as you can. Then submit your list to scrutiny using the dot points from experiment one. If you feel comfortable doing so, you can swap lists with a peer and critique each other. Bear in mind that it is incredibly difficult, if not impossible, for ten texts to reflect everybody's perspectives and interests. Don't feel bad if you fail. Instead, contemplate the challenges, complexities, and potential other approaches to this problem. Use these as the basis for an essay or a piece of creative writing (e.g. a story about an educator struggling to find ways to make all their students feel seen and valuable).

Experiment three: canonical re-placing

Choose a canonical text or genre and creatively rewrite it using strategies discussed in chapter six (see section on textual re-placing). This might include telling the story from a different character's point of view, imagining in characters who were absent in the original, or transporting the story into a different time and place (which could also involve a speculative fiction approach).

PART THREE

AESTHETICS AS (POLITICAL) CONTENT

7 AESTHETICS AS CONTENT

Walking/writing out of style

I'm getting old. I know this because my interior monologues are increasingly interrupted by silent outcries of shock and befuddlement at the fashion choices of women younger than myself. The current trend in activewear – or at least, what the twenty-somethings in my town are sporting for hikes – is tight fluorescent crop tops and Lycra shorts that seem no more than underwear. *Get some clothes on!* the outraged biddy inside my head screams – to my shame. These are thoughts I don't want to have, thoughts contradicting the version of intersectional queer feminism towards which my more conscious, rational self otherwise gravitates. Everyone should have the right to wear what they choose. Human bodies are nothing to be prudish about. I remind myself, in my teens I used to go about flashing midriff too – a smaller amount, mind, but risqué by previous generations' standards. Indeed, *Get some clothes on!* was precisely what my mother used to yell at me as I flounced out the door, rolling my eyes as some of these young women perhaps do with their own mothers now. And no doubt, some of these women as they pass me must be looking on my own clothing choices with equal horror (or perhaps pity).

Choices was an ambitious word selection: most days I barely glance at myself before heading out the door. When the morning alarm goes, I groan, mumble, stumble from bed, swill a big hot mug of tea, throw on whatever, and set out before I'm tempted to just crawl back under the covers. More than once I've returned to discover a white dribble of toothpaste caked like a snail trail down my chin. My go-to look is crinkled shorts and baggy T-shirts, many of them speckled with paint or tile adhesive from the DIY renovations my partner and I did last year. My hiking attire thus sits squarely in the realm of 'non fashion', which fashion sociologist Anna-Maria Almila defines within a system also including 'fashion' and 'anti-fashion' (2016, p. 83). Fashion indicates dressing in line with what is 'considered fashionable or stylish' (p. 83) according to 'constantly changing' trends (p. 85). Anti-fashion entails 'consciously "against fashion"' (p. 86). Non-fashion differs from anti-fashion as less an active rejection and more a 'lack of interest' or inability to participate due to constraints of time, energy, and/or funds (p. 92).

Fashion, anti-fashion and non-fashion co-exist in an interrelational dynamics, rather than as categorical oppositions. Mutually formative, they together weave a complex system of 'social behaviour' wherein 'comparisons between individuals and groups' mediate social status hierarchies of 'differentiation *and* belonging' (Almila, 2016, p. 85, original italics). In these ways, the fashion system is intricately bound with capital – cultural and symbolic as well as economic varieties. Most obviously, adhering to fashion can garner cultural capital by showing one is up with the times and possesses disposable economic resources – fashion being after all a 'system' that 'requires certain economic and material conditions' (p. 85). However, fashion afficionados risk being viewed as 'superficial' (p. 85). Displays of anti-fashion and non-fashion can become an assertion of superiority (p. 86). Some women (myself included, at times) also reject fashion in efforts to reduce the 'male gaze' of unwanted sexual attention (p. 89).

Regardless of whether one seeks to fit in, rebel or opt out, the parameters of what constitutes fashion, anti-fashion and non-fashion are neither timeless nor universal but culturally contextual and ever in flux (Almila, 2016). What represents anti- or non-fashion in one situation may become fashion in another and vice versa. Often, the ways in which the fashion system changes reflect its entanglements with broader socio-cultural and economic relations of power (p. 85). The same point pertains to notions of physical beauty in general (Reischer & Koo, 2004). There are those who would have us believe certain factors represent timeless universal traits of attractiveness, but differences in beauty ideals across cultures and within the same culture at different points in time reveal beauty standards to be strongly subjective and socially conditioned (p. 300). In line with chapter two's points about subjectification, illusions of beauty as a universally objective measure arise via cultural, symbolic and discursive processes that surreptitiously assimilate human subjects into the norms and value systems of their given social situations (Jarrin, 2017, p. 11). Notions of what constitutes beauty emerge 'from accumulated layers of historical and cultural patterns that give meaning to the body' and which 'become habitual at a preconscious level', making perception of beauty seem natural and instinctive when in fact 'perception itself emerges as an embodied response to social relationships' (p. 11).

Socially conditioned beauty ideals typically reflect ideologies bearing underlying economic and/or power-related forces (Reischer & Koo, 2004). In western cultures during times when food was scarce, plumpness was preferred over thinness because plumpness indicated socio-economic status evidenced by access to food (p. 300). Now, low-calorie foods are more expensive, while cheap high-calorie options abound, and mainstream western body size ideals are largely reversed (p. 300). Skin tone is another example: where tanned skin suggests the need to labour outdoors due to low socio-economic standing, pale skin is preferred, but if a tan is associated with resources for enjoying outdoor leisure, it becomes desirable (Martin et al., 2009). Skin tone ideals may also reflect racial hegemonies (Jarrin, 2017). Judgements about people's appearances thus often facilitate unconscious judgements of social class, race and other intersecting axes of identity. But beauty's 'preconscious' affect masks the discrimination at play (p. 11). Some people even believe it is 'moral' to judge physical bodies as external reflections of 'internal capacity for commitment and self-control' (Reischer & Koo, 2004, p. 300). Beauty thereby 'produces forms of affect that condense race, class, and gender inequalities onto and through the body, generating an aesthetic hierarchy that produces a scale of value ranging from the beautiful and normative to the ugly and abject' (Jarrin, 2017, p. 4). This aesthetic hierarchy in turn reproduces intersecting hegemonies.

Beauty's hegemonic force is highly evident in Brazil, where beauty as 'affective capital' (Jarrin, 2017, p. 13) represents a means towards 'upward mobility' (p. 3). For many Brazilians, cosmetic surgery becomes a strategic investment towards improved employment prospects in a job market where 'if one's looks signify humble origins, there are few chances of getting a white-collar job that pays better than average' (p. 3). Brazilian beauty ideals are thus strongly connected with social class and race, for the dominant version of beauty prized in contemporary Brazil is one formed in and through medico-aesthetic 'discourses' of a plastic surgery industry strongly 'informed by eugenic thought and by a desire to produce a racially homogenous population' (p. 8). In Brazil, beauty operates as a Foucauldian 'biopower' that 'instrumentalizes notions of empowerment to render certain bodies as legible and others as premodern, barbaric, or in need of liberation, affecting 'forms of governmentality that manage the body in particular ways' (p. 8). In the broader global context, Reischer and Koo show 'personal management of the body' to be 'intimately connected with the management of the larger "social body" through consumer culture', for 'the ideal gendered body does not remain merely in the realm of the symbolic; its power lies in its ability to directly influence behaviour within the social domain' and 'attractiveness is that which is found ideologically appealing within an overarching set of values' (2004, p. 300). They pose the body as a 'text that can be "read" as a symbol or signifier of the social world that it inhabits' (p. 300).

This notion of bodies as texts people unconsciously read for social meanings resonates with me. I perceive parallels between how aesthetic readings of bodies and clothes obscure the reproduction of intersecting hegemonies, and how judgements of literary merit insidiously reinforce the values of hegemonically privileged groups (as discussed at the end of part two). I wonder, what sorts of insights might arise by reading this analogy in reverse? In other words, where Reicher and Koo (2004) pose bodies as readable texts, might it not equally be suggested that western cultures have over the course of history mapped our power-implicated aesthetic hierarchies of physical beauty onto texts as bodies whose cells are letters, whose organs words?

Compass

Part one of this book explored writing's connections with knowledge and power. Contemporary western cultures' failures to recognize the force of writing-knowledge connections doesn't mean they fail to operate, only that they do so in unchecked, potentially problematic ways – for instance, how creative writing representations help maintain uneven power relations both amongst humans and of humans with beyond-human being. This raised the issue of representative imbalance – creative writing's historic and ongoing domination by hegemonic groups. Understanding how representative imbalance arose and how to combat it became the focus for part two, which examined the western literary canon and publishing industry. Both bear longstanding ties with institutions of religion, education, imperialism, and capitalist economics, which explains how the imbalances arose and also why change remains difficult – though not impossible, for change *has* occurred, and remains ongoing. The end of chapter six noted literary merit as one particularly insidious mode of gatekeeping via which the canon and publishing often continue privileging white western values – even through the works of so-called diverse voices massaged to sing in the dominant key.

The complexities of literary merit prompt part three's explorations of aesthetics as content – definition of which is this chapter's focus. I begin by clarifying my use of the notoriously slippery term aesthetics. Paradoxically, this slipperiness is part of what makes aesthetics politically meaningful, as I explain via discussion of the political potentials in troubling aesthetic boundaries and Jacques Rancière's (2011) theories of consensus and dissensus. In this way, I move towards clarification of the phrase *aesthetics as content*. I then broach historical approaches to textual aesthetics as a site of political struggle towards increased equity, including Marxian and anarchist approaches. These, however, have proven easily co-optable into commercial and totalitarian agendas. Hence no universal political valence can be ascribed to any given aesthetic style. Rather, readers and writers must continually reconsider aesthetic strategies in relation to changing contexts. To frame these reconsiderations, I recommend Timothy Bewes's (2010) strategy of reading with, against, and beyond the grain of texts.

Defining aesthetics

As cultural theorists widely observe, the term aesthetics bears multiform, complex and contested meanings (Jay, 1992; Highmore, 2004; Mangrum, 2015). By Ben Highmore's account, the slipperiness of aesthetics arises because it is 'constantly negotiating' two main modes of definition: ones evoking 'its origins as a philosophical project directed at those sensual, creaturely aspects of life that are not subsumed by rationalist thought', and ones related to 'production of artworks'

(2004, p. 312). This book primarily uses aesthetics in the latter sense, to indicate textual features of form and style. My approach partly aligns with Arne De Boever's notion of the 'aesthetic decision' – '*a decision taken with respect to an aesthetic situation or state, a regime of representation . . . a particular aesthetic*' (2014, p. 4, original italics). Examples include novelists' decisions about perspective, narrative modes (e.g. 'autobiographical' versus fictional or other non-fictional modes), paratextual materials and pacing, among other factors (pp. 5–7). For creative writers, aesthetic decisions may be habitual, accidental, coincidental or otherwise automatic as well as consciously deliberated (Hecq, 2015). Both conscious and unconscious aesthetic decisions are frequently steered by culturally constructed aesthetic value judgements conditioned by the writer's subjective standpoint, whether the writer knows this or not.

Like de Boever, I wish to distance my approach from Kantian notions of 'aesthetic judgement' – 'a judgement of aesthetic value that would, through reflective contemplation, rise above personal preferences' (de Boever, 2014, p. 4; see also Kant, 1790/1952). My interest lies with the subtle implications of meaning various aesthetic techniques can manifest, particularly political implications. In other words, my focus concerns how aesthetics may represent and re-present the interests of various social groups in ways that on one hand often serve the hegemonic status quo, but on the other, raise possibilities of change. This still includes attention to aesthetic schemas of 'judgement' (de Boever 2014: 4) or 'assessment' (Highmore, 2004, p. 312). However, unlike aesthetically oriented theorists of creative writing who seek to elucidate universal aesthetic criteria of strong versus weak writing (e.g. see discussion of New Criticism in chapter six), my aim is not to affirm, reify or recommend such schemas. Rather, I broach systems of aesthetic judgement as sites requiring scrutiny – potential sites of contestation. I seek to reveal their hidden involvements in reproduction of inequitable power relations, and to illuminate opportunities for troubling established hegemonies and promoting change via 'linguistic disobedience': strategic renegotiation of dominant standards in radical ways (Kinsella, 2007, p.11).

My approach to aesthetics recognizes the extensive modes of 'slippage' the term's artistic and textual meanings bear with its more 'philosophical', 'sensual' and 'creaturely' ones (Highmore, 2004, p. 312). Reading and writing are emotively and intellectually engaged activities: as Highmore notes, 'describing sensate, emotional life' is something 'artwork is seen as peculiarly adept at addressing' (2004, p. 312). Aesthetics bears strong links with *affect* – '[t]he subjective or evaluative dimension in human experience', which encompasses 'emotion or feeling, mood, or desire' and 'leaks into all human behaviour and cognition' (Chandler & Munday, 2020, p. 178). However, aesthetics as a 'complex figuration' involving 'values of beauty' has historically been pitched as a 'high-cultural' concern (Highmore, 2004, p. 312), meaning the modes of affect typically understood in terms of aesthetics have been those associated with rarefied experiences of privileged social groups. Meanwhile, affective experiences of 'real life in all its tumbling profusion and messiness' (Willis, 1990, cited in Highmore, 2004, p. 312) – particularly everyday life experiences of non-privileged social groups such as domestic labour and mundane work routines – have historically been 'ranked as decidedly non-aesthetic', and thus 'shorn' from the aesthetic regime (Highmore, 2004, p. 312). As with notions of physical beauty, this sustains a covert form of 'aesthetic hierarchy' in which 'affective capital' serves reproduction of intersecting hegemonies (Jarrin, 2017, p. 4). Therefore, Highmore poses that troubling the bounds between those affective experiences the aesthetic regime incorporates and those it denies can enact modes of political intervention (2004, p. 312). The next section considers this idea in focus.

Troubling aesthetic boundaries

For Highmore, troubling aesthetic boundaries involves revaluing that which aesthetics previously excluded (2004, p. 313). Such revaluations are politically charged because they resist hegemonic associations of art with 'alienation and elitism' by playing up 'the potential of ordinary creativity', which muddies boundaries between art and everyday life (pp. 313–14). Furthermore, remembering how 'aesthetics as it was initially conceived was concerned with areas of experience that were, precisely, difficult to make sense of' (p. 312), redefining aesthetics' boundaries potentiates expression of things previously foreclosed from articulation including 'formless', 'inchoate' and 'unfinished' experiences of 'partial significance', 'incompleteness' and 'contingency' (pp. 316–17). This provides a means for raising subjugated knowledges (see chapter two), via 'cultural resistance "from below"' – art that resists dominant frameworks of aesthetic judgement to validate the aesthetic forms and techniques of culturally oppressed groups (Millner, 2021, p. 402).

For instance, domestic labour (which is often gendered and classed) is 'constantly beginning again, full of repetitions, red herrings, distractions, unfulfilled wishes, and so on' (Highmore, 2004, p. 317). This contributes to its social invisibilization and non-remuneration in western societies wherein completeness, progression, and originality are ideologically reified (p. 317). Artistic techniques of montage and non-linear temporal representation – which resist completion, progress, and originality – have often been similarly dismissed as aesthetically inferior (p. 317). Reclaiming these techniques and asserting their aesthetic worth can facilitate expression of 'the dense and often invisible worlds' domestic labourers inhabit, which enacts '[a]n ethics of remembering, of making a textual space for those who have been denied a public voice' (pp. 319–20). Aesthetic boundary blurring processes are also evident in 'tout-fait/readymade' art, which raises mundane objects to an aesthetic level, questioning regimes of value judgement (Chow & Rohrhubrt, 2011, p. 45). The Situationists likewise blurred boundaries between art and everyday life via practices of public performance, installations, graffiti and other situated enactments of art outside the gallery space, typically for political purpose (Sholette, 2021, pp. 21–9). Ecologically oriented activism promoting human concern for beyond-human being often takes similar approaches (Millner, 2021, p. 402). Particularly notable are 'indigenous performative critiques' that 'rethink aesthetics as a category' towards 'a gathering or worlding of care', which 'worlds forms of sociality and ethical relation outside the colonizing domains of the [mainstream white western] aesthetic and the subject that it requires for political recognizability' (Jackson, 2016, p. 20).

By asserting value in aesthetic decisions the dominant frameworks exclude and dismiss as aesthetically inferior, culture from below politically 'challenges the regime of the worthwhile' (Highmore, 2011, pp. 99–100). This enables 'new collective and democratic experiences to come into being on the grounds that older forms of significance have been disorganized and superseded' (pp. 99–100). In 'taking aesthetics away from a world of fussy deliberation about "art and beauty" into a lively social world animated by the full range of passions' (p. 108), it can be seen to enact a form of engagement with Jacques Rancière's *distribution of the sensible* (2011, pp. 6–7, original italics).

From consensus and dissensus to aesthetics as content

Rancière's distribution of the sensible evokes space 'thought of in terms of distribution: distribution of places, boundaries of what is in or out, central or peripheral, visible or invisible' (2011, p. 6). It indicates ways in which 'the abstract and arbitrary forms of symbolization of hierarchy are embodied as perceptive givens, in which a social destination is anticipated by the evidence of a perceptive universe, of a way of being, saying and seeing' which constitutes 'a certain framing of time and space' (pp. 6–7). When the distribution of the sensible seems unified and unquestioned, there is *consensus*: people share a similar sense of things, with *sense* here indicating an articulation of bodily, affective, and intellectual phenomena encompassing both the physical and emotive *sensations* people feel, and the meanings people form or ways we *make sense* of these *sensory* experiences. Contrasting with this is *dissensus*, which Rancière characterizes at its 'most abstract level' as 'a difference between sense and sense: a difference within the same, a sameness of the opposite' (p. 1). More directly put, dissensus emphasizes situations wherein the radically different senses of things experienced and perceived by different groups and individuals mean 'speaking is not the same as speaking, because there is not even an agreement on what a sense means' (p. 2). Resultingly, dissensus becomes 'a conflict about who speaks and does not speak' (p. 2). The distribution of the sensible thus becomes a site of contestation.

For Rancière, the distribution of the sensible is strongly political. To grasp how, it is important to note Rancière's bespoke treatment of the term politics, which signifies not 'the exercise of power or the struggle for power' but instead 'the configuration of a specific world, a specific form of experience in which some things appear to be political objects, some questions political issues or argumentations and some agents political subjects' while others are excluded from the political realm (Rancière, 2011, p. 7). For Rancière, politics arises 'when the boundary separating those who are born for politics from those who are born for the "bare" life of economic and social necessity is put into question' (p. 3). In other words, 'there is politics when there is disagreement about what is politics' via dissensus as a process of 're-partitioning the political from the non-political' (p. 4).

The inclusions and exclusions that mark the (constructed and contestable) boundaries of the so-called political and non-political bear much in common with those earlier discussed in relation to the aesthetic and non-aesthetic. Dominant constructions of politics and aesthetics have treated them as necessarily distinct, even incompatible realms, championing attention to texts divorced of context (Cruz, 2017, p. 7). But as earlier parts of this chapter have shown, both art and the judgements around it can bear distinctly political implications – including repressive ones that maintain hegemonic power relations as well as subversive ones that call out injustices and push for change. This reflects Rancière's notion of the 'politics of aesthetics' – a theory of how 'the existence of the political and the existence of the aesthetic are strongly interconnected', but these interconnections become obfuscated by suspension of the aesthetic as category of 'exceptionality' and 'autonomy' distinct from *both* politics *and* everyday life (2011, p. 8). To raise 'the meaning and import of the configuration of … the sphere of aesthetics' in 'the political distribution of the perceptible' is to enact a mode of dissensus (pp. 7–8). To trouble boundaries of the aesthetic/non-aesthetic engages the distribution of the sensible as a site of contestation.

Where creative writing is concerned, one means of troubling aesthetic boundaries involves questioning the established order of approved 'poetic operations' (such as 'description, narration, metaphorization, [and] symbolization') via which literature can 'make its objects appear and give sense and relevance to its propositions' (Rancière, 2011, p. 14). This engages the distribution of the sensible as a site of contestation, opening scope to express things previously foreclosed by the discursive constraints dominant aesthetic regimes enforced – in other words, possibilities of raising subjugated knowledges and enacting cultural resistance from below. For writers and readers, this means there are significant political implications embedded in aesthetic decisions – conscious or not. Opting for certain aesthetic decisions over others can indicate alignment with and support for the social groups whose values and interests those decisions are best suited to represent and re-present. Textual forms and styles don't just *frame* textual content but may themselves be read *as* a mode of content bearing significant political force. This is what I mean when I refer to the idea of *aesthetics as content.*

In addition to the sources already discussed, my treatment of aesthetics as content is informed by theories insisting there can be 'no form without content and no content without form' (Léger, 2006, p. 152). Allen Guttmann insists on '"form *as* content" rather than "form *and* content" because how we say what we say is always a part of what we say ... sometimes the most important part' (2013, p. 2007, original italics). Guttman adds, '[t]heoretically, we can separate form from content', but 'practically, the two are inseparable' (2007). Marc James Léger similarly poses the idea of '*aesthetic content*', raising the oft-political nature of this content by calling for critique of how texts 'express through their form a rich conception of the world' that 'opens onto the history of social and cultural foundations' (2016, p. 153, original italics).

Treating aesthetics as content raises questions about links between aesthetic techniques and political agendas. For instance, could there be a certain combination of aesthetic techniques that especially suit political projects oriented towards the dismantling of oppression and pursuit of enhanced social equity? And likewise, are certain other aesthetic techniques or combinations thereof inherently linked with regimes of hegemonic domination and oppression? Marxian and anarchist literary critics have historically debated possibilities of this kind. The next two sections consider their approaches in turn.

Marxian debates about realism

The question of whether certain aesthetic techniques are better suited than others for pursuing social equity was a site of keen interest among theorists of what later came to be called the Frankfurt School. The Frankfurt School was 'a heterogenous set of thinkers' including Georg (György) Lukács, Theodor Adorno, Ernst Bloch, Walter Benjamin and Bertolt Brecht (Mussell, 2017, p. 17). Many, but not all Frankfurt school associates were connected with the Institute for Social Research [Institut für Sozialforschung] at the University of Goethe in the 1920s and 1930s (p. 15). They shared broadly Marxian political affiliations, but of different varieties, leading to a dialectical community of 'intellectual independence and political non-conformity' (p. 17). They weren't an 'actual "school" ... in the sense of a shared, agreed-upon set of theoretical positions, nor a physically localized group of people'; the 'productive and provocative pieces of research' they generated seem to have benefited from healthy debates (pp. 16–17).

One significant debate among associates of the Frankfurt school was realist versus non-realist and/or avant garde styles. As Tyrus Miller (2022, pp. 86–8) relays, Lukács was particularly passionate about this topic. For Lukács, form and genre expressed 'the work's intrinsic intentional relation towards meaningful objects, actions, bodies, and ideas in the world', pointing 'beyond itself, towards a meaningful world' wherein 'formed work is thus necessarily "about" – intentional of – worldly states of affairs' (Miller, 2022, p. 86). In Lukács's view, realism represented the form best suited to Marxian agendas of dismantling social class hierarchies and reconfiguring associated capitalist modes of production (Miller, 2022, p. 87). Realism – or indeed, 'Great realism' – in Lukács's (1938/1980) terms signified literature that:

> does not portray an immediately obvious aspect of reality but one which is permanent and objectively more significant, namely man [sic] in the range of his relations to the real world, above all those which outlast mere fashion. Over and above that, it captures tendencies of development that only exist incipiently and so have not yet had the opportunity to unfold their entire human and social potential. (p. 48)

In connection with this exalting of realism, Lukács (1938/1980) exhibited strong scepticism about '[s]o-called avant-garde literature … from Naturalism to Surrealism', which he critiqued for its 'growing distance from, and progressive dissolution of, realism', and pitted in binary opposition against the 'authentic modern literature' of realism as the only movement capable of giving 'effective and lasting form' to 'social and human content' bearing 'the breadth, the profundity and the truth of the ideas' necessary to inspire social change (p. 48). Lukács also attacked abstract art as promoting a 'dangerous worldview' of 'ultra-formalistic . . . vacuous subject matter' that 'depended on a discursive supplement furnished by questionable philosophies' (Miller, 2022, pp. 87–8).

Other members of the Frankfurt School argued back against Lukács's pro-realist dogmatism. For instance, Adorno charged Lukács with '[o]perating reductively, imperiously distributing labels such as critical or socialist realism . . . like a Cultural Commissar' (Adorno, 1961/1980, p. 153). Yet Adorno, too, though more flexible than Lukács, still often tended to charge many experimental or avant-garde forms of modern art with 'accelerated disintegration of artistic conventions, styles, and genres . . . intensified reflexivity of artistic form . . . extreme individualization of form and idiom at the cost of the communicability of experience . . . diremption between raw materiality and extreme intellectualization' and bearing 'no evident aesthetic qualities traditionally understood' (Miller, 2022, p. 105).

Rejection of abstraction by Lukács, and to a lesser degree Adorno, broadly aligned with the 'socialist realist' aesthetics promoted by the Soviet Union and other dominant modes of socialism of their time (Miller, 2022, p. 87). Indeed, Lukács's critique of abstract art was taken up by the Hungarian Communist Party as 'theoretical ammunition' towards 'imposition of socialist realism' and attendant repression of 'tendencies' the party's 'cultural leadership wanted to sideline and suppress' (Miller, 2022, p. 91). Miller suggests 'Lukács probably did not anticipate how successful this essay would be in torpedoing emergent abstract tendencies nor the repressive means by which their marginalization would take place' (p. 91). An observable irony is that very similar aesthetic regimes of creative censorship or censure have also at various points in history been imposed by capitalist governments including the United States (Cruz, 2017, p. 11) and the French Third Republic, which 'supported art forms that reflected republican values such as harmony, order, clarity' as an 'edifying art . . . accessible to all' (Shyrock, 2019, p. 19).

As Miller also notes, 'unbiased historical and theoretical reflection' shows abstract art to be 'anything but intrinsically hostile to socialism' (p. 92). Indeed, Benjamin and Brecht both defended – and in the latter case, practiced – abstract and avant-garde aesthetic techniques, for instance, Brecht's theatrical use of *verfremdung* (alienation, defamiliarization, or making-strange), alongside aspects of expressionism, absurdism, caricature, and the grotesque (see discussion in Esslin, 1963; Mitchell, 1974). Yet both simultaneously maintained commitment to realism, which they believed could be practiced through experimental forms. They discouraged conflation of realism with naturalism or verisimilitude (believability). Brecht identified as a realist whose chief aim was 'unmasking' real social issues via techniques that strategically rejected naturalism to shock theatre viewers into new awareness of social and political issues (1967/1980, p. 82). Realism in this case becomes defined via engagement with social realities, which sometimes requires so-called avant-garde techniques to break through habitually conditioned desensitization and renew affective investment in the pursuit of change. In Brecht's (1967/1980) words:

Even the realistic mode of writing, of which literature provides many very different examples, bears the stamp of the way it was employed, when and by which class, down to its smallest details. With the people struggling and changing reality before our eyes, we must not cling to 'tried' rules of narrative, venerable literary models, eternal aesthetic laws. We must not derive realism as such from particular existing works, but we shall use every means, old and new, tried and untried, derived from art and derived from other sources, to render reality to men in a form they can master. (p. 81)

Anarchism and avant-gardism

Reflecting stances similar to those of Benjamin and Brecht, anarchist literary theory has long argued avant-gardism's radically realist and political potentials. Carolin Kosuch emphasizes the 'aesthetic, social, and political cross-pollination that took place between the avant-gardes and the anarchists of the nineteenth and early twentieth centuries' (2020, p. 1). While 'anarchism was a political philosophy with strong leanings towards practical implementations directed against the status quo of heteronomy, be it in a monarchical state, a highly regulated and unjust political system, a bourgeois culture, or in party politics', avant-gardists 'strove for a new art that merged with life and was conceived as a revolutionary act' (p. 1). As specific examples, Richard Shyrock notes how poets of the symbolist movement, though commonly dismissed as 'decadent' (2019, p. 18), participated in popularizing anarchist ideas via the cross-pollination of publishing across symbolist and anarchist journals, their shared resistance to the French Third Republic, and aesthetic strategies of poems wherein a 'lack of rules' implied 'the anarchist goal of a society without laws' (pp. 29–30).

Daniela Padularosa raises a similar case regarding Dada, which 'often appeared apolitical' but 'was closely linked to the political thought of its time' (2020, p. 99). As Padularosa observes, 'Dadaism was conceived as an international, apolitical movement mocking politics as well as the arts', but 'in spite of professing to be nothing but an "anti-art" movement, its apolitical credo was clearly political' (p. 101). Padularosa cites an interview from Dadaist Marcel Janco:

> At the beginning, we had no political ideas. But the war made us understand the importance of brotherhood among men . . . The war – the worst crime against humanity – was the reason for our battle over the destruction of old art and the creation of a new art, which was intended to found friendship between men [sic] and nations.
>
> **JANCO**, 1958, cited in **PADULAROSA**, 2020, p. 101

Contesting 'traditional interpretations of Dada art as "foolish" experimentation or "childish" distraction', Padularosa attests to 'Dada's radical artistic, philosophical, and political implications in response to the perceived decline of Western society and the crisis of modernity' (2020, p. 102). To illustrate, she notes how politically pacifist Dadaists flocked to Zurich – which was neutral in the war – where they could create anti-war art, often performing at Cabaret Voltaire, an arts space that 'not only aimed at breaking with modern society but intended to propose a new, different and alternative way of approaching politics . . . furthered by new aesthetic values and a new and unconventional art practice' (p. 108). Pandularosa also notes the activities of Dadaists in Weimar Germany, relaying how '[w]hen Dada moved to Berlin, it lost its idealistic [anarchist] outline and adopted a more pragmatic and Marxist stance in its struggle against post-war hardships and the defective predominant culture' via 'artworks or performances . . . intended to incite the spectator politically and to carry out revolutionary acts' (p. 121).

One final example of arguments from anarchist literary theory for the politicality of avant-garde aesthetics is Patricia Leighten's (2020) account of radical techniques engaged by the visual art movement known as the fauvists (the beasts, a name given by a disparaging critic, but embraced by the group in resistance to mainstream artistic principles). As Leighten explains, '[a]rtists within this radical milieu rejected academic at and theory as well as state-sanctioned art institutions that promoted academic art as yet another manifestation of … bourgeois corruption', developing a 'stylistic vanguardism' that 'signified a rejection not only of the bourgeois commodification of art, but also of a set of values and institutions implicated in bolstering a Republic that deployed the military to attack striking workers and maintained gross economic inequalities' (p. 73). Leighten cites the example of Maurice de Vlaminck, who outwardly proclaimed his avant-garde style as 'an expression of anarchist antimilitarism' and whose 'political choices went hand in glove with aesthetic ones' including 'rough and open brushwork, antinaturalistic color, and lack of formal structure' via which 'Vlaminck obliquely confronted political subjects in his art' (pp. 73–5).

However, the oblique nature of Vlaminck's political aesthetics may ultimately have contributed to his work later being commodified and recuperated into the very institutional artistic structures he contested (Leighten, 2020, p. 95). As Leighten muses, '[a]rtists politicizing their work by virtue of style clearly run the risk of being misunderstood by later generations who are unable to share the values encoded in their violation of inherited forms' (p. 78). While the practices of Vlaminck and other fauvists may have 'positioned the artists in a critical relation to bourgeois norms' in their own times, and why they radically altered the art of the twentieth century', the 'social and aesthetic theories that fostered these movements were all but lost from view after the First World War':

> In the postwar era such formalist language lived on while the politicized content that gave birth to this art was willfully forgotten, hence the ease with which modernism became a bourgeois commodity in the 1920s and after … The final ambivalence of this history offers a disturbing precedent for our own society, stuck now in a loop of 'avant-gardism', commodified before it is made, no matter how critical its expression of the market that consumes it.
>
> **LEIGHTEN**, 2020, p. 95

Potentially even more disturbing is how the same aesthetic techniques used by anarchist avant-gardists were incorporated into the fascist art movement futurism. The next section broaches this uncomfortable co-option via consideration of Benjamin's (1935/1969) critique of fascism's *aestheticization of politics*.

Fascism and the aestheticization of politics

Benjamin (1935/1969) used the phrase 'the aestheticization of politics' to describe how twentieth century fascist movements adopted techniques of poetry and art to stir affect, enlist followers, and rally support for war. Hannah Arendt similarly observed fascism's reliance on poetic catchphrases and mythological allusions to conjure senses of glory (1951/2017, pp. 304–5). Reflecting how uprootedness often renders people vulnerable to totalitarian regimes that purport to grant voice and representation they have otherwise been denied (see chapter one), Benjamin posed fascism was 'attempt[ing] to organize the newly created proletarian masses without affecting the property structure which the masses strive to eliminate' by 'giving these masses not their right, but instead a chance to express themselves . . . while preserving property' (1935/1969, p. 19):

> The logical result of Fascism is the introduction of aesthetics into political life. The violation of the masses, whom Fascism, with its *Führer* cult, forces to their knees, has its counterpart in the violation of an apparatus which is pressed into the production of ritual values. (p. 19)

Benjamin added, '[a]ll efforts to render politics aesthetic culminate in one thing: war. War and war only can set a goal for mass movements on the largest scale while respecting the traditional property system' (1935 [1969], p. 19). To illustrate his argument, he cited the support for war given by fascist-identifying poets of the Italian futurist movement, particularly Filippo Tommaso Marinetti, who in a manifesto promoting Italy's colonial war upon Ethiopian people raged 'against the branding of war as anti-aesthetic', pitching war as

> beautiful because it establishes man's dominion over the subjugated machinery by means of gas masks, terrifying megaphones, flame throwers, and small tanks . . . because it initiates the dreamt-of metallization of the human body . . . because it enriches a flowering meadow with the fiery orchids of machine guns . . . because it combines the gunfire, the cannonades, the cease-fire, the scents, and the stench of putrefaction into a symphony . . . because it creates new architecture, like that of the big tanks, the geometrical formation flights, the smoke spirals from burning villages, and many others . . .
>
> **MARINETTI**, 1912, cited in **BENJAMIN** 1935/1969, p. 19

Marinetti subsequently urged futurist poets and artists to 'remember these principles of an aesthetics of war so that your struggle for a new literature and a new graphic art ... may be illumined by them' (Marinetti, 1912, cited in Benjamin, 1935/1969, pp. 19–20). Elsewhere, Marinetti (1909) clearly aligns futurism with support for fascism, alongside misogyny, racial oppression, and the celebration of speed – fast new technologies symbolizing masculine dominance, authoritative power, and violent conquest.

Marinetti had previously been trained in symbolist art, which advocated art for art's sake ,see discussion in Leung 2009; Cioli, 2015). The stylistic techniques of futurism also shared many similarities with the avant-garde movements anarchists often associated with activism towards liberation from hegemonic domination – but deployed these techniques towards the opposite agenda. For instance, regarding expressionism, Ernst Bloch noted that although '[w]hat the Expressionists intended was undoubtedly the very opposite' of the 'atavistic' tendencies fascism exploits, their style's tendencies towards 'emotive, rhetorical, vacuous manifesto' and 'declamatory pseudo-activism' rendered them 'unable to free themselves intellectually from an imperialist parasitism' (Bloch, 1938/1980, p. 17). Expressionism was therefore easily 'pressed into the service of that synthesis of decadence and atavism which is the demagogy of Fascism' (p. 18).

Returning to the question I posed earlier – of whether certain aesthetic techniques might be better suited than others for political agendas involving pursuit of enhanced social equity, and others inherently linked with oppression – I posit aesthetics themselves bear no intrinsic political affiliations persisting across all times and places. Indeed, to imagine they do risks falling into 'the implicit assumption' white western thinkers often make regarding 'an appropriate correspondence between content and form' (Chow & Rohrhuber, 2011, p. 49). Instead, political meanings – indeed, all meanings – of aesthetics as content are contingent on where, when and how works are produced and presented. Creative writers cannot rely on one particular aesthetic technique always producing the same political effects and must reconsider their approaches to aesthetic content afresh with each new work. Readers must similarly keep rethinking aesthetic implications in relation to contexts. This produces challenges because writing is often read in contexts vastly removed from those of its creation, where the aesthetic decisions may take on vastly different implications.

The need for reading with, against and beyond aesthetics as content

As the previous section noted, a key challenge of aesthetics as content is that writing and reading occur in different times and places. What is radical in the writing context may be recuperated into the status quo by the time it is read and may even appear to support the very ideologies the writer sought to rage against. Need exists for strategies of critical reading attending to the socio-political factors shaping contexts of both textual production and reception. One such strategy is outlined by Timothy Bewes, who poses merging 'Benjaminian habits of reading against the grain' with 'a reading that suspends judgment, that commits itself, rather, to *the most generous reading possible*', which means reading 'with the grain' as well as against it to go beyond it (2010, p. 4, original italics).

Bewes's strategy entails 'a process of deep historicization', which 'begins by historicizing its own temporal positionality with respect to its object of study' (2010, p. 6). A reader pays close attention not only to the ideological and discursive circumstances that limited and enabled the text's ability to take on political meanings (intended or otherwise) in the time and place where it was penned, but also critiques their own ideological and discursive limits towards recognizing how these connect with and/or diverge from those of the text at hand. Rather than critiquing texts from other contexts by the standards of one's own, a reader critiques their own context via what the text in its original context can make recognizable in and about the here and now (p. 11).

The importance critical reading bears to the political impact of aesthetics as content – and indeed, all political elements of representation – may seem to place writers in a deeply fraught position. After all, we have little say over who will read our works, and how. Does this render us fully devoid of agency in how our aesthetic decisions will be interpreted? Despite the trickiness of the situation, I argue we *do* still retain agency, for there are strategies we can deploy to promote contextualized readings of our works. One is to make the context of production visible via intra-textual markers that explicitly remind the reader of our socio-historic positions and/or reflexively probe the subjective limits and ideological problems these positions seem to entail. In this book, I have aimed to make my subjective position (and limitations) visible via the chapters' opening vignettes on 'walking/writing'.

The production of meta-textual and/or exegetical materials outlining the political positions that inform our aesthetic and other approaches is another strategy writers can employ to encourage careful readings of our works. Articles, reviews, interviews, blogs and maybe even manifestoes offer modes via which to broach this task. For instance, the meta-textual writings left behind by figures like Vlaminck and Marinetti make it possible for contemporary literary critics to revive recognition of the fact that the former engaged avant-garde aesthetics to express anarchist ideals of antimilitarism and non-hierarchism while the latter promoted fascist agendas of war and hierarchical domination on bases of race and gender. The actual actions we undertake (such as participating in political rallies) matter similarly, as do personally politically practices (such as ecologically aware eating).

The key point for writers with political aims is, in my view, that we cannot ignore or underestimate the political impact of the aesthetic decisions we make – or fail to make because we automatically follow given frameworks of literary merit or aesthetic ideals towards which we should aim. Whether grounded in traditions of supposed universal appeal or appealing to the excitement of innovation and new trends, such frameworks often present themselves as apolitical, oriented only towards the creation of good literature to appease publishers, dazzle readers and garner literary success (see discussion of New Criticism in chapter six). But as this chapter has argued, textual aesthetics always represent and re-present political impulses of their contexts. If we ignore this fact, we place ourselves at risk of adopting aesthetic techniques that politically undermine our other aims. If we recognize it, we manoeuvre towards the greatest chance of aesthetically realizing our desired ethico-political ideals.

Re-orienting

This chapter outlined key concepts of aesthetics as content, including my treatment of the notoriously slippery term aesthetics and the political valences it bears. As I have acknowledged, multiple precedents exist for mobilizing aesthetics as a site of and for political struggle, including but not limited to the Marxian and anarchist approaches considered here. The key lesson I drew from considering these approaches is that no aesthetic technique or set of techniques can be universally associated with any specific political valence: rather, their valences depend on context, meaning politically oriented readers and writers must ongoingly reconsider shifting implications of aesthetics as content across changing situations. The next question is, where to focus these reconsiderations? Chapter eight raises conceptual metaphor as one (though by no suggestion the only) site worthy of interest.

8 CONCEPTUAL METAPHORS IN FIGURATIVE LANGUAGE

A cockatoo ignores me walking/writing

It's not a tree, but it has a trunk, and at its top, branches of a kind – just two, short and leafless, poking in opposite directions like outstretched wings stripped of feathers and form, like the spindly not-wings that dangle off the torsos of those ground-dwelling creatures who sewed this not-tree, and all the others. They form a line, the not-trees. Countless lines upon lines. And each line forms part of a square that in turn joins other squares to form grids and systems, squares within squares, meeting and merging like the gullies of a river, except in patterns far cruder, simultaneously more predictable and less sensible. Water flows with land, tracing it like fingers exploring flesh with care and consent. Real trees, too, have a flow to them, a respectfulness, for they are tied to water, and they feel the blows of winds, of storms. Thanking the hillsides that bring them shelter, they grow from roots, from systems that stretch further underground than above: they grow up from land, are part of it. By contrast, the not-trees grow down: they dig into land, tower over it, forcing their lines and squares upon it. You know this because you have seen from above. You have seen at night how these squares of not-trees light up, as if on fire. Mostly, they are not, but fires do seem to light more easily in their presence. They are connected by vines, black vines that are not vines, for they never grow yet are somehow always overgrown and strangling. The not-vines hold something somewhat like fire, or maybe lightning. You know this because you have witnessed the violence that erupts when they come unravelled, when they snap. You know these things are frightening. And yet, you refuse fear. You perch on the line, the not-vine, you and your friends, a row of you laughing through song. Of your group today, you are the loudest, the brightest, at least in the eyes of a ground-dwelling creature who has paused to gaze up from below. You have the creature awestruck. Do you know it? You don't only sing, but dance, turning acrobatics as you clamp your feet round the risky vine and spin – upside down, and around, and down, and around, again, and again, and again, and again. Sunlight catches in your white and yellow feathers, making you a living beacon, filled with a fire so different from that of the not-vines and not-trees at night: a fire that feeds, a fire of warmth – and defiance, for in making a perch on this tree that is not a tree, you claim back something that has snatched so much from you. In the eyes of the mouth-agape creature still gazing up, you glow. It has stayed a long time, the creature, in a silence radically uncommon for a species normally even more racketsome than yours – the species that sewed the not-trees and strung the not-vines. Poor brute. It cannot fly. Having never seen or felt half of what you know, it cannot even creep towards imagining the sensations flooding through you now as you spin and twirl and sing and laugh. You cannot guess its thoughts and you do not care. Do such creatures even think? Can they feel? The hold of this one's frame suggests surprise. Its silence echoes stunned wonder. Perhaps there are seeds of sentience in them after all. Not that it matters. Your song and your dance are for many things. This creature is not among them.

Compass

Chapter eight introduced the notion of aesthetics as content, emphasizing the oft-overlooked political implications in the aesthetic decisions writers make. This chapter foregrounds political implications of aesthetic decisions involving conceptual metaphor. The next section distinguishes conceptual metaphors from linguistic ones. I then consider the political implications both cognitive and linguistic metaphors entail, explaining why this area forms one of concern for politically oriented readers and writers. Subsequent sections probe examples of conceptual metaphor's operations via specific metaphor sub-variants and related devices. These include personification, anthropomorphism, zoomorphism, chremamorphism, metonymy, synecdoche and symbolic imagery. This chapter thus shows multiple ways in which conceptual metaphors can manifest political implications via micro-textual aspects of aesthetics as content.

Conceptual and linguistic metaphors

In creative writing and literary theory, metaphor is typically defined as the literary technique of representing one thing in the form of another (Abrams & Harpham, 2015, p. 133). For instance, to say someone is a shining light is not to suggest they literally radiate like the sun or a globe, but rather to associate them with the joys light can bring. To say someone has fallen upon hard times is not to suggest a literal tumble upon time as a physical object, but rather a phase of difficult circumstances. These are examples of what this chapter refers to as linguistic metaphor. Linguistic metaphor is typically differentiated from other forms of analogy such as simile, which differs from metaphor because its phrasing uses comparison rather than direct substitution: to state someone *is* a shining light is use of metaphor; to state they are *like* a shining light, or *as bright as* one is use of simile (Webb, 2009, p. 127).

Conceptual metaphor involves a broader set of practices involving mental linkages wherein 'the locus of metaphor is in concepts' and thus more than just 'a matter of words' (Lakoff & Johnson, 1980/2003, p. 236). Beyond mere substitution of one thing for another in linguistic phrasing, conceptual metaphor refers to cognitive linkages, emphasizing how '[o]ur ordinary conceptual system, in terms of which we both think and act, is fundamentally metaphorical' and metaphor located 'not just in language but in thought and action' (p. 13). Conceptual metaphor remains strongly connected with linguistic metaphor because use of the latter activates the former, and conceptual metaphor is easily recognizable via linguistic metaphor. For instance, linguistic metaphors for time as a resource that can be spent, saved or wasted reflect and reinstate the ways in which many people in western cultures understand time – and budget it (p. 16). By contrast, calling time a cycle, flow or set of linkages may encourage stronger tendencies towards attention and appreciation for temporal experiences in and of themselves and/or one's interrelatedness with past and future generations of beings, both human and beyond-human (Stroude, 2022, pp. 366–7).

The ways in which different linguistic and conceptual metaphors for time promote differing attitudes is one example of how metaphor as a conceptual system 'plays a central role in defining our everyday realities', meaning 'the way we think, what we experience, and what we do every day is very much a matter of metaphor' (Lakoff & Johnson, 1980/2003, p. 13). Metaphors of saving and spending time are also examples of 'dead metaphors' – ones so familiarized we typically forget they are metaphors, such as 'the leg of the table' (Abrams & Harpham, 2015, p. 230). Dead metaphors form an incredible portion of everyday language, but largely pass unnoticed unless we call active attention to them (Lakoff & Johnson, 1980/2003, p. 208). This is among the reasons why conceptual metaphor is so 'ubiquitous in our mental life' while remaining primarily 'unconscious' (p. 235). Conceptual metaphor's operations extend beyond linguistic metaphor – indeed, beyond language – for conceptual metaphor effectively involves any textual and cognitive operation involving association between two or more distinct ideas. For instance, 'more is up and happy is up' lead to 'MORE is HAPPY', which, like time as money, reflects western cultural values – in this case, specifically those of consumer culture (p. 149).

Defined as a cognitive process of linking otherwise separate notions, conceptual metaphor may operate via literary devices typically considered distinct from linguistic metaphor, including most forms of figurative language – textual enactment of a 'conspicuous departure from what competent users of a language apprehend as the standard meaning of words, or else the standard order of words, in order to achieve some special meaning or effect' (Abrams & Harpham, 2015, p. 118). Varieties of figurative language include but exceed linguistic metaphor and simile alongside '*allusion; ambiguity; anaphora; antithesis; aporia; conceit; epic simile; epithet; hyperbole and understatement; irony; kenning; litotes; paradox; pathetic fallacy; periphrasis; pun; symbol; synesthesia . . . alliteration; onomatopoeia;* [and] *rhyme*' (pp. 121–2, original italics). These can all form connections between distinct concepts, and thus facilitate conceptual metaphor. As there is not space to here discuss each in detail, later sections of this chapter foreground a selection I pose bear particular interest for politically oriented readers and writers.

Conceptual metaphor's capacity to shape thought by connecting disparate sites reflects metaphor's etymological origins. It comes from the Ancient Greek '*meta*', which signals change, and '*pherein*' for 'to carry, to bear' (Lossi, 2009, p. 222). In contemporary Greek, metaphor can be used to mean 'transport' or 'transfer' (p. 222). Translator Mary Zournazi relays, '[i]n Greece, the vehicles of mass transportation are called *messa metaphorai*' and '[t]o go to work in Greece, or to come home, one can take a metaphor — a bus or a train' (2005, p. 141). A metaphor is thus something that transforms and/or transports. These two acts are prone to blur, for shifting something from one place to another creates 'new spacings and relations to place that involve the crossing of boundaries': what is carried over is frequently changed by the process and may in turn change its new context (p. 141). Representations involving metaphors 'do not simply make connections, relationships and identities *visible*; they actually *make* those connections, relationships, and identities' (Webb, 2009, p. 15, original italics). Contrary to commonplace assumptions metaphor is usually 'based on similarity' or natural association, 'cross-domain correlations' of conceptual metaphor established via linguistic metaphor and other connective representations themselves 'give rise to the perceived similarities' (Lakoff & Johnson, 1980/2003, p. 236).

Similarities and perceptions thereof do not pre-exist the links conceptual metaphors represent but are actively produced (re-produced) via 'persistent use' (Lakoff & Johnson, 1980/2003, p. 236). Conceptual metaphors rarely operate in isolation but come together to form complex conceptual systems. The earlier example of 'more is up and happy is up' leading to 'MORE is HAPPY' shows how two correlations may combine to form a third (p. 149). In everyday practice there are usually even more linkages constantly at play, largely unconsciously. These continually form and reform conceptual systems of understandings about 'time, causation, events, morality, emotions', and more (p. 246). This idea articulates with Hall's remarks about representation's reliance on 'classifying systems' or 'conceptual maps' (Hall, 1997, p. 18) (see chapter three). Conceptual metaphor thus bears on social values, norms and ideologies in ways that matter for politically oriented reading and writing, as the next section shows.

Metaphor's political implications

Because it shapes thought, conceptual metaphor bears on ideology and politics, producing material, affective, and ideological 'implications for all aspects of our lives, including war and peace, the environment, health, and other political and social issues' (Lakoff & Johnson, 1980/2003, p. 237). However, because conceptual metaphors are predominantly 'learned unconsciously and automatically . . . simply by functioning in the everyday world' (p. 246), we are frequently unaware of how metaphorical systems 'determine questions of war and peace, economic policy, and legal decisions, as well as the mundane choices of everyday life' (p. 235). Metaphor's ubiquitous yet oft-unnoticed nature combined with the fact 'so much of our social and political reasoning makes use of this system' produces a strong potential for people to 'be mystified by its effects' (Lakoff, 1995, p. 1). For readers and writers, this means we can remain largely unaware of conceptual metaphor's political operations via aesthetics as content unless we actively bring it into deliberate focus via critique of other writer's works and/or our own. It is important to consider how common conceptual metaphors come into use and the ideologies they promote.

Conceptual metaphors and the systems they form are neither universal nor arbitrary but 'shaped and constrained by our bodily experiences in the world', which 'depend on the nature of our bodies, our interactions in the physical environment, and our social and cultural practices' (Lakoff & Johnson, 1980/2003, p. 238). As a result, linguistic and conceptual metaphors differ between cultures. Within a given culture, dominant conceptual metaphors typically reify conceptual linkages derived from embodied experiences of people from social groups with greatest capacity to influence language formation (for instance, those with greatest access to publishing). As one example, the previous section noted how the conceptual metaphor of time as money shapes western cultural attitudes to and uses of time. Such attitudes to time reflect and reinstate capitalist systems wherein 'work is typically associated with the time it takes and time is precisely quantified', for instance via payment 'by the hour, week, or year' (p. 8). As chapter four noted, the publishing industry was among the first to introduce such labour practices.

Hourly rates for some workers are higher than for others. This implies some people's time is worth more, reflecting hegemonic social systems. Often, such discrepancies are justified on the basis that the higher-paid workers perform supposedly more skilled forms of labour and/or achieve more within the same time. This reflects conceptual metaphors associating more with happiness (as earlier discussed). It also reflects the emphasis on linear progress over time reified in common conceptual metaphors about life as a journey that 'must have a beginning, proceed in a linear fashion, and make progress in stages toward that goal' (Lakoff & Johnson, 1980/2003, p. 95). The conceptual metaphors for time as money, more as happy, and progress as a journey thus reflect and reinstate material processes via which 'industrial capitalism transformed the conceptions and experiences of time by imposing a propaganda of time-thrift to the working people' (Stroude, 2022, p. 361).

Further examples of conceptual metaphor's political implications are observable in the rhetoric of conservative politics, which conceptualizes 'well-being as wealth' and vice versa (Lakoff, 1995, p. 1). Combined with a conceptual system that attributes positive associations to 'up' and negative ones to 'down' – for instance, the idea of being at the '*peak* of health' (Lakoff & Johnson, 1980/2003, p. 23, original italics) – this promotes correlation of 'moral strength' with one's capacity to be 'upstanding' in the sense of financial independence (Lakoff, 1995, pp. 5–7). Via these metaphorical conceptualizations, 'rich people and successful corporations are model citizens' while those who seek financial support are perceived as morally weak and deserving of their misfortune (pp. 7–9). Such ideological perspectives not only eclipse the forms of harm corporations often inflict on workers and the environment in the name of turning profits but position social programs as 'immoral . . . because they are seen as working against self-discipline and self-reliance' and 'rules out any explanations in terms of social forces or social class' (p. 7).

Associations of strength and morality with physical upstandingness bear implied attitudes of ableist judgement against people who use mobility aids such as wheelchairs. Similar forms of ableism are evident in common dead metaphors associating knowing with sight, such as *see what I mean* (which suggests blind people are less capable of understanding) and the idea of *words falling on deaf ears* to suggest the recipient of a message did not pay attention (which belies the fact deaf people often listen very hard via non-auditory means, such as lip reading). Many metaphors also convey systems of gendered injustice, for instance the association of courage with masculinity via *having balls*, which bears both misogyny and transphobia. General western cultural associations of goodness with light and badness with darkness – for instance, being in a *black mood*, or expressing *black humour* – can be taken as racially discriminatory. In addition to social discrimination amongst humans, metaphors often reflect and reinstate human exceptionalism via ecophobic expressions like using *beastly* to describe something awful or calling someone a *bitch* (female dog) as an insult.

The ableist, racist, misogynistic, transphobic, ecophobic and other discriminatory connotations buried in many dead metaphors used daily without conscious thought affirms Lakoff's point about how metaphors may reinforce 'strict us-them moral dichotomy[ies]' of evil versus good that dehumanize those perceived as 'them' and justify violence, for '[y]ou do not emphathize with evil . . . [y]ou just fight it' (1995, p. 7). In extreme situations, '[m]etaphors can kill' – as Lakoff explains in relation to metaphorical justifications of war by governments and media via 'political cost-benefit analysis', settling 'moral accounts', and 'the fairy tale of the just war' (1991, pp. 5–8). Hannah Arendt similarly noted how the German Nazi party's used aphorisms (repetitive catchphrases) to make genocide seem normal, reasonable and even morally defensible as a hygienic necessity

(1951/2017, pp. 304–5). Metaphors – linguistic and conceptual – are thus deeply entangled with power relations of domination, oppression and exploitation bearing significant material consequences for human and beyond-human life.

On the flipside of metaphors' oft-violent operations are potentials to expose these problems and/or promote alternative ways of being and relating. Readers can help expose problems via literary analysis to expose ideologies inherent in common metaphors and raise dialogues about how to think and act beyond given ideological constraints. Creative writers can help promote alternatives by avoiding the use of problematic metaphors and generating fresh ones promoting new possibilities. For instance, in western cultures, argument is commonly conceived as a warlike struggle wherein the goal is to win by defeating one's opponent, which reinforces us/them divisions and reduces the likelihood of finding common ground (Lakoff & Johnson, 1980/2003, p. 14). Lakoff and Johnson issue an invitation to instead think argument as a 'dance' wherein 'the goal is to perform in a balanced and aesthetically pleasing way' without any need for one party to prove themselves right and the other wrong (p. 14). As earlier noted, metaphors for time as a cycle, flow, or linkages typically promote greater feelings of environmental responsibility than those that treat time as a resource and/or a linear journey in which the aim is progress for its own sake, without necessary care for side-effects.

The conceptual metaphors writing conveys – via linguistic metaphor and other means – thus matter for politically oriented reading and writing. Analysis of figurative language use provides a way to bring the unconscious ideologies conveyed via aesthetics as content into conscious scrutiny. The remaining sections of this chapter consider a non-exhaustive range of examples, signalling some key areas to which readers and writers can attend.

Personification and anthropomorphism

In personification, 'either an inanimate object or an abstract concept is spoken of as though it were endowed with life or with human attributes or feelings' (Abrams & Harpham, 2015, p. 121). Examples include stating that the wind howled, and the old house moaned, or that fate scorned someone. The first two ascribe living qualities to things conventionally understood as non-living, but material. The third ascribes material action to something commonly perceived as immaterial, blurring not only living and non-living, but also abstract and concrete. Anthropomorphism involves describing animals with human-like qualities, which is common in children's stories featuring animal characters, but may also occur in writing aimed at general readers where human emotions are projected onto animals – for instance, by suggesting a dog mourned its owner (which could be possible but can't be known for sure, as we don't possess language to ask dogs about their emotional states) (Nanay, 2021, p. 171).

Personification and anthropomorphism are sometimes promoted as 'ecocentric' devices that contest human 'egocentric' or anthropocentric western cultural representations of nature as 'an unfeeling, soulless sphere of objects, existing to be consumed, destroyed and exploited' (Müller, 2018, p. 46). Ecocentric practices of personification and anthropomorphism contest human exceptionalism by depicting nature as 'imbued with personhood' (p. 47). From this perspective, '[l]iterary personifications of nature are political in so far as they can motivate people to understand and assume non-anthropocentric perspectives', promoting 'cultural attitudes and social practices' of care and responsibility for beyond-human kin (p. 47).

There is, however, a counterargument to personification and anthropomorphism as ecocentric devices: projection of human emotions onto beyond-human beings and entities can itself reflect and reinstate of anthropocentric thinking (O'Connor, 2018, p. 187). The case for personification and anthropomorphism as ecocentric desires rests, after all, on a premise of elevating the beyond-human to 'an equal footing with humans', in which persists an implied assumption of 'morality based on presumed human superiority over the nonhuman' (p. 187). Egocentric personification and anthropomorphism may also impose 'hyper-individualistic, radically egotistical [human] desires' on beings and entities that potentially feel and think quite differently from us (p. 188). Such projections ignore possibilities of attempting to genuinely empathize with beyond-human being in ways that might force us to expand our perspectives and humbly learn from things that confound us – or, to acknowledge our own perceptive limitations and develop greater caution about the forms of violence to which these limitations leave us prone (p. 188).

This is not to discount the political potentials of personification and anthropomorphism to promote empathy with beyond-human beings and entities, but it signals the need to approach these devices carefully, with awareness of their capacities to reinstate anthropocentric thought. It is important to consider the specific metaphors one uses, the conceptual systems they operate within, and the forms of human behaviour they reflect. In the opening vignette to this chapter, I have tried to imagine the terms and metaphors a cockatoo might use to describe human constructions – specifically, powerlines as *not-vines* strung between *not-tree* poles. While I recognize this approach still ultimately projects human understandings onto a fellow animal who no doubt thinks quite differently, the exercise of centring the cockatoo as 'you' and referring to myself as a third person 'creature' at least prompted me to shift some distance beyond my habitual assumptions and better appreciate the strangeness of my own species.

Zoomorphism and chremamorphism

Zoomorphism and chremamorphism work in the opposite direction to personification and anthropomorphism – by attributing humans with qualities conventionally associated with beyond-human beings and entities. Zoomorphism means depicting humans in animal-like ways, for instance by stating a person barked orders or was feathering their nest (Nanay, 2021, p. 171). Chremamorphism is when 'characteristics of an object are ascribed to humans' (Ross & Rivers, 2019, p. 282). This can include non-living natural objects, for instance saying someone has been blown through life like a leaf or has a heart of stone. It often involves machine-like depictions of humans. For instance, cycling commentators liken riders to 'artillery' whose energy levels are measured in terms of having or *running out of firepower*' (p. 198, original italics). Though most definitions of chremamorphism specify its application to humans, it sems equally possible to discuss o/Other animals and living things as objects or machines – for instance, the underground mycelium networks formed by trees and fungi, among other actors, are sometimes referred to as the 'wood wide web' (Angrish, 2022).

Zoomorphism and chremamorphism might seem to provide ways beyond the problems of personification and anthropomorphism because their reversals blur conventional western cultural divisions between living / non-living, human / animal, and nature / technology. This bears potential to trouble the ideologies of human exceptionalism by promoting perceptions of fluidity and relationality between human and beyond-human beings. However, zoomorphism bears problematic potentials as Jeanine Leane (2010) observes in her critique of Mary Durack's remarks about Australian Aboriginal author Colin Johnson (Mudrooroo). Durack 'described the Aboriginal community which [Mudrooroo] came from as '*breeding* among themselves . . . a *drifting* coloured minority *caught* in the vicious circle of lack of opportunity and their own lack of stamina' (Durack, 1965, cited in Leane, 2010, p. 35, italics added). Leane observes how these verbs are 'closer to animal behaviour rather than human behaviour', reflecting historic treatments of Aboriginal and Torres Strait Islander peoples in subhuman ways by white invaders (Leane, 2010, p. 35). Harriett Gaffney (2017) also notes zoomorphism in the form of a 'much racist caricature' from a letter by Charles Joseph La Trobe, the first Governor of the Victorian colony (1851–4), to friends in Britain. La Trobe 'described Aboriginal Victorians as more akin to Opossums than humans', an analogy that 'fed directly into the growing cult of theories about natural selection and "survival of the fittest"' (Gaffney, 2017, p. 6), contributing to a 'Literature of Extinction' which 'trivialises the transformation [settlement] represents . . . as a form of misdirection in which the brute power of colonialism is rendered utterly matter-of-fact' (McCann, 2006, cited in Gaffney, 2017, p. 6, alteration in Gaffney).

Chremamorphism can also dehumanize people in ways conducive to violence and exploitation – for instance, by positioning workers as cogs in a machine, easily discarded and replaced. Especially problematic are forms of chremamorphism engaging machines of warfare – for instance, the earlier-noted metaphors for cyclists as artillery connects with a 'cycling is war' metaphor that in turn forms part of a 'sport is war' conceptual system reifying 'competition, strategy, power, [and] teamwork' in connection with 'national pride' and competition between nations (Ross & Rivers, 2018, pp. 176–7) – a set of values that, in sporting contexts, are usually relatively benign, but if taken beyond the sporting arena, can promote us/them mentalities of xenophobia, or even help rally support for actual war. The glorification of war, speed and technology by Filippo Tommaso Marinetti and the futurists is again notable here (see discussion in chapter seven).

For all four devices discussed in this chapter so far, the question is not of whether the devices are themselves politically sound or unsound. The point is that all can be used to promote problems like human exceptionalism and dehumanization as well as to contest these same things. The question is one of context and perspective – of who is re-presenting whom, and how, with what implications. If I choose to re-present myself using zoomorphism, then this is more likely to affect recognition that I as a human being am myself an animal, not separate from my ecology but part of it – and thus compelled towards responsible interactions with and in that system. But if I re-present someone else via animalistic depictions without explicitly figuring myself and all other humans in the same animal category, and without otherwise signalling a challenge to the human/animal divide, then the re-presentation could be problematic indeed.

Metonymy, synecdoche and selective description

Metonymy is when 'one thing is applied to another with which it has become closely associated', for instance use of 'the crown' to signify the monarchy, or 'Hollywood' for the film industry (Abrams & Harpham, 2015, p. 120). In synecdoche, 'part of something is used to signify the whole, or (more rarely) the whole is used to signify a part' (p. 120). Examples where a part stands for a whole include 'hands' to mean workers, 'sails' to mean ships or 'wheels' for a car (p. 120). Examples where a whole signifies a part include using the name of an author to indicate their oeuvre of writings (p. 120) or stating 'the press' has arrived to indicate the arrival of one or more journalists (Lakoff & Johnson, 1980/2003, p. 41). For Lakoff and Johnson, who treat synecdoche as a metonymy sub-variant, metonymy is 'not just a poetic or rhetorical device', nor 'a matter of language': as with metaphor, '[m]etonymic concepts' form 'part of the ordinary, everyday way we think and act as well as talk' (pp. 41–2).

However, the ways metonymy and synecdoche shape conception differ from those of metaphor. As the previous section noted, metaphor reflects and reinstates conceptual connections between otherwise disparate things. With metonymy and synecdoche, a connection already exists, but the device steers attention towards certain connections or 'certain aspects of what is being referred to' while minimizing others (Lakoff & Johnson, 1980/2003, p. 42). Metonymy and synecdoche thus perform categorizing operations that signal 'a kind of object or experience by highlighting certain properties, downplaying others, and hiding still others', for '[f]ocusing on one set of properties shifts our attention away from others' (pp. 163–4). These categorizations are in turn involved in power relations. To exemplify, Lakoff and Johnson relay '[w]hen we say 'The Times' hasn't arrived at the press conference yet,' we are using 'The Times' not merely to refer to some reporter or other but also to suggest the importance of the institution the reporter represents (p. 42). By contrast, a slang term for journalist is 'legman', which emphasizes the idea of journalists being on their feet chasing after stories while downplaying the other forms of intellectual and ethical labour the acts of news reportage may involve (Merriam-Webster, 2024a). Frequently used in reference to younger journalists and/or those assigned to undertake 'subordinate tasks (such as gathering information or running errands)', the term suggests far less importance and respect (Merriam-Webster, 2024a). Furthermore, while referring to a journalist by the name of their newspaper may emphasize the publication's prestige, it downplays the individual, suggesting any reporter from the same newspaper would be just the same – all are interchangeable and replaceable, which plays a dehumanising function much like that chremamorphism can affect (see previous section).

Metonymy and synecdoche's involvements in power relations are also evident in the examples given earlier. Referring to the monarchy as the crown raises thought of grandeur and respect without mention of the historic violences on which royal privilege rests or the huge disparities between contemporary monarchs living luxurious lifestyles without needing to work versus ordinary people working multiple jobs to scrape rent, yet still too poor for basic dental care. Referring to a car by its wheels emphasizes speed, engineering and the freedom of being on the road without acknowledgement of environmental costs. What other thoughts would come to mind if I referred to my new petrol tank or exhaust pipe? Why is it we refer to the Indian film industry as Bollywood instead of as Mumbai (formerly Bombay)? That's the main city in which it is based, and would be consistent with Hollywood as the main city of the American film industry. That India's film industry needs to reference America's to become legible in western culture's systems of language and conceptualization reflects the ongoing force of western ethnocentrism and white privilege.

When it comes to synecdochic descriptions of people using a part to signify a whole, the choice of what feature will be selected performs an act of categorizing that 'involves our perceptions and our purposes in the given situation' in politically problematic ways. This applies not only for synecdoche in the strict sense, but any description that picks out a particular feature over others (selective description). Lakoff and Johnson illustrate by noting how 'I've invited a sexy blonde to our dinner party', 'I've invited a renowned cellist', 'I've invited a Marxist', and 'I've invited a lesbian' could all potentially refer to the same person (1980/2003, p. 162). Each version re-presents a specific aspect of the person in ways that erase the others.

'Sexy blonde' seems particularly problematic because it objectifies them, foregrounds their appearance ahead of their skills and political commitments, and suggests their openness to sexual advances without noting they are only interested in same-sex relationships – or, if they are in a committed relationship, may not be interested in anyone.

As with personification, anthropomorphism, zoomorphism and chremamorphism, these potential issues of metonymy, synecdoche and selective description don't mean the devices themselves are problematic but raise the need for readers and writers to critique how they are used. This means paying attention to contexts – both that in which the device is presented, and the contextual implications evoked via connections to broader conceptual systems. It also means actively thinking about which potential connections or additional features have been hidden or downplayed to highlight the one in use. There is scope to use metonymy and synecdoche to actively call out the problems of their commonplace usages. For instance, a writer could introduce a character as 'a suit' – thereby suggesting someone caught in and dehumanized by the corporate world – then proceed to flesh the character out in ways that contest and problematize the stereotypes the suit implies.

Symbolic imagery

A symbol in the broad sense 'is anything which signifies something else', meaning 'all words are symbols' – as are all letters, punctuation marks, and the spaces between them (Abrams & Harpham, 2015, p. 358). However, in creative writing theory, the term 'is applied only to a word or phrase that signifies an object or event which in its turn signifies something, or suggests a range of reference, beyond itself' (p. 358). A symbol is 'a concrete image that stands in for a larger idea' (Tracey et al., 2023, p. 43). Symbolism differs from linguistic metaphor: with the latter, the actual subject or object of reference remains present, whereas a symbol fully replaces the referent, leaving it to the reader to interpret its deeper meaning. For instance, the line '[s]he was our queen, our rose, our star' (Praed, 1802–39, cited in Abrams & Harpham, 2015, p. 358) uses metaphor: the referent, 'she', is present; 'rose' and 'star' are clearly metaphorical analogies being used to signal qualities of beauty and brightness. In contrast, 'The Sick Rose', a poem that opens 'O Rose, thou art sick', then proceeds to lament how an 'invisible worm . . . Has found out thy bed . . . [and] Does thy life destroy' (Blake 1794, cited in Abrams & Harpham, 2015, p. 359). As Abrams and Harpham observe, '[t]his rose is not the vehicle for a simile or metaphor, because it lacks the paired subject . . . Blake's rose is a rose – yet it is patently also something more than a rose' (p. 359). To offer another example, if I were to write, *after the storm, a dove of peace landed*, I would be using a metaphor because the reference to peace is explicit, but if I were to simply write, *after the storm, a dove landed*, I would be using symbolism and relying on the reader to interpret the implied meaning of peace based on western cultural frameworks wherein '[t]he dove is conceived of as beautiful, friendly, gentle, and, above all, peaceful' (p. 45).

Symbolism often operates through imagery that might otherwise seem simply part of a scene or character description (Tracey et al., 2023, p. 43). The term imagery is in my view an unfortunate one, as it can mislead writers to overemphasize visuals while forgetting other senses. I therefore emphasize, imagery in writing encompasses *all* sensory mechanisms, including sound, taste, smell, sensations, sight, and more (p. 46). Sensations may involve felt contact with external stimuli (the smooth bark of a tree, the chill of a cool breeze, the lapping of water and so on), internal bodily sensations (one's pulse, breathing, hunger, pain, fatigue or arousal), or combine both (for instance, an increased pulse rate brought on by cold water). Engaging multiple senses in writing is more inclusive for readers who may have one or more sense inhibited but can relate to the others. It also makes sense for writing craft and involvement for all readers, because, as humans 'the world comes to us through the body, through our skin, our ears, our nose, our tongue, our eyes' in ways that shape 'our inner psychic lives', meaning our thoughts and emotions as things 'influenced by chemicals in our brains and bodies' such that '[w]e feel them, viscerally and immediately' (p. 46). Imagery thereby provokes affective engagement and conveys symbolic meaning via the associations sensory experiences evoke. For instance, a turn from sunny weather to cold may for many readers affect a shift from optimism to despair; a character's physical pain or weakness may emphasize lack of agency in other areas; a bird's pleasant song might suggest hope or relief.

While symbolism remains distinct from linguistic metaphor in the ways I have already explained, it retains operations of conceptual metaphor because it still links otherwise disparate sites (such as the dove with peace; an increased pulse rate with panic or excitement; sunny weather with joy; cold weather with despair; and singing with hope). It simply does so by naming one thing, but not the other, and leaving it to the reader 'to come to their own understanding of what is being represented' (Tracey et al., 2023, p. 43). Lakoff and Johnson treat symbolism as closer to metonymy than metaphor, for as with metonymy, it involves referencing one thing via evocation of another bearing a recognizable association (1980/2003, p. 45). The difference is that with metonymy, the association is usually quite direct and physical (the crown is something monarchs wear; wheels are a part of a car) whereas with symbolism the association is more oblique and typically relies on existing cultural frameworks (p. 45). Abrams and Harpham refer to these kinds of symbols as 'conventional' or 'public' symbols – ones where a writer exploits 'widely shared associations between an object or event or action and a particular concept', some instances of which include 'association of a peacock with pride . . . the rising sun with birth . . . the setting sun with death . . . climbing with effort or progress and descent with surrender or failure' (2015, p. 358). They contrast public symbols with personal or 'private' ones writers 'largely generate themselves' (p. 358).

A challenge with both kinds of symbols is that the reader might not always recognize or interpret them as the writer intended. Apparently, '[t]he eagle clearly represents freedom in the United States but not necessarily in Mexico' (Tracey et al., 2023, p. 43). This makes it a public symbol in the US, but not in Mexico, meaning US readers would likely grasp its intended significance but Mexican readers might not. For me as someone raised in Australia, the symbol of an eagle brings an immediate shudder because I associate it fascist iconography and the horrors of the Nazi regime. That public symbolism can misfire like this illustrates the ways in which its interpretation strongly depends on the reader's familiarity with a given cultural system of reference. In other words, symbols are 'culture-bound' (p. 43). This is true for most of the examples I have offered in this section so far. For instance, that doves symbolize peace is a specifically 'Abrahamic' notion – one derived from religious scriptures of Judaism, Christianity and Islamic faiths – but this does not carry into other religions, like Buddhism (p. 43). Abrahamic religions also tend to treat snakes as symbols of sin and evil, but in Hinduism, the ability of snakes to shed and regrow new skin represents creativity, rebirth and transformation (Neto et al., 2019). In many First Nations Australian cultures, the Rainbow Serpent is associated with water and prosperity (McKinnon, 2021, p. 329).

Use of culture-bound symbols therefore bears capacity to draw boundaries between insiders and outsiders – those who bear the cultural background knowledge required for recognizing and interpreting the symbolic meaning being implied, and those who lack this background. Ability to recognize the symbols of the dominant culture may also be understood in terms of cultural capital: in educational settings, symbolism may contribute to invisible reinstatement of inequalities because students from the dominant culture will understand a set text more readily while those without the required cultural capital will feel frustrated by things that don't make sense. However, the political problems of cultural symbolism go beyond mere understanding. For instance, Christianity's links with colonization have made dove symbols for peace and snake symbols for evil discernible to most people from cultures colonized by Britain and other European nations. Yet this understanding relies on how the symbolic systems of colonizing cultures have been forcefully imposed on many people whose longstanding spiritual knowledges and ways of life have been violently suppressed in this process. If as a writer from a background of white western privilege, I use a dove as a symbol of peace and expect First Nations peoples to interpret it as such because I know they have historically been forcibly removed from their families as children and forced into white western schooling, am I not inadvertently approving these historic violences and their ongoing effects today?

For politically oriented writers who come from culturally dominant backgrounds, the issues of cultural dominance enacted via symbolism bear no simple solutions I can perceive. Using symbols from colonized cultures to keep them alive and counter dominant associations might be an option for those themselves from those cultures. But for those not, it would involve problematic acts of cultural misappropriation.

This brings me to personal or private symbols, the ones writers generate themselves (Abrams & Harpham, 2015, p. 358). As Abrams and Harpham note, 'these pose a more difficult problem in interpretation' because the writer can't depend on their reader being able to directly and easily recognize a symbol based on existing cultural knowledge (p. 358). Rather, the writer must provide additional information that enables readers to glean meaning via how the symbol is presented and contextualized in their text itself (p. 358). One way is via motif: 'a conspicuous element, such as a type of event, device, reference, or formula, which occurs frequently' (p. 205). For instance, if the colour blue is repeatedly mentioned in connection with a particular idea that also recurs within a narrative, the reader can come to link the two and recall the idea whenever blue is mentioned, even if the idea no longer is. However, even when writers strive to contextualize their personal symbols so readers can grasp them, the scope for disparities of interpretation remains vast, as Abrams and Harpham observe in relation to debates between literary critics defending different interpretations of the same poem (p. 359).

Potential disparities of interpretation are not necessarily a problem. For politically oriented writing, they may even bear certain benefits. Roland Barthes (1977/2011) rejected the idea of authors as authorities whose intentions readers should slave to correctly discern, arguing this hierarchical writer-reader relationship acts as a model that naturalizes hierarchies in other contexts – such as those of workers and employers – encouraging obedience rather than the questioning of exploitative systems and commands. The openness of personal symbolism is in this sense oriented towards a more egalitarian sharing of agency between reader and writer as co-creative meaning makers. Citing Goethe, Abrams and Harpham observe how personal symbolism 'transforms the phenomenon into idea, the idea into an image, and in such a way that the idea remains always infinitely active and unapproachable in the image, and even if expressed in all languages, still would remain inexpressible' (Goethe, 1824, cited in Abrams & Harpham, 2015, p. 360). The 'indefinite' nature of personal symbolism can therefore be 'richly – even boundlessly – suggestive in its significance' (Abrams & Harpham, 2015, p. 360).

Once again, the ultimate point to make about symbolic imagery's political problems and potentials is that the device itself is not intrinsically problematic, but becomes so when used in certain ways, and/or contexts. For creative writers, it is important to consider how and why we are using various symbols. If we have been raised in a particular culture, then it may be habitual for us to use the symbols of that culture in problematic ways without thought. In editing and rewriting we can question these habits and seek alternative modes of expression. With literary analysis, it is important also to question symbols in context. However, I revive chapter seven's point about reading with, against and beyond the text. The point should not be to condemn a writer if they have used a symbol problematically, as in many cases, this habit will be unintentional, driven by their situated cultural conditioning and constraints. The point is to ask what the presence of problematic symbolism can reveal about those cultural constraints, both as they existed in the context of writing, and in terms of how they may still bear on the context of interpretation – and thus, the scope for thinking beyond our own constraints towards expanded possibilities of imagination.

Re-orienting

This chapter considered how aesthetics as content may manifest political implications via conceptual metaphors at the micro-textual level. As examples, I have considered personification, anthropomorphism, zoomorophism, chremamorphism, metonymy, synecdoche and symbolic imagery – a far from exhaustive selection, but one I hope has illustrated cognitive metaphor's force. I also hope this selection may prompt thinking about other micro-textual devices such as rhyme, assonance, and alliteration, all of which forge sonic linkages between words and ideas (see discussion in Gibbons, 2015). In each of the cases discussed here, I have noted ways in which the focal literary devices can become politically problematic by reifying cognitive associations that support existing ideological systems of inequity, oppression and exploitation. I have also noted potentials for challenging oppressive ideologies by creating fresh metaphors or reconfiguring existing ones in novel ways. Chapter nine extends these discussions by considering conceptual metaphor's political operations via macro-textual features of form and content.

9 CONCEPTUAL METAPHORS THROUGH FORM AND STRUCTURE PART ONE: JOURNEY AND ARC NARRATIVES

Walking/writing in the shadows of an epic

Some hikes are journeys, even epic quests. There are goals, rewards and struggles to achieve them. Maybe it's a fitness challenge, or navigating treacherous terrain, encountering rare wildlife, or snapping that perfect shot of a waterfall, lookout or canopy. People plan, pack, dream and train for such hikes. They study maps, practice survival techniques, post a million photos on social media, and consider themselves forever changed by the experience.

I am not that kind of hiker.

In the mornings, when I set out, I'm usually still half asleep. There are no target destinations, real or symbolic. I walk to be in the act of walking, and so let my feet start falling, trusting them to take me where they will.

Today, my feet bring me to an artificial valley of young trees and flat ground, hugged by a craggy cut rock semicircle. The air always feels cooler here, the way it does in graveyards. Red and white streaks of different minerals ripple through the exposed earth, reminding me of keloid tissues in this hurt and healing flesh. In the 1890s, this was a quarry, mined for road-building aggregate. Operations closed in 1927, nearly a century ago now. Plants are reclaiming ground, animals returning, transforming this place from a barren crater into a valley of green contemplation. Recovery is a far slower process than destruction, though. One hundred years is barely a beginning, and this place will never be what it once was. By my guess, it's less than 1 per cent the size of the smallest quarry within the old Highbury Mine. I shiver to think how long healing will take for that aching place.

In the 1980s, this site was used for theatre performances, including a nine-hour production of *The Mahabharata* (Brook, 1985/1989), a Hindu epic about two warring sets of brothers, the Kauravas and the Pāṇḍavas. I was a child then – too young to know about the show, let alone attend. But I've seen the filmed version. Very close to where I now stand, an actor playing poet sage Vyasa narrated the tale while another playing the god Ganesh sat and scribed. What must the spirits of this place have thought of Ganesh with his elephant head? Did it seem just one invasive imposition of yet another culture's beliefs? Or did they maybe invite him to sit, share some tea, and swap notes on similarities and differences between colonization's effects in India and here?

In my early twenties, I read the *Bhagavad Gita* (Vyasa, 200 BCE/2015) – a key episode within *The Mahabharata* (Vyasa, 200 BCE /1999) – while backpacking round India. At first, I just wanted to better understand the cultures of the places I was travelling through. But I was fast entranced by the strange mix of drama and philosophy in the richly-spun story, and subsequently all the Hindu literature as I could get my hands on. Back then, train rides between Indian cities often went for days and nights on end, so there was plenty of time for losing myself in gods, warriors and their wild antics. Having then only recently renounced the Catholic faith in which I was raised, I was surprised to discover many familiar themes – like babies sent down rivers in baskets, and gods who are at once singular and multiple – amid differences offering a refreshing counterpart to the spirituality I'd previously known.

As a Catholic, I grew up on stories of the saints believers pray to as patrons of various causes. There's a patron saint of travel, of music, of animals, of mothers, babies, dogs, cats, lost keys, you name it. Hindu gods bear parallels in that they're each the god of something. Ganesh, for instance, is the god of education and obstacles. Perhaps that's why he's my favourite – because I'm passionate about empowerment through learning, and often work with students from backgrounds of struggle, for whom getting to and through study involves obstacles of all kinds. A key contrast I perceive between Hindu gods and Catholic saints is that the Catholic saints almost invariably come in two varieties: those who were always impossibly good, and those who were initially very wicked, but then repented and purged all the badness from their systems, becoming even more impossibly better. There's always a clear moral to the story, a lesson for naughty children to learn. The Hindu gods, by contrast, feel paradoxically far more human in their relatable weaknesses and foibles. They react to things for petty reasons, throw tantrums, wreak mischief and succumb to lusts. Hindu stories are thus far less didactic, more open to individual queries and interpretations. Catholicism always left me feeling guilty about my failures to be *good* in the most black and white of terms, encouraging a judgemental attitude towards others' actions as well as my own. Hindu literature instead provided frameworks for broaching complexity, sitting with things that feel uncomfortable or don't make sense, and sensing deeper empathy for other people's ethical ambiguities as well as my own.

I love Ganesh because his story feels relatable and transferable to common life experiences, big and small. He wasn't born with an elephant head. To begin, he had a human face – apparently a very attractive one. His stepfather, Shiva, decapitated him in a fit of rage, then replaced his head with an elephant's. There are various accounts of Shiva's motivations, but the general consensus is that Ganesh was punished unfairly (Krishnaswami, 1996: 1–6). Not only does he have an elephant head, but one of his tusks is broken. The struggle to live with these newfound challenges helped Ganesh become wise. In some stories, he uses the tusk to write (p. 30). That's why he's god of both obstacles and education. But in contrast to a Christian figure like Job, who was temporarily punished then later rewarded with greater riches than ever before, Ganesh is never set free of his own obstacles: he lives with them eternally in constant coming to acceptance. Perhaps this is why praying to Ganesh for assistance with obstacles is different from praying to St Anthony of Padua to reveal those damn keys. While St Anthony will comply and make the keys show up (so Catholics claim), Ganesh is just as likely to place obstacles in one's path to prompt learning through struggle (Subramaniyaswami, 1996, pp. 5–6). I think of this whenever I get stuck in traffic. Why did Ganesh put me here? What is there I need to reflect on and learn from? I don't genuinely believe an invisible deity is directing traffic just to force my solitary existential reckonings. But there's invariably something to reflect on, and the idea helps me find calm when I might otherwise get cranky and honk the horn. Ganesh's story becomes a kind of metaphor I map onto daily events to perceive what are otherwise frustrations in less hopeless ways.

The Mahabharata (Vyasa, 200 BCE/1999) was among the legends early twentieth century American mythographer Joseph Campbell studied when he devised his theory of the monomyth or hero's journey. By Campbell's (1949/2004) account, the monomyth is a narrative pattern bearing compelling appeal because it speaks to supposedly universal human dreams, fears, and desires. The hero's journey was across the twentieth century taken up by screenwriters as a dominant model for how stories should be told to engage audiences (Vogler, 1998/2007). It significantly influenced the *Star Wars* franchise (Lucas, 1977–present) among other major blockbusters (Thompson, 2015). These have in turn influenced the teaching of mainstream screenwriting and creative writing generally (Berry & Batty, 2016), making Campbell's claims seem retrospectively true. As a *Star Wars* fan, I recognize the monomyth's charms, and agree it deserves a place in writing theory – but I worry about its dominance. For writers, it threatens to overshadow the many other ways narratives can unfold. For readers, it encourages singularly focused interpretations and a confirmation bias via which other interpretations get missed.

For instance, while the basic patterns of the monomyth can be interpreted into *The Mahabharata* if one looks for them as Campbell did, to read it solely through a monomythic lens is to miss the many other complexities at play through its micro-tales and tangential anecdotes. Such a reading also overlooks the provocative moral ambiguities in a text where most of the so-called heroes fall on their way to heaven, and the final chapter undoes earlier ones by noting failings of the characters we have been positioned to view as protagonists while compelling empathy for those presented as villains. Even Krishna (among the most revered of Hindu gods) ultimately appears a trickster whose antics are neither purely good nor bad (Das, 2010). There are so many alternative senses in which this epic can be appreciated (see discussion in Thompson, 2015).

The monomyth pattern as it is now applied in mainstream films and writing treats life struggles as journeys, providing an example of how conceptual metaphor manifests not only at the micro-textual levels chapter eight considered, but also at macro-textual levels of textual form and structure. The chapter ahead probes these macro-textual operations of cognitive metaphor, using the monomyth as an example of the political implications tangled in aesthetic decisions about form and structure.

Compass

Chapter eight demonstrated ways in which aesthetics as content may operate via conceptual metaphors expressed at micro-textual levels via figurative language and symbolic imagery. This chapter considers conceptual metaphor's operations at macro-textual levels of form and structure. The opening vignette has already signalled the monomyth as a key example I here use to illustrate why form and structure matter for politically oriented readers and writers. The next section summarizes the monomyth's history and key features, including connections with arc narratives. I then examine problematic political implications of both the monomyth and arc narratives – namely, how they re-present conceptual metaphors associated with dominant white western ideologies of extreme individualism and human exceptionalism, thereby helping sustain intersecting modes of injustice both between humans and of humans with beyond-human being. Recognition of these problems leads me to consider various attempts to reinvent the monomyth, including the heroine's journey, the black hero's journey, and the queer hero's journey. While all these approaches bear some benefits, they remain limited in ways reflecting the reasons why efforts to redress creative writing's representative inequities can bear greater impact by focusing not only on *who* writing represents, but *how* representation is mediated by culturally constructed notions of so-called literary merit. This sets the direction for chapter ten, which looks beyond the journey towards o/Other equally valid but less recognized textual forms and structures.

The monomyth: Joseph Campbell and archetypal criticism

In overview, the monomyth involves a hero who leaves their familiar world to undertake a journey or quest, then returns, having overcome challenges and won a reward to help resolve problems that prompted their journey in the first place (Abrams & Harpham, 2015, p. 16). The monomyth is commonly attributed to early twentieth century American mythographer Joseph Campbell (1949/2004), who studied stories from a vast array of global cultures, seeking to identify common patterns, based on which he posed the monomyth as a universal schema for what makes a story powerful and engaging. However, Campbell's pursuits were not isolated and may best be understood as part of an early twentieth-century movement called 'archetypal criticism' (Abrams & Harpham, 2015, pp. 15–16).

Archetypal criticism worked from the premise that 'recurrent narrative designs, patterns of action, character types, themes, and images' can be identified across 'a wide variety of works of literature, as well as in myths, dreams, and even social rituals', and this recurrence results from 'elemental and universal patterns in the human psyche, whose effective embodiment in a literary work evokes a profound response from the attentive reader', who 'shares the psychic archetypes expressed by the author' (Abrams & Harpham, 2015, p. 15). Archetypal criticism drew strongly on psychoanalytic theory, particularly the works of Carl Jung. In Jungian theory, the term 'archetype' indicates 'primordial images' reflecting a 'psychic residue' of 'repeated patterns of experience in our very ancient ancestors', which persist in humanity's 'collective unconscious' and find expression through 'myths, religion, dreams, and private fantasies, as well as in works of literature' (Abrams & Harpham, 2015, p. 16).

Key figures of archetypal criticism included Maud Bodkin, G. Wilson Knight, Robert Graves, Philip Wheelwright, Richard Chase, Leslie Fiedler and Northop Frye (Abrams & Harpham, 2015, p. 16). In Bodkin's *Archetypal Patterns in Poetry* (1939), heroes play a major role (see discussion in Pandey, 2021, p. 59), which likely provided influence for Campbell. Additional precursors of note include British amateur anthropologist Lord Raglan, who, prior to Campbell, conducted a study identifying twenty-two themes supposedly common to heroes across world literatures including departure and return, struggles with adversaries, and victory leading to rewards (Raglan, 1936/1949), and Austrian psychoanalyst Otto Rank, whose even earlier *Myth of the Birth of the Hero* (1909/2015) emphasized similar themes. Indeed, for archetypal criticism, 'death/rebirth' was 'the archetype of archetypes . . . grounded in the cycle of the seasons and the organic cycle of human life' (Abrams & Harpham, 2016, p. 16).

Campbell's *The Hero with a Thousand Faces* (1949/2004) relays the monomyth across three broad phases entailing seventeen stages. These are reflected in table 9.1.

Phase	Stages
Departure	Call to adventure
	Refusal of the call
	Supernatural aid
	Crossing the first threshold
	Belly of the whale
Initiation	Road of trials
	Meeting with the goddess
	Woman as temptress
	Atonement with the father
	Apotheosis
	The ultimate boon
Return	Refusal of the return
	The magic flight
	Rescue from without
	Crossing the return threshold
	Master of the two worlds
	Freedom to live

Campbell presented the stages in a cyclical diagram, accentuating the departure and return pattern (1949/2004, p. 227). He emphasized the necessarily simplified, general nature of his model, and the diversities of ways in which individual tales might alter, skip, add to, re-order, repeat and/or otherwise reinvent the basic patterns he outlined:

> The changes rung on the simple scale of the monomyth defy description. Many tales isolate and greatly enlarge upon one or two of the typical elements of the full cycle . . . others string a number of independent cycles into a single series . . . Differing characters or episodes can become fused, or a single element can reduplicate itself and reappear under many changes.
>
> **CAMPBELL**, 1949/2004, p. 228

The monomyth's stages constitute the first of two parts in *The Hero with a Thousand Faces* (Campbell, 1949/2004). Part two opens with discussion of time as cyclical and 'the cosmogonic cycle': 'the passage of universal consciousness from the deep sleep zone of the unmanifest, through dream, to the full day of waking; then back again through dream to the timeless dark' – a pattern Campbell posed as manifest not only in the sleep/wake cycles of 'every living being', but through 'the grandiose figure of the living cosmos' where 'in the abyss of sleep the energies are refreshed, in the work of the day they are exhausted; the life of the universe runs down and must be renewed' (p. 247). Campbell then considered creation tales from various cultures, followed by tales of virgin births, after which he surveys eight categories of variations on 'Transformations of the Hero', each of which entails multiple different ways in which the monomyth may unfold. In his epilogue, Campbell again emphasized there can be 'no final system for the interpretation of myths' (p. 353), proceeding to reflect on the collectivist nature of the societies in and for which many of the myths he studied were created, associating the monomyth with '[r]ites of initiation and installation' that taught 'the essential oneness of the individual and the group . . . As the individual is an organ of society, so is the tribe or city – so is humanity entire – only a phase of the mighty organism of the cosmos' (p. 355). He contrasted this collectivist attitude with the dominant culture of his own time, which he characterized as radically transformed by ideals of 'the self-determining individual . . . the power-driven machine . . . [and] the scientific method of research' (p. 358). Campbell thus seemed to critique issues of extreme individualism similar to those raised in earlier parts of this book:

> The problem of mankind today . . . is precisely the opposite to that of men in the comparatively stable periods of those great co-ordinating mythologies which now are known as lies. Then all meaning was in the group, in the great anonymous forms, none in the self-expressive individual; today no meaning is in the group – none in the world: all is in the individual.
>
> **CAMPBELL**, 1949/2004, pp. 358–9

These contrasts between past and present cultures in my reading suggest a need for different patterns of writing to serve changed needs. *The Hero with a Thousand Faces* (1949/2004) is about studying myth, not producing it, with no suggestion creative writers replicate the monomyth pattern in new works. Despite this, Hollywood screenwriters have transformed the monomyth into a formula for producing engaging scripts (Vogler, 1998/2007) – a formula creative writing educators often recommend too (Berry & Batty, 2016). The next section considers these adaptations and their impact on real-life contexts.

The hero's journey: Hollywood's merging of the monomyth with arc narratives

As the previous section noted, the monomyth was intended for studying stories, not producing them, with no suggestion creative writers replicate its patterns in new works. Yet George Lucas (1977–present) did just that when he took the monomyth as a model for the *Star Wars* films (see discussion in Thompson, 2015).

In *The Writer's Journey: Mythic Structure for Writers,* American screenwriter Christopher Vogler went even further, arguing for 'The Hero's Journey' as a set of 'principles that govern the conduct of life and the world of storytelling the way physics and chemistry govern the physical world' (1998/2007, p. xiii). Emphasizing that the journey need not be literal and most crucially represents a meaningful struggle of self-development – for instance, through education, illness, heartbreak, and/or towards self-actualization – Vogler characterized the hero's journey as 'an eternal reality, a Platonic ideal form, a divine model' from which 'infinite and highly varied copies can be produced, each resonating with the essential spirit of the form' (p. xiii). Vogler's account thereby the hero's journey's operations of conceptual metaphor at macro-textual levels of form and structure.

Where Campbell cautioned that seventeen stages could not adequately capture the myriad complexities at play, Vogler reduced the stages to twelve. He related these to an Aristotelian three act structure of rising conflict and resolution, as reflected in table 9.2:

TABLE 9.2 *Three act structure and the hero's journey*

Three Act Structure	Hero's Journey Stage	Description
Act One: 'the hero's decision to act' (Vogler, 1998/2007, p. 12)	Ordinary World	Portrayal of the hero in their ordinary world offers a contrast with the new world they will soon enter (Vogler, 1998/2007, p. 10)
	Call to Adventure	A problem or challenge arises and compels the hero towards their adventure (p. 10).
	Refusal of the Call	The hero expresses reluctance to embarking on their adventure. It will require a worsening of the problem and/or encouragement from a mentor to motivate them past their fear (p. 11).
	Meeting with the Mentor	The mentor is encouraging figure who helps the hero prepare to embark on their adventure. The mentor may provide advice, encouragement, and/or equipment for the journey (p. 12).
	Crossing the First Threshold	The hero finally overcomes their fears and embarks on their adventure into the unknown world (p. 12).

Act Two: 'the action itself' (p. 12)	Tests, Allies, Enemies	Having begun their adventure, the hero faces new challenges and tests. They make allies and enemies as they begin learning the rules of the unknown world (p. 13).
	Approach to the Inmost Cave	The hero approaches a dangerous place, wherein the object of the quest is to be found. This may be their enemy's headquarters, or an especially dangerous place. Heroes will often pause to prepare as they begin their approach (p. 14).
	The Ordeal	The hero directly confronts their greatest fear. There may be a possibility of death (literal or symbolic) as they grapple with hostile forces. For the audience, there is tension, suspense and uncertainty whether the hero will succeed or fail (pp. 14–15).
	Reward	Having faced their ordeal, the hero claims the reward they have been seeking. This could be a special weapon, token or elixir. It could also be knowledge and experience. Additionally, 'the hero may also become more attractive [and] has earned the title of "hero" by having taken the supreme risk on behalf of the community' (p. 16).
Act Three: 'the consequences of the action' (p. 12)	The Road Back	The journey is not yet complete: the hero must still negotiate 'the consequences of confronting the dark forces of the Ordeal' as they begin their return to the ordinary world. There may be reconciliations to make, and 'there are still dangers, temptations, and tests ahead' (p. 17).
	The Resurrection	As warriors of ancient times 'had to be purified before they returned to their communities', the hero 'must be reborn and cleansed in one last Ordeal of death and **Resurrection** before returning to the Ordinary World of the living' (p. 17, bold in original).
	Return with the Elixir	Returning to their ordinary world, the hero comes bearing an elixir: a 'treasure, or lesson from the Special World', such as 'a magic potion with the power to heal', 'a great treasure', or 'knowledge or experience that could be useful to the community someday' (p. 18).

Though Vogler continues to represent the hero's journey in circular diagrams (1998/2007: 206), by connecting it with a three-act structure, he reveals how it can also be viewed as a linear arc narrative of rising conflict building towards crisis and resolution (pp. 157–8). As Jane Alison notes, an arc narrative is one in which 'a situation arises, grows tense, reaches a peak, subsides', forming a 'wave' with a discernible 'beginning, midpoint, and end' (2019, p. 6). In addition to Aristotelian drama, arc narratives are commonly associated with Freytag's pyramid (Abrams & Harpham, 2015, p. 267). Both approaches insist a story needs 'an obstacle, some drama, a crisis' that unfolds via 'exposition, rising action, climax, falling action, and resolution' (Tracey et al., 2023, p. 163). M. H. Abram and Geoffrey Harpham similarly emphasize the arc narrative as a linear 'sequence of beginning, middle, and end' with a 'pyramidal shape, consisting of a rising action, climax, and falling action' leading towards 'resolution' (2015, pp. 267–8).

The cultural influence of the *Star Wars* franchise (Lucas, 1977–present) and Vogler's (1998/2007) reconfiguration of the hero's journey in synch with arc narratives has been significant, influencing theories and approaches not only in screenwriting but creative writing generally (Berry & Batty, 2016). Beyond creative writing, it is also adapted into discourses of psychology (Williams, 2019), organizational leadership (Varney, 2020), marketing (Sanders & von Krieken, 2018), and property investment discourses (Martin, 2018). These usages reflect Vogler's assertion that, in addition to 'design principles of storytelling', the hero's journey provides 'a set of principles for living … nothing less than a handbook for life, a complete instruction manual in the art of being human' (1998/2007, p. xiii). In healthcare, Arthur Frank's *The Wounded Storyteller* (1995/2013) mirrors the hero's journey by posing that people struck by serious illness or injury find strength to process their experiences and persist with life by framing their life experiences in terms of 'quest' and 'restitution' narratives via which they tame the 'chaos' of illness with its uncertainties and disruptions (p. xiv). As Frank relays, a 'quest narrative' is one of 'being transformed', which in the case of illness narratives 'implies that the teller has been given something by the experience, usually some insight that must be passed on to others' (Frank, 1995/2013, p. 118).

The ways in which the hero's journey is transferred beyond writing to real life contexts wherein people use it to make sense of their struggles reflects its operations as a conceptual metaphor at the macro-textual level. That people evoke this conceptual metaphor when making potentially big decisions involving relationships, careers, investments, identity, goals and more is telling of how conceptual metaphors at the macro-textual level can shape thinking and values in politically consequential ways.

Political implications of arc narratives and the hero's journey

As a conceptual metaphor expressed via form and structure, the hero's journey is one example of aesthetics as content at the macro-textual level. This section focuses on the political implications thereof. Because the hero's journey bears arc narrative features, I begin by considering the political implications of arc narratives generally, before broaching the hero's journey as a specific sub-variant.

That arc narratives are problematically dominant in contemporary writing and writing theory is a driving premise of *Meander, Spiral, Explode* by Jane Alison (2019), whose critique partly informs my own. With references to how the 'rising action' of an arc narrative inevitably builds towards a 'climax' followed by 'falling action' and 'resolution' (Abrams & Harpham, 2015, pp. 267–8), Alison remarks, 'something that swells and tautens until climax, then collapses? Bit masculo-sexual, no?' (2019, p. 6). Later, Alison cites critic Robert Scholes's remark that '[t]he archetype of all fiction is the sexual act . . . the fundamental orgastic rhythm of tumescence and detumescence, of tension and resolution, of intensification to the point of climax and consummation' (Scholes in Alison, 2019, p. 13). Both Alison and Scholes interpret the arc narrative as a macro-textual metaphor for a certain kind of sexual experience – the kind dominant in mainstream media and heteronormative porn representations of sexual pleasure as though it applied 'only to limited sexual experience, most often to reaching orgasm', belying the 'complex and multifaceted . . . physiological, psychological, relational, and cultural domains' sexual pleasure also often involves (Ashton et al., 2019, p. 410). While Scholes appears quite satisfied with stories that blow their loads and fall asleep, Alison objects, remarking, 'Well. Is this how *I* experience sex? It is not' (2019, p. 13, italics in original). She proceeds to observe extensive critiques of arc narratives by feminist scholars who point out how 'beginnings, middles, and ends in traditional narrative and traditional narratology never seem to accrue directly to the account of the woman' (Winnett, n.d., cited in Alison, 2019, pp. 13–14).

Alison's point is not to denigrate the arc as inherently problematic or suggest it should be fully discarded. She notes how it 'makes sense' for certain stories (2019, p. 15). She also notes its capacity to combine with other patterns in generative, fascinating ways (p. 242). Her argument is not against the arc itself, but its dominance – the ways theories of creative writing and literary theory have prized the arc to such degrees it eclipses other equally valid alternatives, and the ways this dominance of the arc as a macro-textual conceptual metaphor of 'masculo-sexual' pleasure reflects and reinstates patriarchal dominance in bedrooms and beyond (Alison, 2019, p. 6). I agree with Alison that the arc's dominance is problematic and need exists to diversify the range of approaches recommended to aspiring creative writers. I also agree with the need for more diverse representations of the many forms sexual pleasure can take beyond just reaching orgasm. However, as a queer bisexual woman I question the binary opposition of male versus female pleasure: my impression is that many men are also dissatisfied with orgasm-centred sex, while some women and non-binary people are all for it. I also perceive problems with the arc in relation to conceptual metaphors beyond just sex, the political implications of which entail intersectional concerns including but well exceeding those of gender.

For me, a key problem of the arc as a macro-textual evocation of conceptual metaphor is its rising and falling nature, which is commonly represented in a literally up and down graph pattern. These visual mappings suggest the conceptual metaphor 'more is up' (Lakoff & Johnson, 1980/2003, p. 149). Although conflict and crisis may not be happy experiences for the heroes themselves, common insistence in creative writing advice books that conflict is the way to titillate readers associates 'more is up' with 'happy is up', thus suggesting that 'MORE is HAPPY' (p. 149). As noted in chapter eight, this set of associations reflects and reinstates white western values of consumer culture (p. 149). It also aligns with conceptualizations of 'well-being as wealth' (Lakoff, 1995, p. 1) in conservative political discourses that associate 'moral strength' with financial independence (pp. 5–7). Such discourses encourage rich people to perceive themselves as 'model citizens' (p. 9) who feel no guilt, only pride in their success – even if success is won via exploitation of other people and/or environmentally damaging practices. As chapter eight relayed such discourses also enable people in positions of privilege to judge those in less fortunate situations as undeserving of empathy or support, because it is assumed they just aren't working hard enough – a view that eclipses longstanding inequities of race, gender, social class and intersecting factors, thereby allowing conservatives to justify (in their own minds) ongoing lack of action towards change. In this way, arc narratives as conceptual metaphors reflect and reinstate ideologies of extreme individualism.

Further problematizing the arc is that its vertical rising and falling action follows a single trajectory, mapped against a horizontal axis of time proceeding from the beginning, through the middle, to the end. The arc as conceptual metaphor thereby promotes a 'linear and cumulative understanding of time' as 'moving only forwards, or backwards', which is also often reflected in representations wherein time becomes an 'arrow' and the future a 'target' (Stroude, 2022, p. 361). This understanding of time as linear is but one among many, other examples of which include time a cycle, flow or set of linkages – conceptualizations of time that may encourage stronger tendences towards attention and appreciation for temporal experiences in and of themselves and/or one's interrelatedness with past and future generations of beings, both human and beyond-human (pp. 366–7). Linear conceptualizations of time are strongly associated with dominant white western cultures wherein progress entails incrementally working towards having more and more, and time becomes a resource to be mined for maximum returns – time becomes money (Lakoff & Johnson, 1980/2003, p. 95).

Chapter eight already observed how conceptual metaphors of time as money reflect and reinstate the labour practices of industrial capitalism by 'imposing a propaganda of time-thrift to the working people', thereby reinforcing inequities of social class and naturalizing economic inequalities by suggesting those with more wealth have used their time more wisely and encouraging exploited workers to work harder rather than question systemic injustices of the labour and production systems at play (Stroude, 2022, p. 361). Beyond social class, linear time bears unfairly on women, whose opportunities for occupational success remain compromised by historic divisions between forms of work deemed suitable and unsuitable for female workers, ongoing pay discrepancies, stresses of workplace sexual harassment, and in many cases, career interruption due to pregnancy, childrearing and/or other caring responsibilities (Di Niro & Walker, 2018). Conceptual metaphors of linear time and progress additionally bear problematic implications for bisexual people, transgender people and o/Other queer people whose life trajectories and temporal experiences tend towards repetition and fragmentation – what Jack Halberstam terms living in 'queer time' – in comparison with heteronormative and homonormative models of maturation over time (for instance, because bisexual people may find themselves coming out not once but repeatedly; because transgender people may undergo puberty in adulthood; etc.) (Halberstam, 2005). Similar points are raised in relation to theories of 'crip time' (temporal experiences of living with disability) (Saunders, 2020, p. 1), 'fat time' (temporal experiences associated with fatness) (Dickman, 2022, p. 65), neurodiverse ways of being in time (Saunders, 2020, p. 1) and the temporal fragmentations that often form part of living with trauma (Richardson et al., 2023).

Perhaps most problematic about white western conceptualizations of time as linear are their racial and colonial implications. As Riyad Shahjahan observes, western associations of time with 'linear history, progress, and … Darwin's evolutionary theory' have long served as 'an epistemic tool through which a chronology of difference was created by colonial logic' (2015, p. 490). Arianne Stroude similarly critiques how linear progress-oriented ideologies of time have historically been used to spread colonization and justify western nations' domination over so-called 'developing' countries supposedly 'trying to catch up' with the west, thus solidifying 'global economic and political structures based on imperialist arrangements' while eclipsing the 'resource-intensive consumption' and ecological damage unbridled progress often affects (2022, pp. 361–2). In these ways, arc narratives as conceptual metaphors reflect and reinstate not only extreme individualism, but human exceptionalism, and are thus politically implicated in the maintenance of inequitable power relations both amongst humans and of humans with beyond-human being.

As an arc narrative sub-set, the hero's journey inherits these conceptual metaphors of more as better and progress over linear time – becoming also politically implicated in representation and re-presentation of extreme individualism, human exceptionalism, intersectional inequities amongst humans, and human violence against beyond-human being. The hero's journey indeed amplifies problems of extreme individualism by emphasizing the progress of a sole figure who, by virtue of being *the* hero, is identified as special and more worthy of attention than o/Other characters who exist to enable the hero's story to unfold. Human exceptionalism is also often amplified because the journey involves venturing into a wild unknown world, the challenges of which may include struggles against nature as a dangerous, unpredictable force. Furthermore, the hero in question is mostly either human, or anthropomorphized with human traits. Historically, this human hero has also been by implication cis-male, racially privileged, able-bodied, straight and hegemonically privileged across most other axes of intersectionality.

I recognize that the final claim of the above paragraph might appear contentious. Campbell's (1949/2004) monomyth was based on analyses of stories from global cultures, including ones featuring female protagonists, and Vogler carefully alternated between 'he' and 'she' pronouns when outlining the hero's journey stages (1998/2007, pp. 10–18). Many mainstream narratives use the hero's journey for stories with protagonists who are female, African American, or otherwise beyond the hegemonic hero norm. The next section clarifies my claim by attending to these narratives, noting both their possibilities and limits.

Subverting the monomyth?

Chapter six considered efforts to redress creative writing's representative inequities by promoting so-called diverse voices. I noted that such efforts have made important and ongoing gains but remain limited if they do not also address pressures on writers to align with aesthetic standards of so-called literary merit defined by hegemonically dominant patriarchal white western tastes. As the examples considered in this section illustrate, similar limitations apply to hero's journey stories that simply swap out the able-bodied, straight, white cis-male hero for a protagonist who exceeds these conventions in some way, without redress to the hero's journey model.

Portrayals of female heroes in mainstream films exemplify how focusing on the *who* of writing without attention to the *how* enables persisting reinforcement of ideological frameworks that maintain subordination of the very groups such stories superficially seem to empower. Though such stories feature women in heroic roles, thereby seeming to provide feminist role-models, they typically 'subordinate gender issues that might affect the protagonist to the story blueprint' (Jacey, 2010, p. 312). One illustration is Rey, who features in the *Star Wars* films *The Force Awakens* (Abrams, 2015), *The Last Jedi* (Johnson, 2017) and *The Rise of*

Skywalker (Abrams, 2019). Rey's first appeared soon after Disney appropriated the *Star Wars* franchise in 2012, seemingly reflecting Disney's 'alleged commitment to depicting empowered female characters' by reinventing 'the passive Disney Princess through a feminist revamping that sees the modern Princess taking on the mantle of an action heroine' (Giannelli, 2020, p. 97). Rey is often celebrated as a positive portrayal of a female hero bearing 'skills usually associated with *Star Wars* male characters . . . making the point that the new Disney Princess simulacra are as capable as men: they fight and use the Force, repair and operate vehicles, and plan on-the-spot successful rescue missions' (pp. 103–4). Yet even these superficially positive traits are problematic because they position Rey as a '"Mary Sue," an impossibly perfect type who excels at any task . . . contrasting with other girls who are portrayed as weak, needy, and imperiled' (Larabee, 2016, p. 8). Though Rey encounters patriarchal oppression, she easily speaks up against it in ways most other female *Star Wars* characters do not (Meneses & de Alenca Costa, 2023, pp. 4–5). This implies gender inequities could be easily solved if women simply toughened up and became more like men, thereby downplaying the systemic, structural, and symbolic forces of hegemonic gender still at play.

Rey's impossible perfection and imperviousness to systemic injustices seems particularly problematic given her promotion to young girls and parents as 'a new kind of popular feminist hero and role model' (Wood et al., 2020, p. 546). As a 'girl who can do anything', the figure of Rey easily plays into 'a deterministic project through which parents aim to cultivate the "right" kind of girls' (p. 546). Rey 'uses capitalist mechanics when she sees fit to fight the oppressions of the patriarchal system endured on Jakku', thereby 'messaging to young audiences that if they are unable to defeat the system, they must use it for their own gain' (Giannelli, 2020, p. 112). As feminist critics note, 'Disney's more inclusive character development is not a genuine effort toward diversity', but rather 'a marketing strategy exploiting female audiences' desire to recognize themselves in movie characters and products' (p. 97). Young girls who identify with Rey are encouraged to 'invest in an individualized idea of doing "good" through consumption', becoming drawn into the 'project of participating in and consuming culture . . . as a consumer in neoliberalism' (Wood et al., 2020, p. 546).

The rise of Rey also 'intersects with recent representations of women in combat roles in the wake of the Pentagon's decision to eliminate restrictions on them', rendering Rey 'thoroughly embedded in a comic-book war and a national militarism' (Larabee, 2016, p. 8). This aligns with Jacey's point about how stories that insert female heroes into the conventional hero's journey model typically continue to reify values associated with patriarchy – for instance, by celebrating individualist, warlike competition via the singular hero who goes out into the world to conquer enemies, meanwhile downplaying the worth of alternative values such as collectivism, care and efforts towards overcoming adversarial them/us divisions (Jacey, 2010, p. 313). In response to these problems of the conventional hero's journey, feminist theorist Maureen Murdock proposed a 'heroine's journey' (1990). However, most versions of the heroine's journey still imply 'an innate masculinity and femininity' (Jacey, 2010, p. 314). This reflects binary, essentialist views on gender as masculine or feminine and attached to cisgender male and female bodies respectively, often with added implications of heteronormative sexual orientation – views that sustain ongoing oppression of LGBTQIA+ people while also undoing the feminist cause by pigeonholing women into traditional submissive roles (Sadri, 2020).

To get beyond the heroine's journey's gender essentialism, queer theorists have posed a queer hero's journey (Sadri, 2020). This is frequently identifiable in young adult fiction to convey stories about 'coming out' (publicly revealing one's sexuality or gender) as a 'rite of passage' (Bowden, 2021, p. 67). However, reflecting how gay and lesbian fiction has often facilitated ongoing erasure of bisexuality, asexuality, transgender people and non-binary people (see chapter six), queer hero's journey narratives of coming out are typically problematic for the latter groups because 'the queer is prevented from articulating itself' (p. 67). For instance, transgender characters are frequently 'robbed of the right to come out for themselves, instead being outed by an antagonistic figure who projects that character into a space of victimization and marginalization' (p. 67). Such narratives fulfil the requirements for 'drama and conflict' hero's journey and arc narrative forms impose by bringing transgender characters to a 'low point . . . stripped of the things they usually depend on – such as support, self-confidence and certainty about their identities', re-iterating 'repetitive and predictable' stories wherein queer people are 'inevitably presented as victimized, internally conflicted, mentally unwell, isolated and out of place . . . voiceless and without autonomy' (p. 67). Bowden therefore argues that queer narratives which engage hero's journey models 'give the appearance of celebrating the diverse ways it is possible to experience queer gender but ultimately collaborate with the very stereotypes they claim to resist' (p. 67).

Regarding disability, while the quest and restitution narratives recommended by Frank (1995/2013) prove helpful in some cases, they are for many people directly detrimental because the social pressure to generate a coherent linear tale of insight won through struggle belies ongoing feelings of chaos, trauma and non-linear re-living of the so-called past as present and persisting experiences of physical and psychological pain (Smith & Sparkes, 2005). Similarly for neurodiversity, narratives like Mark Haddon's *The Curious Incident of the Dog in the Night-Time* (2003) – wherein an autistic boy solves a murder mystery using his unusual 'mathematical genius' – may seem to provide a positive 'anti-hero's journey' (Siegelman, 2005, p. 47). However, they do so by evoking problematic 'savant' tropes (see discussion in Murray, 2008, p. 65). The hero's journey likewise seems troublesome for positive representations of fatness, because it tends to encourage stories wherein the fat protagonist's quest is all about losing weight, which promotes fatphobia rather than acknowledging fat bodies and lives as equally valid (see discussion in Nolfi, 2011, p. 55).

Returning to Rey, another problem the above examples raise is her story's lack of intersectional nuance. As Ann Larabee notes, the 'Mary Sue' figure Rey embodies is 'almost always white and heterosexual' (2016, p. 8). Rey stays faithful to this trope, also appearing as cis-gender, able-bodied, thin and conventionally attractive by white western standards. Though she is raised in poverty and in some ways represents social class struggle, this is largely undone by the later revelation her ability to use the Force stems from a hitherto-obscured noble lineage, which plays into the deeply problematic idea some people are eugenically born superior others (Giannelli, 2020, p. 110). Rey thus bears hegemonic privilege on basically all fronts other than gender, where she still retains privilege relative to transgender, non-binary, and intersex people. Her imperviousness to patriarchal injustices not only downplays the ongoing challenges patriarchal culture produces, but makes invisible how these challenges are enhanced for women simultaneously combatting intersecting injustices. Regarding race, for instance, the characters Rose, played by Vietnamese American actor Kelly Marie Tran, and Finn, played by British Nigerian actor John Boyega, bear minor roles compared with Rey's. Their scant characterizations have been criticized as 'poorly written' and 'bland' – in other words, tokenistic (Reysen et al., 2024, p. 256). Even so, the mere presence of these non-white characters outraged a certain toxic component of the *Star Wars* fanbase to such degrees they launched 'racist and sexist' social media attacks against Tran, Boyega, and the films' producers (p. 256).

In making this shift towards race and the hero's journey, I again acknowledge Campbell's monomyth was based on analyses of stories from global cultures. However, much like traditional white western ethnographers – and despite his aforementioned critique of individualism – Campbell interpreted these stories via his own cultural lens, projecting '[w]hite ways of knowing and being' steeped in 'individualism, meritocracy, and Western paternalism', which Hollywood's adaptation of the monomyth into the hero's journey seemingly amplified (O'Connor, 2022, p. 92). Cait O'Connor signals the problematics of using the conventional hero's journey model for stories with African American protagonists, noting how poorly its individualistic frameworks accommodate 'collective effort, reverence for ancestral guidance, and . . . culture and community' – all of which represent crucial values in traditional African societies and contemporary African American movements of 'collective struggle rooted in Black political and literary tradition' (p. 92). As collective community values of kinship also feature strongly in many First Nations cultures (Wyld, 2025), the points O'Connor makes could also apply to stories about protagonists from many First Nations cultures globally. For instance, in America, Pocahontas 'was turned into a legendary figure by non-

Native writers as a means of justifying their occupation of Native lands and assuaging their guilt after killing off the original inhabitants of the United States' (Wilmer, 2009, p. 8). In these non-Native narratives, Pocahontas is 'constructed as a virtuous and virginal figure who fell in love with a white man, adopted the values of his culture, and helped him overcome the hostile Native population', thus promoting 'a non-Native discourse that implies that the "good Indian" is one who rejects her own people' while '[b]y contrast, many Native Americans have regarded Pocahontas as a traitor to her people' (p. 8).

On a more hopeful note, O'Connor (2022) suggests the possibility of adapting the hero's journey model to tell stories featuring African American characters via analysis of the Marvel film, *Black Panther* (Coogler, 2018). By O'Connor's account, this film 'offers an appealing counter story, a disruption of genre, a disruption of the hero's journey and White ways of existing in time and space' because of the ways it foregrounds 'relationship between hero and society', reclaiming and reshaping the hero's journey model to 'honor collective effort' (2022, p. 92). It also 'creates a place where Black leaders, Black women, and Black genius are cultivated' (p. 92). These suggestions are in line with other critiques praising the film's presentation of 'experiences of Black people that disrupted stereotypical tropes' as 'an example of how positive media representation can increase the self-esteem and empowerment of Black people' (Dogan et al., 2022, pp. 183, 192).

However, *Black Panther* (Coogler, 2018) has been criticized for pandering to white audiences' demands for 'visual spectacle that entertains and sells' while 'distancing them from the actual content of what they are viewing', via 'unrealistic portrayal of Africans' belying 'the lived conditions and social issues' of people living in Africa today (Viljoen, 2023, para. 3). African American viewers meanwhile report mixed responses: while the film offered enjoyable 'escapism' from day-to-day experiences of racism, this largely entailed 'avoidance coping' – 'hope at the expense of active coping strategies' or action against ongoing issues of racism such as police brutality (Dogan et al., 2022, pp. 191–2). In parallel with how the female hero's imperviousness to gender inequity downplays the ongoing injustices of patriarchalism, black hero's journey tales thus risk downplaying the significant injustices racism continues to enforce at social, structural, systemic, and symbolic levels, letting white audiences superficially imagine 'enough has been done about diversity' (Viljoen, 2023, para. 4).

While using the hero's journey model to resist the intersecting hegemonies with which it has traditionally been associated is therefore possible and bears some capacity to increase representative equity, the examples this section explored illustrate the persisting limitations such approaches entail. As the critiques of Jacey (2010, p. 313) and O'Connor (2022, p. 92) reflect, many of these problems seem related to the ways in which the hero's journey continues to figure a single human or anthropomorphized hero, reifying ideologies of extreme individualism and human essentialism, regardless who that individual hero might be.

Re-orienting

This chapter has considered the ways in which macro-textual features of textual form and structure may convey conceptual metaphors bearing political implications. Via examination of hero's journey and arc narratives, I have demonstrated the problematic ways in which conceptual metaphors of form and structure may reflect and reinstate ideological values of hegemonically dominant groups. While it is possible to use the hero's journey model to represent groups historically subordinated by the intersecting hegemonies with which the model has traditionally been associated – for instance, via the heroine's journey, the queer hero's journey and the Black hero's journey – such approaches remain limited, reflecting why efforts to redress creative writing's representative inequities can bear greater impact by considering *how* representation is aesthetically mediated as well as *who* it represents. There is therefore a need to think beyond the journey. Chapter ten takes up this objective, examining alternative forms creative writing can take.

10 CONCEPTUAL METAPHORS THROUGH FORM AND STRUCTURE PART TWO: BEYOND THE JOURNEY

A walking/writing encounter with a Brown Snake

hushed shimmer   you are
                                             gone

        before I've really seen
you
        let alone thought to fear   you

                        as I've been taught   to fear

your poison whisper   – one bite
                        and in a shimmer, I'd be   gone, gone,

                        beyond
                        the grass where you now hide

                        gone forever, dust
                          and bone
                                        –
                                yet

somehow, I don't fear
you, somehow   I long
                                again   to glimpse   you

                                                      – a shooting star
                                                      a futile wish –

your shimmer   is now   long gone

and so,   alone   with my footfalls

                                      – loud, clumsy echoes –

I breathe   slow
                                      new
                                            dread

                                      wondering why
                                      you streaked so fast

            like a tear down earth's dry cheek

  – barely   a shimmer

                        then   gone

            as though you were the one with reason
                              to fear me
                              and my loud feet

Compass

Chapter nine demonstrated how conceptual metaphor can operate at macro-textual levels via form and structure. I used journey and arc narratives to illustrate the problematic political implications form and structure can affect by re-presenting conceptual metaphors associated with dominant white western ideologies of extreme individualism and human exceptionalism. Attempts to reinvent the monomyth, including the heroine's journey, the black hero's journey, and the queer hero's journey bear some benefits, but remain limited, signalling a need to think beyond the journey and the arc. There are after all near endless forms and structures creative writing can take (Alison, 2019, p. 4). All of them present different conceptual metaphors involving different evocations of aesthetics as (political) content. In this chapter, I discuss a selection chosen because they unsettle individualism and/or human exceptionalism, offering scope for promoting more dialogic, interrelational ways of being with each other and the earth. These include ecologically informed patterns, braided texts, short story cycles and experimental traditions of poetic form and formal play in sonnets, villanelles, ghazals and pantoums.

Ecologically informed patterns

In chapter nine, I considered Alison's (2019) argument for creative writing teachers and theorists to promote a more diverse range of story patterns beyond the currently dominant arc form. Though Alison does not address the hero's journey specifically, many of the problems relating to it are as chapter nine observed related to its arc features. The possibilities Alison raises are therefore relevant for thinking beyond the hero's journey, too. Likening writing to architecture, Alison poses writers can build stories as structures in virtually endless shapes and ways (p. 4). She then suggests looking to ecological patterns such as those of 'living creatures', 'organic beings', 'a crystal', 'an orange', 'a puzzle' or any one of the multiple 'patterns' recurring 'at every scale in our world, atomic to galactic' (pp. 19–21). From a human essentialist perspective, leaping from architecture to nature might seem contradictory, but from a perspective that recognizes humans as animals, the things we build – with bricks and mortar as with words – are likenable to nests, hives and burrows, giving pause to recall, 'eco' comes from 'oikos', which means 'home' and signals collective responsibilities involved in sharing and maintaining living spaces (Zandvliet, 2016, p. 83).

The ecologically-inspired textual patterns Alison suggests include the 'SPIRAL', which she likens to 'a fiddlehead fern, whirlpool, hurricane . . . or a chambered nautilus'; a 'MEANDER', which unfolds like 'a river curving and kinking' or 'a snake in motion'; a 'RADIAL or EXPLOSION', resembling 'a splash of dripping water' or 'petals growing from a daisy's heart'; 'BRANCHING and other FRACTAL patterns' of 'self-replication at a lesser scale' such as those of 'trees, coastlines, clouds'; and 'CELLULAR' patterns of 'repeating shapes' such as those in 'honeycomb' or a 'foam of bubbles', which might 'look like cells or, inversely, like a net' (2019, pp. 21–2).

Another ecological form of relevance is Ursula Le Guin's 'carrier bag' (1986/1989) (for by the same reasoning that architecture is ecological, so too are bags and the things we human animals gather in them). Observing the dominance of stories 'about bashing, thrusting, raping, killing, about the Hero', Le Guin argues for the novel as 'a fundamentally unheroic kind of story' (p. 168), yet observes:

the Hero has frequently taken it over, that being his imperial nature and uncontrollable impulse, to take everything over and run it while making stern decrees and laws to control his uncontrollable impulse to kill it. So the Hero has decreed through his mouthpieces the Lawgivers, first, that the proper shape of the narrative is that of the arrow or spear, starting *here* and going straight *there* and THOK! hitting its mark (which drops dead); second, that the central concern of narrative, including the novel, is conflict; and third, that the story isn't any good if he isn't in it. (pp. 168–9)

In contrast, Le Guin poses 'that the natural, proper, fitting shape of the novel might be that of a sack, a bag' – for '[a] book holds words' and '[w]ords hold things', raising possibilities of the novel as 'a medicine bundle, holding things in a particular, powerful relation to one another and to us' (1986/1989, p. 169). This suggestion bears resonances with Alison's 'branching', 'fractal' and 'cellular' patterns, all of which emphasize connections between smaller parts and greater phenomena (2019, pp. 21–2). It also articulates with Gilles Deleuze and Felix Guattari's concept of books as 'assemblages' that can take 'arborescent' or 'rhizomatic' forms (1987, pp. 3–8).

By Deleuze and Guattari's account, arborescent forms reflect the main trunk and branches of a tree, forming 'hierarchical systems with centers of significance and subjectification' that naturalize hegemonic privilege and subordination (1987, p. 16). Rhizomatic forms meanwhile reflect the 'very diverse forms' of extension and interconnection 'in all directions' of potatoes, burrows, grass and other 'subterranean' forms wherein there is typically no privileged centre or unifying pattern other than collective interaction and diversification (p. 7). While arborescence, for Deleuze and Guattari, is associated with problematic linear forms singularly proceeding from beginning through middle to end, '[a] rhizome has no beginning or end; it is always in the middle, between things, interbeing, *intermezzo*'; while arborescence evokes 'filiation' and 'imposes the verb "to be"', 'the rhizome is alliance, uniquely alliance', projecting 'the conjunction, "and ... and ... and..."' (p. 25). Critiquing an overemphasis on arborescence in western culture and thought, Deleuze and Guattari (1987) argue for rhizomatic forms because they

> know how to move between things, establish a logic of the AND, overthrow ontology, do away with foundations, nullify endings and beginnings ... The middle is by no means an average; on the contrary, it is where things pick up speed ... a perpendicular direction, a transversal movement that sweeps one and the other away, a stream without beginning or end that undermines its banks. (p. 25)

In the light of more recent research indicating the strong collective entanglements trees bear with fungi, soil, bacteria, animals and each other (Angrish, 2022),

Deleuze and Guattari's (1987) critique of arborescence ironically underestimates the rhizomatic qualities trees themselves already bear. This noted, their emphasis on the need for forms emphasizing non-hierarchical interconnectivity aligns with the arguments Alison (2019) and Le Guin (1986/1989) separately present, while the notion of rhizomatic systems (including those in which trees participate) offers another ecological pattern for macro-textual conceptual metaphors via which creative writing can unsettle human essentialism and extreme individualism.

Braided narratives and short story cycles

Braided narratives and short story cycles seem well suited for generating branching, fractal, cellular, carrier bag and/or rhizomic forms based on non-hierarchical connections between multiplicities. In braided narratives, writers 'plait together different narrative threads' – for instance via 'multiple narrators who tell distinct, sometimes incommensurate, stories', in ways that 'grapple with both the poignant fissure that fractures the most intimate attachments between individuals and the chasm that historical violences carve between social groups' (Bancroft, 2018, p. 262). A short story cycle is 'a volume of "autonomous" yet "interrelated" stories' wherein 'each of the stories can function and be understood independently', yet 'the meaning of the cycle is generated by reading it in order, as a whole' (Wood, 2022, p. 44). While braided narratives and short story cycles are often confused (Bancroft, 2018, p. 262), a key distinction is that each story in a short story cycle can be read as a stand-alone work, which is typically not the case for all threads of braided narratives. In both cases, however, the assemblage creates a whole encompassing more than the sum of its parts, and the foregrounding of multiple distinct yet interconnecting stories produces rhizomatic interconnections that refuse the singular, hierarchical conceptual metaphors of hero's journey and arc narratives, instead emphasizing diversity, collectivity and collaboration. Short story cycles are frequently 'cyclical, iterative, and incomplete' (Wood, 2022, p. 43), and braided narratives similarly 'acknowledge their interdependence and contradictions', inviting 'a way of reading and relating that strives to be open to different experiences, aware of the tensions between them, and accountable to these sometimes conflicting claims' (Bancroft, 2018, p. 264).

Niamh Wood pitches short story cycles as 'particularly well-positioned' for stories about climate change because of their 'capacity to create a sense of community, defamiliarize climate change discourse, [and] generate ecological enchantment' without becoming 'overtly didactic' (2022, p. 43). Corinne Bancroft meanwhile notes how braided narratives can 'help train readers to hold multiple, often incommensurate, subjectivities in our minds simultaneously, pushing us to embrace new channels of responsibility that recognize many distinct subjects'

(2018, p. 263). *The Overstory* by Richard Powers (2018), which straddles the boundaries of braided narratives and short story cycles, exemplifies the potentials both Wood (2022) and Bancroft (2018) signal. The book is divided into four parts – 'Roots', 'Trunk', 'Crown' and 'Seeds' – evoking the form of a (rhizomatic) tree. 'Roots' introduces the book's wide cast of characters via eight distinct stories, the only obvious connection between which is that each story features trees in some way. In 'Trunk', the separate stories begin coming together: some characters meet in real life; others connect indirectly, for instance by reading a book another has written. In 'Crown', these interactions intensify, particularly through characters who become involved in ecological activism. Then in 'Seeds', the characters again separate and scatter, with some succumbing to death, and questions about the ongoing impacts of their actions for the future of trees and all beings remaining open and unanswered.

Another example of textual form drawing on nature to tell interconnected stories with rhizomatic interconnections is *Purple Threads* by Wirradjuri (First Nations Australian) author Jeanine Leane (2011/2023). As Evelyn Araluen notes, *Purple Threads* refuses 'Western teleological narrative' and 'gives us something more radical' via the interwoven stories of 'multiple generations of Wiradjuri women [who] live in defiance of exploitation and displacement' (2023, p. xi). The book 'unfolds not through crisis or conflict, but instead an intricate historical geography' wherein '[n]o story is simply told' – for '[s]tory is an act of radical locality, which rejects the ordering of the world into wide abstract categories for shipping grain and gold and wool from one end to the other of it', and these radical stories 'turn in their own time through their own power just like the land: country floods, country burns, country grows and regrows forever' (pp. xi–xii).

Yet one more example is the creative nonfiction book *Black Duck* by Yuin, Bunurong and Tasmanian Aboriginal (First Nations Australian) author Bruce Pascoe (2024). *Black Duck* comprises six parts: 'Late Summer', 'Autumn', 'Winter', Early Spring', 'Spring' and 'Early Summer'. This six-season approach reflects the highly localized, unique understandings of weather bespoke to different First Nations language groups across Australia, some of which name up to thirteen distinct seasons (Woodward, 2013). While annual progression in chronological order might at first seem a singular linear approach, the multiple short vignettes within each part take a non-chronological, non-hierarchical approach to ecologically oriented interconnections and diversities. Focusing on titular themes such as 'Grasses', 'Boats', 'Dogs', 'Harvest', 'Snakes' and 'Smoke', these vignettes rarely stay fixed in the one year, rather they leap back and forth into near and distant pasts and futures that together feed a present connected with all time. There are also frequent inter-references between vignettes as well as recurring themes and motifs. These continually remind readers of the complex interconnections ever-present between all parts of an ecology, including humans as ecological beings bearing collective responsibilities to live harmoniously with our kin (however violently overlooked these responsibilities might currently be in dominant white western cultures).

The Overstory (Powers, 2018), *Purple Threads* (Leane, 2011/2023) and *Black Duck* (Pascoe, 2024) exemplify ways in which ecologically inspired story patterns can provide macro-textual conceptual metaphors to help subvert the extreme individualism and human exceptionalism promoted by mainstream hero's journey and arc narratives. However, not all textual patterns necessarily involve storytelling. The need to consider texts that do other things remains – such as portraying an image, emotion, question, problem, possibility or compound between multiple instances of one or more of these things, without necessary recourse to characters, events, time-frames or other features of stories and narratives in the conventional white western sense. To redress this need, the next section considers traditions of experimentation in poetic forms. In making this turn, I wish to discourage any oversimplified split between poems and narratives. I therefore emphasize, poems are often used to tell stories (for instance, in epic poems and verse novels) while there is no necessary association of prose with narrative in the sense of events relayed over time, as reflected in the slipperiness of definitions between prose poetry and flash fiction, both of which often abandon conventional narrative in favour of images, emotions, questions, and other possibilities just noted.

Experimental traditions of poetic form and formal play in sonnets

The previous section noted Alison's analogies between stories and architectural structures writers can build in virtually endless ways (2019, p. 4). Paul Valéry similarly called poets 'architect[s]' whose constructions provide spaces for 'discoveries, comparisons, flashes of expression feeling, intellect, memory, and power of verbal action' (1954, pp. 231–2). The discoveries Valéry signals are also evident in Alison's remarks about how reading and writing become ways of travelling through texts – invisible motions via which 'our way of "seeing" shifts', sparking creative thinking and fresh realizations (2019, p. 5). Links between writing, spatial structures, and thought are likewise commonly raised by poets and poetic theorists (Webb, 2012; Gibbons, 2015; Hanna, 2020, p. 198). Indeed, the word 'stanza' means 'room' (Addison, 2003, p. 124), and stanzas are among the ways in which poetic form enacts a 'determining force on crucial aspects of meaning' including 'types of utterance [that] cannot be made' as well as those that can (p. 140).

The sonnet form is an example of how macro-textual conceptual metaphors expressed through form and structure can steer thinking by both limiting and potentiating what readers and writers may articulate, linguistically and cognitively. Given the associations some poets and theorists draw between formal traditions and conservatism (Hanna, 2020, p. 175–6), my turn to sonnets and traditional forms may seem anathema to this book's radical aims. However, working with traditions does not require slavish adherence to them (Weston, 2016, p. 3). Forms offer rich scope for 'formal innovation' (Hanna, 2020, p. 129). For instance, the Oulipo movement were a 1960s group of French-speaking writers and mathematicians who created literary works using intensive formal constraints (Sainsbury, 2017). Examples of Oulipo techniques include writing an entire book without using the letter e, or replacing every noun in a text with the seventh noun found after it in the dictionary (Frank, 2024). Oulipo writings demonstrated how formal constraints may superficially appear to restrict creative possibility, but can actually promote imagination by barring habituated patterns and necessitating creative problem solving (Sainsbury, 2017, p. 313). For vegan anarchist pacifist poet John Kinsella, formal tradition offers 'a box to be pushed against; to be used pragmatically at times, but ultimately to be tested at every opportunity' (2013, p. 94). I here similarly approach poetic forms as experimental traditions rich with traditions of experimentation.

Sonnets help illustrate what I mean by experimental traditions and traditions of experimentation. A sonnet is conventionally defined as 'a lyric poem consisting of a single stanza of fourteen iambic pentameter lines linked by an intricate rhyme scheme' (Abrams & Harpham, 2015, p. 336). Yet even its dominant iterations it includes two major categories – the 'Italian or Petrarchan sonnet', and the 'English or Shakespearean' version (p. 336). The Italian sonnet 'falls into two main parts: an octave (eight lines) rhyming abbaabba followed by a sestet (six lines) rhyming cdecde or some variant, such as cdccdc' wherein the octave typically states two conflicting perspectives on 'a problem, situation, or incident' that the sestet brings to 'resolution' – a pattern which can be likened to the hero's journey's call to adventure (the problem) and return with the elixir (the resolution) (p. 336). The English sonnet 'falls into three quatrains and a concluding couplet: abab cdcd efef gg' and itself includes another sub-variant, 'the Spenserian sonnet', which links 'each quatrain to the next by a continuing rhyme: abab bcbc cdcd ee' (p. 336). The Italian sonnet is more traditional in the sense of being older. The English versions evolved after the form was brought to England. Although today canonized as dominant and revered, the English sonnet was at its time an aberration purists discouraged or dismissed while enthusiasts found an 'experimental space' of 'freedom, creativity . . . copious wit' and even a 'place of transgression' (Brown, 2004, p. 35).

In addition to adaptations in stanza divisions, metre and rhyme, early English sonnets also expanded subject matter. While early Italian sonnets dealt primarily with romantic tensions between lovers – most specifically, 'the hopes and pains of an adoring male lover' (Abrams & Harpham, 2015, p. 336), later sonneteers in England and elsewhere turned it towards multiple 'other matters of serious concern' (p. 336). They also altered its patten of presenting then resolving two perspectives on a problem, instead offering 'a repetition-with-variation of a statement in each of the three quatrains' and 'an *epigrammatic* turn at the end' (p. 336, original italics). An epigram is 'a concise poem dealing pointedly and often satirically with a single thought or event and often ending with an ingenious turn of thought' that is often 'terse, sage . . . witty . . . [or] paradoxical' (Merriam-Webster, 2024b). An epigrammatic turn is not necessarily a resolution, and bears more potential for open endings. As machines of thinking, the early Italian sonnet and later variations can thereby be seen as presenting different approaches to dialectic as a practice of 'discussion and reasoning by dialogue as a method of intellectual investigation' (Merriam-Webster, 2024c). While resolution in the early Italian sonnet encouraged the winning of one view over the other, or a bending towards harmony via compromise – for instance, in Hegelian dialectic where 'a concept or its realization passes over into and is preserved and fulfilled by its opposite' or Marxian dialectic where 'thesis' and 'antithesis' are brought towards 'synthesis' (Merriam-Webster, 2024c) – later sonnets' repetition patterns allowed for more than two points of view. They also make space for ambiguous endings encompassing persisting differences or entirely new turns, rejecting quick and easy solutions while promoting the need for ongoing efforts of interactive reasoning.

Ongoing experiments with the sonnet across recent centuries entailed even more bending of its so-called rules. By contemporary definitions, sonnets need not contain fourteen lines or follow any firm rules of metre or rhyme but can remain recognizable as sonnets via dialectic processes (Weston, 2016). Ecopoets are increasingly taking to sonnets and 'sonnet-like forms' as machines of thought for thinking through conflicting perspectives on problems without neat resolutions (p. 3). Recognizing how 'form can be harnessed – adapted rather than slavishly adhered to – in creating poetic ecologies', ecopoets repurpose this 'form with a history intimately associated with very human concerns' for 'poems explicitly concerned with nature, place, and environment', promoting a 'warping of expectations' that 'allows these poets to dramatize a shift towards ecologically-aware thinking' (p. 3).

(Ongoing) traditions of experimentation in villanelles, ghazals and pantoums

Moving beyond the dialectical thinking sonnets sustain, villanelles open possibilities for dialogic interplays of more rhizomatic, interconnective variations. Dan Disney ascribes the villanelle 'an unstable canonical history': despite claims of it being an 'antique' form, the earliest known instance appears to be 'J'ay perdu ma Tourterelle', written in 1572 by French writer Jean Passerat (Disney, 2021, pp. 85–6). In the dominant villanelle form, the first and third lines of the first stanza are repeated across subsequent stanzas, with one of the two lines appearing in each stanza in alternate order, before the final stanza reunites them, usually bringing them into closer proximity as a couplet (Abrams & Harpham, 2015, p. 343). Like sonnets, villanelles can enact varying modes of dialectic between the thoughts of the two repeated lines, but they additionally offer scope to repeatedly rework those thoughts by placing each one in a fresh context each time it appears. The final stanza can then forge a new relationship between them, remade within a constellation of all the other ideas middle stanzas have introduced. Villanelle patterns of repetition and interconnection seem vital to the strong 'political possibilities of the form', even in its more conventional iterations (Disney, 2021, p. 86). These include ecological possibilities. For instance, reviewing Kinsella's *Brimstone* (2020), Disney notes how Kinsella 'threads together texts either praising or memorializing nature', thereby 'surveying colonized lands while the planet endures a fourth industrial revolution' in ways revealing 'how sustained, instrumentalizing attacks are causing systemic collapse' (Disney, 2021, p. 86).

Furthermore, like sonnets, villanelles come in multiple variations and bear rich scope for experimentation. Disney's own unpaginated collection *either, Orpheus* (2016), most poems in which 'spring from stray quotes excavated from *Paris Review* interviews' or other quotes from canonical and contemporary writers (Griffin, 2016, para. 2), demonstrates a radical range of potentialities to which the villanelle may give rise. Disney does not remain bound to repeating lines verbatim, instead making repetition 'free game for distortions and teasing-outs of nuance . . . with key repeating phrases shifting in subtle degrees throughout (Griffin, 2016, para. 9). For instance, in a poem responding to the writings of Irish poet Paul Muldoon, the line 'as *all children know, truth* is a snake eating its own tail' morphs into 'and *as all children know, truth* is self-polishing, a bust of bronze', then, 'and *as all children say, truth* is the future's loudest part', before returning to 'where, *as all children know, truth* is a snake eating its own tail' (Disney, 2016, n.p., original italics). Other poems use repetition even more subtly, in ways perhaps closer to motifs. A poem responding to American poet John Ashbury, for example, transforms 'I argue about this with my analyst' into 'I argue / bliss is improbable', then 'I have many arguments with my analyst', and finally 'arguing about this with my analyst' (Disney, 2016, n.p.).

Disney's Ashbury poem eschews conventional villanelle stanza patterns, presenting all lines as a single block. Its repetitions do not always sit neatly on a single line, with some broken across multiple lines – one example of Disney's radical engagements with 'the limitless possibilities of enjambment as a form of making new meanings at the margins' (Griffin, 2016, n.p.). Combined with the dialogic interplays *either, Orpheus* (Disney, 2016) crafts via its assemblage of differing poetic voices, these poetic innovations produce 'a calcification of current moments across spaces' that together illuminate the crises of late capitalism and what Disney terms the 'anthroposcene', thereby making clear 'that the end of the anthroposcene is neither a bang nor a whimper, but the accumulation of a long series of unexamined events and choices' (Griffin, 2016, para. 9). These techniques provided inspiration for the brown snake poem that opens this chapter, which combines villanelle repetition patterns (the motifs of 'gone' and 'fear') with ecopoetic techniques of typeless space and fragmented formatting (see chapter three).

Ghazals and pantoums engage patterns of repetition and recontextualization similar yet different to those of villanelles, each inviting slightly different associations and directions of thought. The ghazal – originally an Arabic form – is comprised of couplets (any number), each of which ends with the same word or phrase (Poetry Foundation, 2024a). Instead of a dialectic between two main ideas, it focuses on one idea brought into multiple different situations, each of which shows the main idea in new ways, potentially opening fresh avenues for exploration. These potentials seem likenable to Alison's notion of radial narratives exploding out from their centres (2019, p. 165). The pantoum – a traditional Malaysian form widely adopted into western literatures – is conventionally made of four-line stanzas (any number) across which each stanza's second and fourth lines recur as the next one's first and third lines, and the final stanza's second and fourth lines revive the first stanza's first and third lines (Poetry Foundation, 2024b). Like villanelles, pantoums involve correspondences between endings and beginnings, with various lines repeated and recontextualized through the poem's body. But more than two lines are repeated and recontextualized in this way, allowing for a wider range of wanderings – always still with some connective thread to bring past into present and future in ways that also unsettle dominant western notions of linear time and progression. The pantoum can thus be said to progress something like the meandering narratives Alison likens to rivers and snakes (2019, p. 117).

It would be possible to make similar comments about virtually every poetic form in existence. Each one builds a different textual space through which readers and writers may move, thus potentiating different thoughts and discoveries. As exhaustive discussion of all forms and potentials exceeds what is possible here, I hope the select examples I have provided can spark thinking about forms and possibilities beyond those I have been able to explore. This includes so-called free verse – in my view, a problematic name and notion, for any use of language (including but exceeding poetry and creative writing across all forms and genres) inevitably involves negotiating the constraints language brings, such as the existing lexicon and scope for lexical expansions that can still convey meaning to others. There are also constraints writers choose for ourselves. Some writers – like the Oulipans – do this in conscious, deliberately difficult ways (for instance, by writing a book without using a nominated letter) (Sainsbury, 2017). More common forms of chosen constraints include selection of topic, genre, perspective and voice, all of which both enable and constrain what the writing can say – and necessarily so: without foreclosing some possibilities, both writers and readers would drown in an overwhelm of word soup. When I write so-called free verse poetry, I produce constraints for myself via patterns of stanza lengths, line lengths, repetition, and sonic resonances of assonance and consonance, among other devices. Only occasionally do I directly base my patterns on a single established form (as in the brown snake villanelle), but the constraints I choose for myself are nonetheless informed – consciously and unconsciously, I think – by formal poems I have read and the influences their patterns bear on poetic practice generally.

The point of exploring sonnets, villanelles, ghazals and pantoums has not been to advocate these forms themselves in their conventional iterations. Rather, I hope this section's discussions can prompt reflection regarding what we as readers and writers might learn from them about new possibilities for building poems as architectural and/or ecological structures that enable fresh scope for thought. Additionally, I suggest these possibilities extend not only to building poems but may be used to devise innovative structures for stories and other texts (for instance, characters within a short story cycle might meet and interact in villanelle, pantoum, or ghazal patterns, or in novel patterns inspired by their repetition schemes). I hope experimental traditions of poetic form can inspire even more possibilities for conceptual metaphor at the macro-textual level, in addition to the ecologically inspired examples in braided narratives and short story cycles discussed earlier.

Re-orienting

Following from chapter nine's observations about the problematic political implications of hero's journey and arc narratives, this chapter sought to think beyond the journey by exploring alternative forms and structures for creative writing. As noted at the outset, it is possible to structure texts in virtually endless ways. I have here considered but a very narrow selection, chosen for their capacities to unsettle the extreme individualism and human exceptionalism that appear key problems of hero's journey and arc narratives. These have included ecological forms, braided narratives, short story cycles and poetic forms including sonnets, villanelles, pantoums and ghazals. There are, however, many more approaches to form and structure conducive to these objectives – and myriad objectives beyond them, too. As earlier noted, rather than an exhaustive account, I have sought to provide just a few examples to prompt reflection regarding ways in which politically oriented readers and writers might identify and develop new possibilities for conceptual metaphor at the macro-textual level via form and structure.

These macro-textual approaches can, I suggest, bear greatest impact if combined with micro-textual considerations of conceptual metaphor through figurative language, as discussed in chapter eight. Equally vital to remember is the point made in chapter seven – that no single aesthetic technique bears any intrinsic political valence applicable across all times and places, and politically oriented readers and writers must ongoingly rethink the political implications aesthetic decisions entail in relation to shifting contexts via practices of reading with, against, and beyond the text. This point is true of the hero's journey too: in previous times, it may have strengthened collective societies by providing each individual with a sense of their place in and responsibilities to the whole, but in a society dominated by extreme individualism, its glorification of a single special figure tends towards the opposite effect (see chapter nine). In future contexts, this could change yet again. So, I wish to emphasize, it is not the model itself I have been critiquing, rather the way its current dominance threatens formal diversity. My argument is not about eradicating the hero's journey altogether, but rather, bringing it onto a more even level with o/Other equally valid ways of telling stories, enhancing re-presentative equity via aesthetics as (political) content.

PRAXIS MODULE THREE: AESTHETICS AS (POLITICAL) CONTENT

Overview of experiments

Like those in modules one and two, these praxis experiments are adaptable across formal and informal learning in groups and independently. They provide examples of ways in which to activate the strategies of creative writing analysis and production theorized in chapters eight to ten – though they are certainly not the only ways, and I hope each one can spark thinking about additional possibilities for experimentation. Main concepts include:

1   Operations of **aesthetics as (political) content** via **conceptual metaphors** at micro-textual levels via devices of **figurative language** (including but not limited to linguistic metaphors, similes, personification, anthropomorphism, zoomorphism, chremamorphism, metonymy, synecdoche and symbolic imagery).

2   Operations of **aesthetics as (political) content** via **conceptual metaphors** at macro-level levels via **form and structure** (for instance, the monomyth pattern, arc narratives, and various so-called fixed forms in poetry, as well as alternatives to these dominant approaches).

3   At both micro- and macro-textual levels, the need for attention to **how culturally dominant conceptual metaphors may reflect and reinstate ideologies** that support existing norms and power relations.

4   Likewise at both micro and macro levels, the possibilities of **generating fresh metaphors** to open new modes of thinking towards possibilities of change.

Experiment one: figurative reconfigurations

Choose a short text or excerpt from a longer text, ideally 1,000–2,000 words. News media articles and opinion blog entries work well. Using different coloured highlighters, go through and mark all the uses of figurative language, using different colours for different kinds (e.g. pink for linguistic metaphor, yellow for simile, blue for metonymy, green for symbolism and so on). Remember to keep an eye out for dead metaphors in commonplace sayings that have become so familiar we tend to forget about the wordplay involved (e.g. when someone's eyes light up, or a new trend is on the rise, or the cat is in the bag).

Choose ten or more examples and analyse each one in relation to the following points:

- What cognitive linkage is being made, or in other words, what conceptual metaphor is at play? (e.g. life as a journey, time as money, or more as up and/or happy).

- Is this a commonplace conceptual metaphor or a fresh one? (Note that commonplace conceptual metaphors can be expressed via inventive figurative language. For instance, 'each tick of the clock sounded like a coin falling from a pocket they could never refill' is a relatively unusual phrase compared with 'they were running out of time', but each one treats time as a limited resource, reflecting the time as money conceptual metaphor.)

- Is the conceptual metaphor at play obviously ableist or discriminatory in some way? (e.g. metaphors that connect sight with knowing or hearing with paying attention, thus discriminating against blind and deaf people).

- What ideologies and/or cultural worldviews does the conceptual metaphor seem to reflect? (e.g. time as money metaphors reflecting western attitudes to time and labour not shared across all cultures, more is happy metaphors reflecting consumerist values, etc.).

- Are there techniques of personification, anthropomorphism, zoomorphism, chremamorphism, metonymy and/or synecdoche at play? If so, what political implications do these suggest?

Draw your findings together to consider how the combination of these conceptual metaphors impacts the text's overall aesthetics as (political) content. This might involve noticing whether a particular type of conceptual metaphor is frequently used and/or whether multiple kinds work together to form systems. What ideological and political effects does this bear? In other words, whose values and ideologies do they represent, and how does their re-presentation relate to established power relations in the context where the writing was produced?

Now try rewriting the text and changing the metaphors to different ones. You may like to use the metaphor generating tool in experiment two. Reflect on how these different metaphors potentially change the text's aesthetics as content, and thus, its political implications.

Experiment two: making fresh metaphors

As chapter eight noted, generating fresh metaphors can spark radical new thinking. Table 9.3 is a metaphor generator. It lists abstract nouns on the left and concrete ones on the right. Abstract nouns indicate things we can't access via our bodily senses. Concrete nouns indicate things we can. There is blank space so you can add more of your own.

Link the nouns on the left with ones on the right. Use these to build metaphors. For instance, 'love is a mosquito', 'fate is a furnace', 'hope is a mountain', etc. As you do so, ask yourself whether the metaphors you are creating seem familiar or unusual. Aim to get beyond commonplace conceptual metaphors. To increase the likelihood of random and unexpected metaphors, you can cut the words up and put them into two hats, then draw them out and pair them that way. This works particularly well in a group setting where everybody contributes a few words to each hat.

TABLE 9.3 *Metaphor generator*

Abstract Nouns	Concrete Nouns
Love	Waterfall
Fate	Astronaut
Hope	Engine
Sorrow	Mosquito
Joy	Bruise
Memory	River
Anger	Flower
Jealousy	Mountain
Forgiveness	Needle
The past	Furnace
The future	Rope

Once you have made your metaphors, choose some that interest you and see if you can extend on them. For instance, if hope is a mountain, describe what kind of mountain it is and/or the experience of trying to climb it. Use this conceptual metaphor as the starting point for a poem, story, or other piece of creative writing. You don't need to stick to linguistic metaphor in your creative writing, but may express the conceptual metaphor via other devices (e.g. simile, symbolism, textual form, etc.)

Experiment three: beyond the journey

Choose a story to analyse. In your analysis, use the following questions to consider how closely this story adheres to or deviates from the dominant monomyth pattern:

- Is there an obvious protagonist (i.e. a hero of the story?).

- Does the protagonist shift from a known world to an unknown one? (This doesn't necessarily mean a literal shift, but could be a change of circumstances in the same location, and/or an internal shift in the context of a personal crisis.)

- Can you identify a call to which the protagonist responds? (e.g. a problem to solve, a desire to fulfil, a struggle to overcome, a point to prove, etc.).

- Does the protagonist refuse the call before accepting it?

- Is there a mentor figure who guides the protagonist?

- List any particular tests, hurdles, or turning points the protagonist faces as they proceed.

- Note any friends or allies who assist the protagonist along their way.

- Note any antagonists or enemies who hinder the protagonist (note that allies and enemies may sometimes switch roles or be hard to distinguish).

- What is the lowest point?

- When and how does the protagonist overcome their lowest point? (If they overcome it.)

- What is the outcome of their struggle? (e.g. achievement of a goal, attainment of new knowledge, the solution to a problem, etc.).

- Do they return to their known world? If so, how is their relationship to this world different upon return?

Based on the above responses, reflect on how many elements of the monomyth are present in the story and how many are absent or subverted. If the story aligns closely with the traditional monomyth pattern, consider the political implications of this aesthetic feature in relation to the content of the text. Also consider how the story and its implications would be different if elements of the pattern were removed or changed to subvert its norms. If the story already resists the dominant monomyth schema, consider the alternative ways you might map its pattern and what conceptual metaphor might be appropriate for a story of this kind. What political implications does this conceptual metaphor bear and how do they compare with those of the monomyth?

Use these reflections as the starting point for an essay about the text you have analysed. Or experiment with rewriting the text in ways that go beyond the conventional monomyth pattern. If the story you analysed already does this, experiment with using its patterns to tell a new story.

Experiment four: un/fixed forms

Experiment with rewriting the same poem in the following poetic forms:

- Sonnet

- Villanelle

- Ghazal

- Pantoum

- Any others you'd like to try

See chapter ten for descriptions of these forms and their variations. Note that you don't have to follow the forms strictly and can be flexible with their rules where you choose. If you need an idea for a poem, consider writing about an encounter with an animal or beyond-human entity, as in the poem about the brown snake at the start of chapter ten. Another option is to use one of the metaphors generated using experiment two.

Reflect on which of the forms was easiest for the poem you were trying to write. And which one do you think produced the best results? Are these findings reflective of the thought processes involved in your poem? (e.g. was the dialectical form of the sonnet less appropriate to these thought processes than the more dialogical approach of the pantoum – or vice versa?) Or did you find each poetic form steering your thinking in different directions? Were there things that surprised you as you wrote?

Draw the best parts of all the poems together and create a new one that could not explicitly be labelled as any single one of the established forms, but which draws influence from all of them. Experiment with formatting and reformatting using space and layout in different ways.

CONCLUDING REFLECTIONS

Walking/writing still in ignorance

The following poem is the oldest 'walking/writing' piece in this book, penned as I was developing awareness about the ethical complexities of producing political writing as a non-Indigenous Australian living on stolen never-ceded Country. My poem bears shortcomings I shall discuss as I reflect on the problems, tools, and theories discussed across this book, and the question, where to from here?

I was born here, decades gone now,
still I have no way of saying where — no words
for this red glory I call dirt.

But that's not one, not any
of the names to which it answers.
Soundless, the mouths of my feet seal over
like they were never
there — here

(true:
they never were — whoever heard
of feet with mouths?)

Unable to converse, they can't connect.
My legs can't walk, can't stand — I hover
over this more-than-dirt,
feet drawing blood with each lurch.

I do not know
why the lark hushes,
why the emu peers at me that way.
I cannot hear, let alone sing
their songs, so loud.

Only years of learning have brought me
at last, to question my stupidity.

Decades gone now,
I was born here (where?)

still I have no way.

First published in Duniyaadaari under the title 'Gone. Now. Still'

Creative writing doesn't simply express thought but enacts it (Webb, 2012; Gibbons, 2015). Composing 'Gone. Now. Still.' facilitated deep thinking about my ignorance as a non-Indigenous white Australian, and the (oft invisible) violences such ignorance entails. That thinking didn't stop with the poem's drafting. Following time, distance and the learning that has unfolded since, I now recognize it as flawed. The opening and closing stanzas lament having 'no way' – falsely suggesting a hopeless, zero agency scenario of consignment to staying in full ignorance. In fact, there are multiple ways to become more educated and aware. Recognizing responsibility and doing the work are key. Some of the practices I have pursued include attending talks by First Nations Elders and figures of lived expertise, reading their books, participating in cultural activities when invited, and seeking consultation in appropriate ways (with proper remuneration for services rendered and respect for knowledge sharing protocols).

Through these practices, I have become a different writer from the one who wrote 'I have no way'. I remain prolifically ignorant, but less so than before, and commit myself to ongoing learning – learning processes of which this book has been part, for it has pushed me towards focused learning, thinking, and reflexion. In the walking/writing pieces presented across chapters one to ten of this book (all of which were composed after 'Gone. Now. Still.'), I have sought to foreground both my ignorance and my responsibility to address it – one key part of writing in solidarity *with* First Nations peoples, but never *for* them. The slogan of Aboriginal activists in the 1970s still holds true: 'If you have come here to help me you are wasting your time, but if you have come because your liberation is bound up with mine, then let us work together' (Lilla Watson and the Aboriginal Activists Group, Queensland 1970s, cited in Verma, 2022, p. 197).

In line with theories of intersectionality, I perceive ongoing injustices of colonization as connected with those of race, gender, heteronormativity, cisnormativity, ableism, social class and more. These include injustices that directly affect me as a queer woman living with an invisible disability. However, as the preface emphasized, I recognize vast difference in scale between challenges I face and those faced by First Nations peoples. I also recognize – and remember my responsibility to redress – the violences entailed in the privileges my whiteness and other hegemonic benefits bring.

As the preface also noted, my grappling with ethically sound political writing as a non-Indigenous Australian living on stolen never ceded Country is a local challenge that resonates globally with problems of creative writing's implications in power, injustice and the need for change. These are the issues this book has confronted. I have sought to provide tools and theories politically oriented readers and writers can put in action towards improved relations between humans, and of humans with beyond-human being. In part one, I mapped the problems, noting first how western cultures have divorced creative writing from knowledge, place and relationality in ways that reflect and reinforce ideologies of extreme individualism and human exceptionalism associated with uprootedness and its many maladies. I then observed how a lost recognition of writing-knowledge connections doesn't mean the connections cease to exist, rather that they persist in unchecked ways that can become particularly problematic given how knowledge in turn connects creative writing with power, privilege, capital, hegemony, ideology, constraints on agency and more. As a most immediate example of writing-power connections and the problems they entail, I noted Hall's (1997) theory of representation as re-presentation, observing how creative writing historically has been – and remains – representatively imbalanced towards the interests of hegemonically privileged groups.

Representative imbalance therefore set the focus for part two, which sought to understand how the imbalances arose – and how best to redress them. Exploration of the western literary canon and publishing showed historic and ongoing entanglements in institutions of white western heteropatriarchy and capitalist economics, which contextualizes persisting inequities of representation today. Both the canon and publishing have, however, improved over the past century – the former via efforts from literary critics, educators and creative writers who have sought to expand the canon and/or generate subversive counter-narratives, and the latter via pressures on publishers to promote so-called diverse voices. Notwithstanding the important gains these movements have made and continue making, the end of part two argued that they remain limited if they don't also address questions of how literary merit is evaluated.

Part three therefore turned towards aesthetics as (political) content – the idea that 'how we say what we say is always a part of what we say' with distinctly political implications (Guttman, 2013, p. 2007). Crucially, no particular aesthetic style or technique bears any intrinsic political valence applicable across all times and places. Rather, writers and readers must constantly reconsider aesthetics as content in relation to shifting contexts. Reading 'with', 'against' and 'beyond' the grain of texts can vitally support these objectives (Bewes, 2010). Conceptual metaphor offers one relevant site of attention for politically oriented readers and writers seeking to activate and/or critique aesthetics as content. Examples of conceptual metaphor explored in this book included micro-textual evocations via figurative language, and macro-textual evocations of textual form and structure. The examples given were necessarily limited – intended to spark thinking about the many other possibilities of cognitive metaphor at micro- midi- and macro-textual levels far beyond those mentioned here, for instance, associations formed via rhyme and other sonic devices, word and sentence ordering, passive versus active voice, syntax, and layout, to name a few. Additionally, aesthetics as (political) content may extend far beyond conceptual metaphor. Textual engagements with time, space, and rhythm are among those I hope to keep exploring in future work.

On that note, I wish to emphasize the unfinished, ongoing nature of the inquiries this book has pursued. In reiteration of remarks from the preface, this book presents but one perspective in what needs to be a varied polyvocal dialogue about creative writing's political potentials. Creative writing has but one role to play in processes of change requiring collective efforts across many fields and practices. As W. H. Auden (in)famously mused, poetry in itself 'makes nothing happen' (1940/2024, part II, line 5) – and I think this holds for other forms of literature too. Reading and writing alone cannot replace vital practices such as rallying, protests, petitions, sending letters to figures of authority, raising funds for those struck by war or other crises, boycotting exploitative brands, demanding change through legal reform, riding bicycles to reduce emissions, considered voting, and ecologically aware eating, to name but a few. However, reading and writing can motivate these practices. By raising subjugated issues and engaging affective responses, writing can become both a 'mouth' and a river that 'flows on' and 'survives' (Auden 1940/2024, part II, lines 5–10), stirring people out of complacency, into action. Words themselves may create little or no change. But what we do with them – that matters.

REFERENCES

Åberg, M. (2013). Liberalism and revivalism. A comparative case study of liberal ideology, individualism, and revivalism in Schleswig-Holstein and Värmland, ca. 1860–1920. *Scandinavian Journal of History*, *38*(2), 154–179. https://doi.org/10.1080/03468755.2013.764924

Addison, C. (2003). Little boxes: The effects of the stanza on poetic narrative. *Style*, *37*(2), 124–143.

Abrams, J. (Director). (2015). *Star Wars: The force awakens* [Film]. Disney.

Abrams, J. (Director). (2019). *Star Wars: The rise of Skywalker* [Film]. Disney.

Abrams, M. & Harpham, G. (2015). *A glossary of literary terms* (11th edn.). Cengage.

Adorno, T. (1980). Reconciliation under duress (R. Livingstone, Trans.). In T. Adorno, W. Benjamin, E. Bloch, B. Brecht, G. Lukács, & F. Jameson (Authors), *Aesthetics and politics* (pp. 151–176). Verso. (Original work published 1961.)

Agard, J. (2006). Listen Mr Oxford don. *Index on Censorship*, *35*(2), 100–101. https://doi.org/10.1080/03064220600744677 (Original work published 1967).

Ahmed, S. (2012). *On being included: racism and diversity in institutional life*. Duke University Press.

Ahmed, S. (2014). Chapter one. In K. Sian (Ed.), *Conversations in postcolonial thought* (pp. 15–34). Palgrave Macmillan.

Ahmed, S. (2020). "I am my own person," women's agency inside and outside the home in rural Pakistan. *Gender, Place and Culture: A Journal of Feminist Geography*, *27*(8), 1176–1194. https://doi.org/10.1080/0966369X.2019.1664420

Alefaio, S. (2022). *Pacific-Indigenous psychology: Galuola, a niu-wave of psychological practices*. Springer.

Alison, J. (2019). *Meander, spiral, explode: Design and pattern in narrative*. Catapult.

Almila, A. (2016). Fashion, anti-fashion, non-fashion and symbolic capital: The uses of dress among Muslim minorities in Finland. *Fashion Theory*, *20*(1), 81–102. https://doi.org/10.1080/1362704X.2015.1078136

Althusser, L. (2006). Ideology and ideological state apparatuses (notes towards an investigation). In A. Sharma & A. Gupta (Eds.) *The anthropology of the state: a reader* (pp. 86–111). Blackwell. (Original published 1970.)

Angrish, R. (2022). The wood wide web: Tree talk in the forest. *Resonance*, *27*(8), 1429–1441. https://doi.org/10.1007/s12045-022-1435-x

Anstey Hill Recreation Park. (n.d.). Park signage. Anstey Hill Recreation Park, Perseverance Rd, Tea Tree Gully, SA 5091, Australia. (Signs viewed January-June 2024, installation date unknown).

Apps, A. (2015). *Intersex*. Tarpaulin Sky Press.

Araluen, E. (2021). *Drop Bear*. UQP.

Araluen, E. (2023). Introduction. In J. Leane (author), *Purple Threads* (pp. ix–xii). UQP.

Arendt, H. (2017). *The origins of totalitarianism* (Penguin Classics edn.). Penguin. (Original published 1951.)

Ashcroft, B., Griffiths, G., & Tiffin, H. (1989). *The empire writes back*. Routledge. https://doi.org/10.4324/9780203402627

Ashton, S., McDonald, K., & Kirkman, M. (2019). Pornography and women's sexual pleasure: Accounts from young women in Australia. *Feminism & Psychology, 29*(3), 409–432. https://doi.org/10.1177/0959353519833410

Aston, R. (2017). A Culture of text: The canon and the common core. *Journal of Curriculum Theorizing, 32*(2), 39–52.

Auden, W. H. (2024). *In memory of W. B. Yeats*. Poets.org. https://poets.org/poem/memory-w-b-yeats (Original published 1940.)

Augustyn, A. (2008). Narratology. In J Abella et al. (Eds.). *Encyclopedia Britannica*. Retrieved January 15, 2024, from https://www.britannica.com/art/narratology

Baker, D. (2010). Monstrous fairytales: Towards an écriture queer. *Colloquy: Text, Theory, Critique, 20*(1), 79–103.

Bancroft, C. (2018). The braided narrative. *Narrative, 26*(3), 262–281. https://doi.org/10.1353/nar.2018.0013

Barbin, H. & Foucault, M. (1980). *Herculine Barbin: Being the recently discovered memoirs of a nineteenth-century French hermaphrodite* (Trans. R. McDougall). Pantheon. (Original written 1800s; published in French in 1978.)

Barcham, M. (2023). Towards a radically inclusive design – Indigenous story-telling as codesign methodology. *CoDesign, 19*(1), 1–13. https://doi.org/10.1080/15710882.2021.1982989

Barthes, R. (2011). The death of the author. In C. Cazeaux (Ed.), *The Continental aesthetics reader* (2nd ed., pp. 519–524). Routledge. https://doi.org/10.4324/9781351226387-35 (Original published 1977.)

Batchelor, P. (2023, October 24). Disability representation in the publishing industry [blog post]. *Professional Writing Academy*. https://www.profwritingacademy.com/disability-publishing-industry

Batzke, I., Espinoza Garrido, L., & Hess, L. M. (Eds.). (2021). *Life writing in the posthuman anthropocene*. Springer.

Beauchamp, S. (2016, December 10). The color purple author Alice Walker: 'Rebellion is close to godliness'. *The Huffpost*. https://www.huffpost.com/entry/the-color-purple-rebellion_b_8754654

Benjamin, W. (1969). The work of art in the age of mechanical reproduction (H. Zohn, Trans.). In H. Arendt (Ed.). *Illuminations*. Schocken Books. (Original published 1935.)

Bennett, M. (2024, May 28). Māori who speak with the dead. *Newsroom*. https://newsroom.co.nz/2024/05/28/maori-who-speak-with-the-dead/

Bennett, T. (2010). Introduction. In P. Bourdieu (author), *Distinction: A social critique of the judgement of taste*. Routledge.

Berry, M., & Batty, C. (2016). The stories of supervision: creative writing in a critical space. *New Writing, 13*(2), 247–260. https://doi.org/10.1080/14790726.2016.1142568

Bewes, T. (2010). Reading with the grain: A new world in literary criticism. *Differences, 21*(3), 1–33. https://doi.org/10.1215/10407391-2010-007

Bhatia, M., Poynting, S., & Tufail, W. (2024). *Racism, violence and harm: Ideology, media and resistance*. Springer.

Bin Salleh, R. & Vaarwerk, A. (2022). Pub talk: Magabala books publisher Rachel Bin Salleh. *Kill Your Darlings New Fiction, Essays, Commentary and Reviews*, Jul-Dec 2022, 126–133.

Birch, T. (2013, November 7). The ghost river. *The Guardian*. https://www.theguardian.com/books/australia-culture-blog/2013/nov/07/tony-birch-melbourne-writer-short-story-ghost-river-culture-books

Bishop, R. S. (1990). Mirrors, windows, and sliding glass doors. *Perspectives: Choosing and using books for the classroom, 6*(3), 1–2. Retrieved June 1, 2024, from https://scenicregional.org/wp-content/uploads/2017/08/Mirrors-Windows-and-Sliding-Glass-Doors.pdf

Blake, M. (2024). *Beautiful people: My thirteen truths about disability*. Hachette.

Bloch, E. (1980). Discussing expressionism (R. Livingstone, Trans.). In T. Adorno, W. Benjamin, E. Bloch, B. Brecht, G. Lukács, & F. Jameson (Authors), *Aesthetics and politics* (pp. 16–27). Verso. (Original published 1938.)

Bloom, H. (1994). *The western canon: The books and school of the ages*. Harcourt Brace.

Bodkin, M. (1934). *Archetypal patterns in poetry: Psychological studies of imagination*. London University Press.

Booth, E., & Narayan, B. (2018). Towards diversity in young adult fiction: Australian YA authors' publishing experiences and its implications for YA librarians and readers' advisory services. *Journal of the Australian Library and Information Association, 67*(3), 195–211. https://doi.org/10.1080/24750158.2018.1497349

Bornstein, K. (2012). *A queer and pleasant danger: The true story of a nice Jewish boy who joins the church of Scientology, and leaves twelve years later to become the lovely lady she is today*. Beacon Press.

Bourdieu, P. (2010). *Distinction: a social critique of the judgement of taste* (R. Nice, Trans.). Routledge. (Original published 1979.)

Bourman, R. P., Buckman, S., Pillans, B., Williams, M. A. J., & Williams, F. (2010). Traces from the past: the Cenozoic regolith and intraplate neotectonic history of the Gun Emplacement, a ferricreted bench on the western margin of the Mt Lofty Ranges, South Australia. *Australian Journal of Earth Sciences, 57*(5), 577–595. https://doi.org/10.1080/08120099.2010.494764

Bowden, C. (2021). Transphobic tropes in contemporary young adult novels about queer gender. *The Australasian Journal of Popular Culture, 10*(1–2), 65–77.

Brady, W. (2014). Indigenous insurgency against the speaking for others. In T. Neale, C. McKinnon, & E. Vincent (Eds.), *History, power, text: Cultural studies and Indigenous studies* (pp. 112–121). UTS ePress.

Brady, A., & Schirato, T. (2011). *Understanding Judith Butler*. Sage. https://doi.org/10.4135/9781446269183

Brecht, B. (1980). Against Georg Lukacs (S. Hood, Trans.). In T. Adorno, W. Benjamin, E. Bloch, B. Brecht, G. Lukács, & F. Jameson (Authors), *Aesthetics and politics* (pp. 68–87). Verso. (Original published 1967.)

Brewster, A., & Scott, K. (2012). Can you anchor a shimmering nation state via regional indigenous roots?: Kim Scott talks to Anne Brewster about "That Deadman Dance." *Cultural Studies Review, 18*(1), 228–246.

Brontë, C. (2022). *Jane Eyre*. Union Square & Co. (Original published 1847.)

Brook, P. (Director). (1989). *The Mahabharata* [film of live stage performance]. MP Productions. (Live performance staged 1985)

Brown, G. (2004). *Redefining Elizabethan Literature*. Cambridge University Press.

Brown, K. (2019). *The pretty one: On life, pop culture, disability, and other reasons to fall in love with me*. Simon & Schuster.

Burawoy, M. (2019). *Symbolic violence: Conversations with Bourdieu*. Duke University Press.

Burger, B. (2020). Engaged Queerness in African speculative fiction. *Scrutiny 2, 25*(2), 1–12. https://doi.org/10.1080/18125441.2020.1859772

Burger, B., Rahm J., & Liebermann, Y. (2016). Introduction: Narrating the nonhuman. In Y. Lieberman, J. Rahm and B. Burger (Eds), *Nonhuman Agencies in the Twenty-first Century Anglophone Novel* (pp. 1–24). Palgrave Macmillan.

Butler, J. (1993). *Bodies that matter: On the discursive limits of sex.* Routledge.

Butler, K. (2009). Review of Jones, Jennifer A., Black Writers, White Editors: Episodes of Collaboration and Compromise in Australian Publishing History, *Melbourne Historical Journal, 37*(1), 147–149.

Carlin, D. (2012). Queer theory and the American novel. In A. Bendixen (Ed.), *A Companion to the American novel* (pp. 342–356). John Wiley & Sons, Ltd. https://doi.org/10.1002/9781118384329.ch20

Campbell, J. (2004). *The hero with a thousand faces.* Bollingen. (Original published 1949.)

Carretta, V. (2011). The emergence of an African American literary canon, 1760–1820. In G. Maryemma & J. W. Ward (Eds.), *The Cambridge history of African American literature* (pp. 52–65). Cambridge University Press.

Centre for Stories. (2024). *Cyril Wong.* Centre for Stories. https://centreforstories.com/stories/singapore-hot-takes/cyril-wong/

Chandler, D. & Munday, R. (2020). *A dictionary of media and communication* (3rd edn.). Oxford University Press.

Chatman, S. (1980). *Story and discourse: Narrative structure in fiction and film,* Cornell University Press. https://doi.org/10.1515/9781501741616

Chatterjee, N., & Chatterjee, A. (2024). Arab world in Hergé's The Adventures of Tintin: Making visible the idea of terra nullius. *Contemporary Review of the Middle East, 11*(1), 9–22. https://doi.org/10.1177/23477989231221348

Cho, S., Crenshaw, K. W., & McCall, L. (2013). Toward a field of intersectionality studies: Theory, applications, and praxis. *Signs, 38*(4), 785–810. https://doi.org/10.1086/669608

Chow, R., & Rohrhuber, J. (2011). On captivation: A remainder from the 'Indistinction of Art and Nonart.' In P. Bowman & R. Stamp (Eds.). *Reading Rancière* (pp. 44–72). Bloomsbury.

Cioli, M. (2015). Art (Italy). *1914–1918: International Encyclopedia of the First World War.* https://encyclopedia.1914-1918-online.net/article/art_italy

Cixous, H. & O'Grady, K. (2014). Guardian of language. Trans. E. Prenowitz. In H. Cixous & S. Sellers (Eds.). *White ink: Interviews on sex, text and politics* (pp. 81–87). Taylor and Francis. https://doi.org/10.4324/9781315711706

Clare, M. (1978). *Karobran: the story of an Aboriginal girl.* Alternative Publishing.

Clark, L. (2011). Fictional geographies: Versions of the Waikato in juvenile fiction, 1874–1907. *Journal of New Zealand Literature, 29*(2), 89–107.

Clements, A. Rando, F., & Smith, S. (2013). Living our lives through their words: Reflections on the marathon reading of work by Audre Lorde and Adrienne Rich at the lesbian herstory archives, November 17, 2012. *Frontiers (Boulder), 34*(2), 261–269. https://doi.org/10.5250/fronjwomestud.34.2.0261

Coccia, E. (2020). Producing intimacy: Queer attachments in workingwomen's writings. *Legacy, 37*(1), 17–41. https://doi.org/10.5250/legacy.37.1.0017

Coleman, C. (2017). *Terra nullius.* Hachette.

Coleman, C. (2019). *The old lie.* Hachette.

Collins, P. H., da Silva, E. C. G., Ergun, E., Furseth, I., Bond, K. D., & Martínez-Palacios, J. (2021). Intersectionality as critical social theory. *Contemporary Political Theory, 20*(3), 690–725. https://doi.org/10.1057/s41296-021-00490-0

Collis, P. (2021). *Nightmares run like mercury.* Recent Work Press.

Colpania, G., Mascataand, J. & Smie, K. (2022). Introduction: Postcolonial responses to decolonial interventions. *Postcolonial Studies, 25*(1), 1–16.

Connell, R. (2020). *Masculinities* (2nd edn.). Routledge, Taylor & Francis Group. (Original published 1993.)

Coogler, R. (Director). (2018). *Black Panther* [film]. Marvel.

Cook, G. (2015). 'A pig is a person' or 'You can love a fox and hunt it': Innovation and tradition in the discursive representation of animals. *Discourse & Society, 26*(5), 587–607. https://doi.org/10.1177/0957926515576639

Copley, I. (Personal Communication, June 14, 2024). Cultural consultation. Private location, Campbelltown, South Australia.

Couser, G. T. (2005). Disability, life Narrative, and representation. *PMLA, 120*(2), 602–606. http://www.jstor.org/stable/25486192

Crenshaw, K. W. (1988). Race, reform, and retrenchment: Transformation and legitimation in antidiscrimination law. *Harvard Law Review, 101*(7), 1331–1387. https://doi.org/10.2307/1341398

Crisp, T., Napoli, M., Yenika-Agbaw, V., & Zapata, A. (2020). The complexities of #OwnVoices in children's literature. *Journal of Children's Literature, 46*(2) 5–7.

Cruz, C. (2017). The (mis)education of the Filipino writer: The Tiempo age and institutionalized creative writing in the Philippines. *Kritika Kultura, 2017*(28), 3–34. https://doi.org/10.13185/KK2017.02802

Cunneen, C. (2020). *Conflict, politics and crime: Aboriginal communities and the police.* Routledge.

Dagenais, N. (2019). Reclaiming Indigenous space through testimonial life writing: Antane Kapesh's Je suis une maudite Sauvagesse as territorial imperative. In R. Rimstead & D. A. Beneventi (Eds.), *Contested spaces, counter-narratives, and culture from below in Canada and Québec* (pp. 188–211). University of Toronto Press. http://www.jstor.org/stable/10.3138/j.ctvd7w83t.13

Dalleo, R. (2016). Introduction. In R. Dalleo (Ed.), *Bourdieu and postcolonial studies* (pp. 1–16). Liverpool University Press.

Daly, M. (1978). *Gyn/ecology: The metaethics of radical feminism.* The Women's Press.

Das, G. (2010). *The difficulty of being good on the subtle art of dharma.* Oxford University Press.

Davis, M., & Williams, G. (2023). *Everything you need to know about The Voice* (1st ed.). NewSouth Publishing.

De Boever, A. (2014). *States of exception in the contemporary novel.* Bloomsbury.

del Pont, R. (2024). Before Amazon: Publishing industry and cultural mutations. *Revista Interamericana de Bibliotecología, 47*(1). https://doi.org/10.17533/udea.rib.v47n1e354358

Deleuze, G & Guattari, F. (1987). *A thousand plateaus: capitalism and schizophrenia* (B Massumi, Trans.). University of Minnesota Press.

Di Niro, C., & Walker, A. (2018). You're doctor what? Challenges for creative arts research in a culture of binaries. In A. Black & S. Garvis (Eds.). *Lived experiences of women in academia: Metaphors, manifestos and memoir* (pp. 32–44). Routledge. https://doi.org/10.4324/9781315147444

Dickman, M. C. (2022). Reproducing fatness and disability: Risk avoidance and the womb. *Fat Studies, 11*(1), 57–69.

Disney, D. (2016). *Either, Orpheus.* UWA Publishing.

Disney, D. (2021). Review of Brimstone: A book of villanelles. *World Literature Today, 95*(2), 85–86.

Dittmar, J. E. (2011). Information technology and economic change: The impact of the printing press. *The Quarterly Journal of Economics, 126*(3), 1133–1172. https://doi.org/10.1093/qje/qjr035

Dogan, J. N., Rosenkrantz, D., Wheeler, P. B., & Hargons, C. N. (2022). Exploring identity and coping among Black viewers of Marvel's Black Panther. *Psychology of Popular Media, 11*(2), 183–195. https://doi.org/10.1037/ppm0000359

Dutoya, V. (2016). Defining the "queers" in India: The politics of academic representation. *India Review, 15*(2), 241–271. https://doi.org/10.1080/14736489.2016.1165570

Doubinsky, S., & Kkona, C. (2024). Introduction. In S. Doubinsky & C. Kkona (Eds.). *Women of horror and speculative fiction in their own words: Conversations with authors and editors* (pp. 1–120. Bloomsbury. https://doi.org/10.5040/9781501384493

Douglas, Y. (2016). The real malady of Marcel Proust and what it reveals about diagnostic errors in medicine. *Medical Hypotheses, 90*, 14–18. https://doi.org/10.1016/j.mehy.2016.02.024

Dowd, M. & Eckerle, J. (2007). Introduction. In M. Dowd & J. Eckerle (Eds.), *Genre and women's life writing in early modern England: re-imagining forms of selfhood* (pp. 1–14). Ashgate.

Eades, Q. (2015). *all the beginnings: a queer autobiography of the body*. Australian Scholarly Publishing.

Eagan, V. (2020). Structural violence in unexpected Indigenous police custody deaths; Canada and Australia. *Salus Journal, 8*(1), 33–61.

Eason, A. E., Brady, L. M., & Fryberg, S. A. (2018). Reclaiming representations & interrupting the cycle of bias against Native Americans. *Daedalus (Cambridge, Mass.), 147*(2), 70–81. https://doi.org/10.1162/DAED_a_00491

Eastman, G. (1973). *Sign me Alice: [a play in sign language]*. Gallaudet College Bookstore.

Eckerle, J & McAreavey, N. (2019). Introduction. In Eckerle, J. A., & McAreavey, N. (Eds.), *Women's life writing and early modern Ireland* (pp. 1–22). University of Nebraska Press.

Eckerman, A. (2023). *She is the Earth*. Magabala.

Enriquez, G. (2021). Foggy mirrors, tiny windows, and heavy doors: Beyond diverse books toward meaningful literacy instruction. *The Reading Teacher, 75*(1), 103–106.

Esslin, M. (1963). Brecht, the absurd, and the future. *The Tulane Drama Review, 7*(4), 43–54. https://doi.org/10.2307/1125018

Ewart, C. (2010). Terms of disappropriation: Disability, diaspora and Dionne Brand's What We All Long For. *Journal of Literary & Cultural Disability Studies, 4*(2), 147–162. https://doi.org/10.3828/jlcds.2010.12

Faiman, P. (Director). (1986). *Crocodile Dundee* [Film]. Paramount Pictures; 20th Century Studios.

Fairclough, N. (2013). *Critical discourse analysis: The critical study of language* (2nd edn.). Taylor & Francis. https://doi.org/10.4324/9781315834368 (Original published 1995.)

Fairfield, C. (2022). The roots of a clear-cut: Tracing feminist orientation and environmental legibility in twentieth century women's life writing. *Interdisciplinary Studies in Literature and Environment, 29*(4), 1190–1208. https://doi.org/10.1093/isle/isaa202

Fanon, F. (1986). *Black skin white masks* (C. M. Lackmann, Trans.). Pluto Press.

Fenton-Hathaway, A. (2022). Apprehensions of a canon: Literature and Medicine 2013–2022. *Literature and Medicine, 40*(2), 235–242. https://doi.org/10.1353/lm.2022.0025

Fernandez-Moya, M. & Puig, N. (2021). Shaping the rules of the game: Spanish capitalism and the publishing industry under dictatorship (1939–1975), *Business History, 63*(8), 1273–1292. https://doi.org/10.1080/00076791.2020.1757072

Fleming, V. (Director). (1939). *The wizard of Oz* [film]. Metro-Goldwyn-Mayer.

Flemming, J. (2021). *How to Be Human: An Autistic Man's Guide to Life*. Simon and Schuster.

Folkerth, W. (2020). Reading Shakespeare after neurodiversity. In L. Dunn (Ed.), *Performing disability in early modern English drama* (pp. 141–157). Springer. https://doi.org/10.1007/978-3-030-57208-2_7

Ford, P. L. (2010). *Aboriginal knowledge, narratives and Country: Marri kunkimba putj puthj marrideyan*. Post Pressed.

Forster, E. M. (1927). *Aspects of the novel*. Harcourt Brace.

Foucault, M. (1980). *Power/knowledge: Selected interviews and other writings, 1972–1977* (C. Cordon, L. Marshall, J. Mepham & K. Sopher, Trans.). Pantheon.

Frame, J. (1957). *Owls do cry*. Pegasus.

Frank, A. (2013). *The wounded storyteller*. University of Chicago. (Original published 1995.)

Frank, G. (2024, 28 February). Grave unseriousness: Experimenting with Oulipo constraints. *The Poetry Foundation*. https://www.poetryfoundation.org/articles/162152/grave-unseriousness-experimenting-with-oulipo-constraints

Frawley, M. (1998). The editor as advocate: Emily Faithfull and "The Victoria Magazine." *Victorian Periodicals Review, 31*(1), 87–104.

Fredericks, B. (2014). 'There is nothing that identifies me to that place': Indigenous women's perceptions of health spaces and places. In T. Neale, E. Vincent, & C. McKinnon (Eds.). *History, power, text: Cultural studies and Indigenous studies* (pp. 291–309). UTS ePRESS.

Freeman, R. (2010). Black and white: In search of an "apt" response to Indigenous writing. *Text: Journal of Writing and Writing Courses, 14*(2), 1–16. https://doi.org/10.52086/001c.31480

Freire, P. (1994). *Pedagogy of hope: reliving pedagogy of the oppressed* (R. Barr, Trans.). Continuum.

Gaffney, H. (2017). Romancing theft. *Text: Journal of Writing and Writing Courses, 21* (SI 41), 1–11. https://doi.org/10.52086/001c.25933

Gardiner, M. (2000). *Critiques of everyday life*. Routledge. https://doi.org/10.4324/9780203130858

Gargaillo, F. (2022). Queer allusion: Wilde, Housman, Cullen. *Modern Language Quarterly, 83*(1), 57–80.

Gates, H. Louis. (1988). *The signifying monkey: a theory of Afro-American literary criticism*. Oxford University Press.

Gates, H. L. (1991). The master's pieces: On canon formation and the Afro-American tradition. In D. La Capra (Ed.). *The bounds of race* (pp. 17–38). Cornell University Press. https://doi.org/10.7591/9781501727481-003

Genette, G. (1980). *Narrative discourse: an essay in method* (J. E. Lewin, Trans.). Cornell University Press.

Giannelli, F. (2020). The princess strikes back: Forces of destiny and the capitalization of the Disney princess. In *The transmedia franchise of Star Wars TV* (pp. 97–117). Springer. https://doi.org/10.1007/978-3-030-52958-1_6

Gibbons, R. (2015). *How poems think*. University of Chicago.

Gilbert, S. M., & Gubar, S. (2020). *The madwoman in the attic: The woman writer and the nineteenth-century literary imagination* (Veritas paperback edn.). Yale University Press. https://doi.org/10.12987/9780300252972

Gilman, C. (2021). The yellow wallpaper. *Project Gutenberg*. https://www.gutenberg.org/ebooks/1952 (Original published 1892).

Gilmore, L., & Marshall, E. (2019). *Witnessing Girlhood: Toward an Intersectional Tradition of Life Writing*. Fordham University Press. https://doi.org/10.1515/9780823285518

Glassman, J. (2012). Stop speaking for us: Women-of-color bloggers, white appropriation, and what librarians can do about it. *InterActions: UCLA Journal of Education and Information Studies*, *8*(1), 1–20. https://doi.org/10.5070/D481000820

Gooden, A., & Hackett, V. C. R. (2020). Encountering the metropole: Stuart Hall, race, (un)belonging, and identity in Canada: Exploring the African Caribbean immigration experience. *Journal of African Diaspora Archaeology and Heritage*, *9*(1), 53–71. https://doi.org/10.1080/21619441.2020.1858387

Gould, P. (2011). Early print literature of Africans in America. In G. Maryemma & J. W. Ward (Eds.), *The Cambridge history of African American literature* (pp. 39–52). Cambridge University Press.

Graham, M. & Ward, J. (2011). Introduction. In M. Graham & J Ward (Eds.), *The Cambridge history of African American literature* (pp. 1–17). Cambridge University Press.

Gramsci, A. (1992a). *Prison Notebooks: Volume One* (J. A. Buttigieg, Trans.) Columbia University Press. (Original written 1929–1935.)

Gramsci, A. (1992b). *Prison Notebooks: Volume Two* (J. A. Buttigieg, Trans.) Columbia University Press. (Original written 1929–1935.)

Gramsci, A. (1992c). *Prison Notebooks: Volume Three* (J. A. Buttigieg, Trans.) Columbia University Press. (Original written 1929–1935.)

Gramsci, A. (2021). *Subaltern social groups: a critical edition of prison notebook 25* (J. A. Buttigieg & M. Green, Trans. & Eds.). Columbia University Press. https://doi.org/10.7312/gram19038 (Original written 1929–1935.)

Green, C. P. (2019). *Nganajungu Yagu*. Cordite.

Green, C. P. & Kinsella, J. (2018). *False tales of Colonial Thieves*. Magabala.

Greene, T. W. (2022). A fourth ideology of individualism: Adding "online individuality" to a theoretical lens. *Theory in Action*, *15*(1), 68–78. https://doi.org/10.3798/tia.1937-0237.2204

Griffin, A. (2016). *A review of Dan Disney's 'either, Orpheus'*. Westerly. https://westerlymag.com.au/review-of-dan-disneys-either-orpheus/

Grubgeld, E. (2020). *Disability and life writing in post-independence Ireland*. Springer International Publishing. https://doi.org/10.1007/978-3-030-37246-0

Guillory, J. (1993). *Cultural capital: The problem of literary canon formation*. University of Chicago.

Guttmann, A. (2013). Form as content, or, it's all style. *International Journal of the History of Sport*, *30*(17), 2007–2015. https://doi.org/10.1080/09523367.2013.854611

Haddon, M. (2003). *The Curious Incident of the Dog in the Night-Time*. Jonathan Cape.

Halberstam, J. (2005). *In a queer time and place: Transgender bodies, subcultural lives*. NYU Press. https://doi.org/10.18574/nyu/9780814790892

Halberstam, J. (2011). *The queer art of failure*. Duke University Press. https://doi.org/10.1215/9780822394358

Halberstam, J. (2020). *Wild things: The disorder of desire*. Duke University Press.

Hall, A. (2014). *Anstey Hill – Newman's Nursery*. The Paranormal Guide. http://www.theparanormalguide.com/photos/test

Hall, S. (1989). Cultural identity and cinematic representation. *Framework: The Journal of Cinema and Media*, *36*(1), 68–81.

Hall, S. (1992). Race, culture, and communications: Looking backward and forward at cultural studies, *Rethinking Marxism, 5*(1), 10–18. https://doi.org/10.1080/08935699208657998

Hall, S. (1997). The work of representation. In S. Hall (Ed.) *Representation: Cultural representations and signifying practices* (pp. 13–74). Sage.

Hallström, L. (Director). (1994). *What's eating Gilbert Grape?* [Film]. Paramount; Myriad.

Hanman, N. (2013, August 22). Eve Kosofsky Sedgwick and Judith Butler showed me the transformative power of the word queer. *The Guardian.* https://www.theguardian.com/commentisfree/2013/aug/22/judith-butler-eve-sedgwick-queer

Hanna, A. (2020). Yeats's stanzas, Yeats's rooms. In J. Griffiths & A. Hanna (Eds.). *Architectural space and the imagination* (pp. 167–179). Springer. https://doi.org/10.1007/978-3-030-36067-2_11

Haraway, D. J. (2016). *Staying with the trouble: Making kin in the Chthulucene.* Duke University Press. https://doi.org/10.1515/9780822373780

Harmon, K. (2020). Challenging phonocentrism: Writing signs and bilingual deaf literatures. In A. Hall (Ed.), *The Routledge companion to literature and disability* (pp. 43–56). Routledge. https://doi.org/10.4324/9781315173047-6

Harper, D. (2024). *Online Etymology Dictionary.* https://www.etymonline.com/

Hecq, D. (2015). *Towards a poetics of creative writing.* Multilingual Matters.

Heiss, A. (2021). *Bila Yarrudhanggalangdhuray.* Simon & Schuster.

Heiss, A., & Minter, P. (2014a). Aboriginal literature. In A. Heiss & P. Minter, Eds). *Macquarie PEN anthology of Australian Aboriginal literature* (pp. 1–8). Allen & Unwin. https://doi.org/10.1515/9780773597174

Heiss, A. & Minter, P. (Eds). (2014b). *Macquarie PEN anthology of Australian Aboriginal literature,* Allen & Unwin. https://doi.org/10.1515/9780773597174

Hemmings, C. (2011). *Why stories matter.* Duke University Press. https://doi.org/10.1215/9780822393702

Henningsgaard, P. (2019). Alexis Wright's publishing history in three contexts: Australian Aboriginal, national, and international. *Antipodes 33*(1), 107–124.

Hergé, G. (26 September 1946 – 29 June 1993). *Tintin* [comic series]. Le Lombard.

Hernández, K., Rubis, J. M., Theriault, N., Todd, Z., Mitchell, A., Country, B., Burarrwanga, L., Ganambarr, R., Ganambarr-Stubbs, M., Ganambarr, B., Maymuru, D., Suchet-Pearson, S., Lloyd, K., & Wright, S. (2021). The creatures collective: Manifestings. *Environment and Planning E: Nature and Space, 4*(3), 838–863. https://doi.org/10.1177/2514848620938316

Highmore, B. (2004). Homework: Routine, social aesthetics and the ambiguity of everyday life. *Cultural Studies, 18*(2–3), 306–327. https://doi.org/10.1080/0950238042000201536

Highmore, B. (2011). Out of place: Unprofessional painting, Jacques Rancière and the distribution of the sensible. In P. Bowman & R. Stamp (Eds.). *Reading Rancière* (pp. 95–108). Bloomsbury.

Hillman, T. (2008). *Intersex (for lack of a better word).* Manic D Press.

Hiraide, L. A. (2021). Postcolonial, decolonial, anti-colonial: Does it matter?, *New Voices in Postcolonial Studies Magazine,* Summer, pp. 11–15. https://newvoicespocostudies.wordpress.com/hiraide/

Hirschmann, J. (2020). Lord Byron's deformed foot: A medical and biographical assessment. *The Byron Journal 48*(1), 57–70. https://www.muse.jhu.edu/article/758749.

Houston, E. (2020). Featuring disabled women in advertisements: The commodification of diversity? In K. Ellis, G. Goggin, B. Haller, & R. Curtis (Eds.), *The Routledge companion to disability and media* (pp. 50–58). Routledge. https://doi.org/10.4324/9781315716008-5

Huggan, G. (2016). Writing at the margins: Postcolonialism, exoticism and the politics of cultural value (from the postcolonial exotic). In R. Dalleo (Ed.). *Bourdieu and postcolonial studies* (pp. 17–52). Liverpool University Press.

Ignatiev, N. (1995). *How the Irish became white*. Routledge.

Jacey, H. (2010). The hero and heroine's journey and the writing of Loy. *Journal of Screenwriting, 1*(2), 309–323.

Jackson, M. (2016). Aesthetics, politics, and attunement: On some questions brought by alterity and ontology. *GeoHumanities, 2*(1), 8–23. https://doi.org/10.1080/237356 6X.2016.1165076

Jacques, J. (2017). Forms of resistance: Uses of memoir, theory, and fiction in trans life writing. *Life Writing, 14*(3), 357–370. https://doi.org/10.1080/14484528.2017.1328301

James, G. LaPoe V., LaPoe, V., & Davis, A. (2023). Missing women news coverage and implications of standpoint theory. *Ethical Space, 2*(3), 1–21. https://doi.org/10.21428/ 0af3f4c0.92066f5a

Jansen, A. M. Y. (2021). "Erasure is a bitch, isn't it?": Deborah Miranda's feminist geographies and Native women's life writing. *Studies in American Indian Literatures, 33*(1), 55–81. https://doi.org/10.1353/ail.2021.0004

Jarrin, A. (2017). *The biopolitics of beauty: Cosmetic citizenship and affective capital in Brazil*. University of California Press.

Jay, M. (1992). "The aesthetic ideology" as ideology; Or, what does it mean to aestheticize politics? *Cultural Critique, 21*(21), 41–61. https://doi.org/10.2307/1354116

Johnston, K. (2020). Canadian disability dramaturgies. In A. Hall (Ed.), *The Routledge Companion to Literature and Disability* (pp. 253–264). Routledge. https://doi. org/10.4324/9781315173047-26

Johnson, R. (Director). (2017). *Star Wars: The last Jedi* [film]. Disney.

Jones, C. (2002). Foucault's inheritance / inheriting Foucault. *Culture and Organization, 8*(3), 225–238.

Jones, J. (2009). *Black writers, white editors: Episodes of collaboration and compromise in Australian publishing history*. Australian Scholarly Publishing.

Joseph, M. (2019). *Victorian literary businesses: The management and practices of the British publishing industry*. Springer. https://doi.org/10.1007/978-3-030-28592-0

Kant, I. (1952). *The critique of judgement* (Trans. J. C. Meredith). Clarendon Press. (Original published 1790.)

Kapila, K. (2022). *Nullius: The anthropology of ownership, sovereignty and the law in India*. HAU Books.

Kelley, J. E. (2008). Power relationships in Rumpelstiltskin: A textual comparison of a traditional and a reconstructed fairy tale. *Children's Literature in Education, 39*(1), 31–41. https://doi.org/10.1007/s10583-006-9039-8

Keneally, T. (1978). *The chant of Jimmie Blacksmith*. Collins.

Kings Park and Botanic Garden. (n.d.). Park Signage. Kings Park and Botanic Garden, Perth, WA, Australia. (Sign viewed March 2024, installation date unknown.)

Kimmerer, R. W. (2013). *Braiding sweetgrass: Indigenous wisdom, scientific knowledge and the teachings of plants*. Milkweed Editions.

Kinsella, J. (2007). *Disclosed poetics: Beyond landscape and lyricism*. Manchester University Press. https://doi.org/10.7765/9781847791740

Kinsella, J. (2020). *Brimstone: A book of villanelles*. Arc.

Kolářová, K. (2016). How Sam became a father, became a citizen: Scripts of neoliberal inclusion of disability. In M. do Mar Castro Varela, N. Dhawan, & A. Engel (Eds.). *Hegemony and heteronormativity: Revisiting 'the political' in queer politics*. Routledge.

Kosuch, C. (2020). Introduction. In C. Kosuch (Ed.), *Anarchism and the avant-garde: A radical arts and politics in perspective* (pp. 1–9). Brill Rodopi.

Kovach, M. (2009). *Indigenous methodologies: Characteristics, conversations and contexts.* University of Toronto.

Krishnaswami, U. (1996). *Broken tusk: Stories of the Hindu god Ganesha.* August House.

Krupat, A. (1983). Native American literature and the canon. *Critical Inquiry, 10*(1), 145–171. http://www.jstor.org/stable/1343410

Kuskin, W. (2008). *Symbolic Caxton: Literary culture and print capitalism.* University of Notre Dame Press.

Lakoff, G. (1991). Metaphor and war: The metaphor system used to justify war in the Gulf. *Journal of Cognitive Semiotics, 4*(2), 5–9.

Lakoff, G. (1995). Metaphor, morality, and politics – Or, why conservatives have left liberals in the dust. *Social Research, 62*(2), 1–22.

Lakoff, G. & Johnson, M. (2003). *Metaphors we live by.* University of Chicago. (Original published 1980.)

Larabee, A. (2016). Editorial: Star Wars and the girl hero. *Journal of Popular Culture, 49*(1), 7–9. https://doi.org/10.1111/jpcu.12348

Latour, B. (2011). Networks, societies, spheres: Reflections of an actor-network theorist. *International Journal of Communication, 5*(1), 796–810.

Lavoie, F. (2021, June 6). *Why We Need Diverse Books is no longer using the term #OwnVoices* [press release]. WNDB. https://diversebooks.org/why-we-need-diverse-books-is-no-longer-using-the-term-ownvoices/

Lawson. H. (2015). Eureka. Best poems encyclopedia. https://www.best-poems.net/henry_lawson/eureka.html (Original published 1889.)

Layle, P. (2024). *But everyone feels this way: How an autism diagnosis saved my life.* Hachette.

Le Guin, U. (1989). 'The carrier bag of fiction'. In U. Le Guin (author) *Dancing at the edge of the word: Thoughts on words, women, places* (pp. 165–170). Grove Press. (Original published 1986.)

Leane, J. (2010). Aboriginal representation: Conflict or dialogue in the academy. *The Australian Journal of Indigenous Education, 39*(1), 32–39.

Leane, J. (2015). Biography: David Unaipon. *Australian Quarterly, 86*(1), 28–30.

Leane, J. (2023). *Purple Threads.* UQP. (Original published 2011.)

Lefebvre, H. (2003). *The urban revolution* (R. Bonnono, Trans.). University of Minnesota Press. (Original published 1970.)

Lefebvre, H. (2014). *Critique of everyday life: the one-volume edition.* Verso.

Léger, M. (2006). Henri Lefebvre and the moment of the aesthetic. In A. Hemmingway (Ed.). *Marxism and the history of art* (pp. 143–160). Pluto. https://doi.org/10.2307/j.cttl8mvp14.14

Leighten, P. (2020). A politics of technique: Fauvism and anarchist individualism. In C. Kosuch (Ed.), *Anarchism and the avant-garde: Radical arts and politics in perspective* (pp. 70–98). Brill Rodopi.

Leonard, K. (2011). "We wear the mask": The making of a poet. In G. Maryemma & J. W. Ward (Eds.). *The Cambridge history of African American literature* (pp. 206–219). Cambridge University Press. https://doi.org/10.1017/CHOL9780521872171.012

Leung, A. (2009). Futurism 100! At the Estorick Collection. *The Art Section: An Online Journal of Art and Cultural Commentary.* https://www.theartsection.com/futurism-100

Leung, C. (2023). Survival of the unfit: Virginia Woolf's crip and eugenic modernisms in *The Voyage Out. Journal of Literary & Cultural Disability Studies 17*(1), 41–57. https://www.muse.jhu.edu/article/881150.

Levinson, B. (Director). (1989). *Rain Man* [Film]. Metro-Goldwyn Meyer.

Lore, C. & Prady, B. (Producers). (2007–2018). *The Big Bang Theory* [Television Series]. Warner Bros.

Lossi, A. (2009). Metaphor. In Sepp, H. R., & Embree, L. (Eds.) *Handbook of phenomenological aesthetics* (Vol. 59, pp. 211–213). Springer Netherlands. https://doi.org/10.1007/978-90-481-2471-8_42

Lowe, D. (2022). Far-right extremism: Is it legitimate freedom of expression, hate crime, or terrorism? *Terrorism and Political Violence, 34*(7), 1433–1453. https://doi.org/10.1080/09546553.2020.1789111

Lowe, L. (2015). *The intimacies of four continents*. Duke University Press. https://doi.org/10.1515/9780822375647

Lucas, G. (Creator) (1977–present). *Star Wars* [film franchise]. Lucasfilm; Disney.

Ludot Vlasak, R. (2012). Canon trouble: Intertextuality and subversion in Queer as Folk. *TV Series (Le Havre), 2*(2), 265–276. https://doi.org/10.4000/tvseries.1479

Lukács, G. (1980). Realism in the balance (R. Livingstone, Trans.). In T. Adorno, W. Benjamin, E. Bloch, B. Brecht, G. Lukács, & F. Jameson (Authors), *Aesthetics and politics* (pp. 28–59). Verso. (Original published 1938.)

MacKellar, D. (1908). *My country*. The Official Dorothea MacKellar Website. Retrieved June 1, 2024, from https://www.dorotheamackellar.com.au/my-country/

Magabala. *Our Partners*. Magabala Books. https://magabala.com.au/pages/our-partners (Viewed 1 June 2024).

Maggio, R. (2014). The anthropology of storytelling and the storytelling of anthropology. *Journal of Comparative Research in Anthropology and Sociology, 5*(2), 89–106.

Mahmood, S. (2006). Feminist theory, agency, and the liberatory subject: Some reflections on the Islamic revival in Egypt. *Temenos, 42*(1), 31–71. https://doi.org/10.33356/temenos.4633

Makereti, T. (2016). Stories: Making soup, baking bread. *Biography (Honolulu), 39*(3), 406–409. https://doi.org/10.1353/bio.2016.0049

Makki, F. (2014). Development by dispossession: Terra nullius and the social-ecology of new enclosures in Ethiopia. *Rural Sociology, 79*(1), 79–103. https://doi.org/10.1111/ruso.12033

Malešević, S. (2011). Ideology. In K. M. Dowding (Ed.) *Encyclopedia of power*. Sage.

Mangrum, B. (2015). Bourdieu, Cavell, and the politics of aesthetic value. *Literature & Theology, 29*(3), 260–283. https://doi.org/10.1093/litthe/fru043

Marinetti, F. (1909). *The futurist manifesto*. Books on Trial. https://www.booksontrial.com/the-full-text-of-the-futurist-manifesto/

Marshall, T. C. (2008). Cultural differences in intimacy: The influence of gender-role ideology and individualism—collectivism. *Journal of Social and Personal Relationships, 25*(1), 143–168. https://doi.org/10.1177/0265407507086810

Martin, A. (1986–2000). *The baby-sitters club* [book series]. Scholastic.

Martin, C. (2018). Clever Odysseus: Narratives and strategies of rental property investor subjectivity in Australia. *Housing Studies, 33*(7), 1060–1084. https://doi.org/10.1080/02673037.2017.1414161

Martin, J., Ghaferi, J., Cummins, D., Mamelak, A., Schmults, C., Parikh, M., Speyer, L., Chuang, A., Richardson, H., Stein, D., & Liégeois, N. (2009). Changes in skin tanning attitudes. Fashion articles and advertisements in the early 20th century. *American Journal of Public Health, 99*(12), 2140–2146. https://doi.org/10.2105/AJPH.2008.144352

Mathews, T. (2014). *Alberto Giacometti: The art of relation*. I.B. Taurus & Co Ltd.

McIntosh, P. (2009). Introduction. In K. Weekes (Ed.), *Privilege and prejudice: Twenty years with the invisible knapsack* (pp. ix–xiii). Cambridge Scholars.

McIntosh, P. (2020). *On privilege, fraudulence, and teaching as learning: selected essays 1981–2019*. Routledge.

McKinnon, C. (2014). From scar trees to a 'bouquet of words': Aboriginal text is everywhere. In C. McKinnon, T. Neale, & E. Vincent (Eds.), *History, power, text: Cultural studies and Indigenous studies* (pp. 371–383). UTS ePRESS. http://www.jstor.org/stable/j.ctv1w36pd7.26

McKinnon, C. (2021). Striking back: The 1980s Aboriginal art movement and the performativity of sovereignty. In B. Hokowhitu, A. Moreton-Robinson, L. Smith, C. Andersen, & S. Larkin (Eds.), *Routledge handbook of critical Indigenous studies* (pp. 324–336). Routledge. https://doi.org/10.4324/9780429440229-28

McLean Davies, L., Truman, S. E., & Buzacott, L. (2021). Teacher-researchers: A pilot project for unsettling the secondary Australian literary canon. *Gender and Education, 33*(7), 814–829. https://doi.org/10.1080/09540253.2020.1735313

McNair, J. C., & Edwards, P. A. (2021). The lasting legacy of Rudine Sims Bishop: Mirrors, windows, sliding glass doors, and more. *Literacy Research, 70*(1), 202–212. https://doi.org/10.1177/23813377211028256

Mellors, A. (2014). Disabled poetry. *Textual Practice, 28*(3), 385–404. https://doi.org/10.1080/0950236X.2013.848927

Meneses, A. C. S., & de Alencar Costa, M. T. (2023). The protagonism of Rey in Star Wars: The force awakens, a feminist reading. *Acta Scientiarum. Language and Culture, 45*(1). https://doi.org/10.4025/actascilangcult.v45i1.64735

Merriam-Webster. (2024a). Legman [dictionary entry]. *Merriam-Webster*. https://www.merriam-webster.com/dictionary/legman

Merriam-Webster. (2024b). Epigram [dictionary entry]. *Merriam-Webster*. https://www.merriam-webster.com/dictionary/epigram

Merriam-Webster. (2024c). Dialectic [dictionary entry]. *Merriam-Webster*. https://www.merriam-webster.com/dictionary/dialectic

Messenger, J. (1964). Joe O'Donnell, "Seanchai" of Aran. *Journal of the Folklore Institute, 1*(3), 197–213. https://doi.org/10.2307/3813903

Met, P. (1996). Of Men and animals: Hergé's Tintin au Congo, a study in primitivism. *Romanic Review, 87*(1), 131–144.

Michaels, B., De Ville, C., Dall, B., Rockett, R. (1988). Every Rose Has Its Thorn [Song]. On *Open Up and Say . . . Ahh!*. Capitol Records.

Miller, T. (2022). *Georg Lukács and critical theory: Aesthetics, history, utopia*. Edinburgh University Press. https://doi.org/10.1515/9781399502436

Millner, N. (2021). More-than-human witnessing? The politics and aesthetics of Madre Tierra (Mother Earth) in transnational agrarian movements. *GeoHumanities, 7*(2), 391–414. https://doi.org/10.1080/2373566X.2021.1973906

Mitchell, M. (1936). *Gone with the wind*. Macmillan.

Mitchell, S. (1974). From Shklovsky to Brecht: Some preliminary remarks towards a history of the politicisation of Russian Formalism, *Screen, 15*(2), 74–81, https://doi.org/10.1093/screen/15.2.74

Moreton-Robinson, A. (2015a, October 26). 'Aboriginal sovereignty, Foucault, and the limits of power' keynote address to 'Indigenous Foucault: A Symposium presented by the Faculty of Native Studies', University of Alberta. [Video]. YouTube. https://www.youtube.com/watch?v=nN5zwy2Y8AY

Moreton-Robinson, A. (2015b). *The white possessive: Property, power, and Indigenous sovereignty*. University of Minnesota.

Moreton-Robinson, A. (2016). Introduction: Locations of engagement in the first world. In A. Moreton-Robinson (Ed.), *Critical Indigenous studies: Engagements in first world locations* (pp. 3–16). University of Arizona. https://doi.org/10.2307/jj.423485.4

Moreton-Robinson, A. (2000). *Talkin' up to the white woman: Aboriginal women and feminism*. UQP.

Moreton-Robinson, A. (2004). Whiteness, epistemology and Indigenous representation. In A. Moreton-Robinson (Ed.). *Whitening race: Essays in cultural criticism* (pp. 75–88). Aboriginal Studies Press.

Morgan, S. (1987). *My place*. Fremantle Press.

Morse, D. R. (2018). Sounding dismodernism in James Joyce's Ulysses. *Journal of Literary & Cultural Disability Studies, 12*(4), 459–475. https://doi.org/10.3828/jlcds.2018.36

Mulford, C. (2007). Writing women in early American studies: On canons, feminist critique, and the work of writing women into history. *Tulsa Studies in Women's Literature, 26*(1), 107–118. https://doi.org/10.1353/tsw.2007.a220821

Mullaney, C. (2019). 'Not to discover weakness is the artifice of strength': Emily Dickinson, constraint, and a disability poetics. *J19: The Journal of Nineteenth-Century Americanists, 7*(1), 49–81. https://doi.org/10.1353/jnc.2019.0002.

Müller, S. (2018). Environmental modernism: Ecocentric conceptions of the self and the emotions in the works of R.M. Rilke and W.B. Yeats. In S. Müller & T. Pusse (Eds.), *From ego to eco: Mapping shifts from anthropocentrism to ecocentrism* (pp. 39–59). Brill.

Murdock, M. (1990). *The heroine's journey: Woman's quest for wholeness*. Shambhala.

Murray, A. (2023). *Unladylike lessons in love*. HarperCollins.

Murray, S. (2008). Idiots and savants. In *Representing autism* (pp. 65–103). Liverpool University Press. https://doi.org/10.5949/UPO9781846314667.005

Mussell, S. (2017). *Critical theory and feeling: The affective politics of the early Frankfurt School*. Manchester University. https://doi.org/10.2307/j.ctv18b5kzp

Nanay, B. (2021). Zoomorphism. *Erkenntnis, 86*(1), 171–186.

Nayar, P. K. (2011). The poetics of postcolonial atrocity: Dalit life writing, testimonio, and human rights. *Ariel, 42*(3–4), 237–264.

Neale, M., & Kelly, L. (2020). *First Knowledges Songlines: The power and promise*. Thames & Hudson.

Neale, T., Vincent, E., & McKinnon, C., (Eds.) (2014). *History, power, text: cultural studies and Indigenous studies*. UTS ePRESS.

Neto, F. T. L., Bach, P. V., Lyra, R. J. L., Borges Junior, J. C., Maia, G. T. d. S., Araujo, L. C. N., & Lima, S. V. C. (2019). Gods associated with male fertility and virility. *Andrology, 7*(3), 267–272. https://doi.org/10.1111/andr.12599

Nettelbeck, A. (2008). Practices of violence/myths of creation: Mounted Constable Willshire and the cultural logic of settler nationalism. *Journal of Australian Studies, 32*(1), 5–17. https://doi.org/10.1080/14443050801993784

Nghikefelwa, J. M., Wyld, F., & Wisker, G. (2022). Creating and curating: Three voices from Namibia, Australia and the UK on decolonising the literary-related doctorate. In M. L. Moncreiffe (Ed.), *Decolonising curriculum knowledge: International perspectives and interdisciplinary approaches*. Palgrave Macmillan. https://doi.org/10.1007/978-3-031-13623-8_4

Nicol, J. C. (2008). Questioning the canon: Issues surrounding the selection of literature for the high school English curriculum. *English Quarterly Canada, 38*(2), 22–28.

Nobitz, N. M. (2018). *History's queer stories: Retrieving and navigating homosexuality in British fiction about the Second World War*. Transcript Verlag. https://doi.org/10.14361/9783839445433

Noble, M. (2010, July 19). I am me and I am OK [blog post]. *Intersex Human Rights Australia*. https://ihra.org.au/18138/opinion-michael-noble/

Nolfi, K. L. (2011). YA fatphobia, *The Horn Book Magazine, 87*(1), 55–59.

Normandin, S. (2018). *Chaucerian ecopoetics: Deconstructing anthropocentrism in the Canterbury tales*. Palgrave Macmillan.

O'Connor, C. (2022). A new odyssey: Finding the hero's journey in Black Panther. *English Journal, 111*(3), 90–97. https://doi.org/10.58680/ej202231573

O'Connor, M. (2018). Dark ecology and black comedy in Patrick McGinley's Foggag. In S. Müller & T. Pusse (Eds.), *From ego to eco: Mapping shifts from anthropocentrism to ecocentrism* (pp. 185–200). Brill.

Odell, J. (2019). *How to do nothing: Resisting the attention economy*. Melville House.

Oettli, S. (2011). Janet Frame's conceptualization of the writing process: From The Lagoon to Mirror City. *Commonwealth Essays and Studies, 33*(2), 98–109. https://doi.org/10.4000/ces.8164

Okorafor, N. (2014). *Lagoon*. Hodder & Stoughton.

Orlowski, P. (2011). *Teaching about hegemony race, class and democracy in the 21st century*. Springer. https://doi.org/10.1007/978-94-007-1418-2

Orwell, G. (1946). *Why I write*. The Orwell Foundation. https://www.orwellfoundation.com/the-orwell-foundation/orwell/essays-and-other-works/why-i-write/

Padularosa, D. (2020). Anti-art? Dada and anarchy. In C Kosuch (Ed.), *Anarchism and the avant-garde: radical arts and politics in perspective* (pp. 99–128). Brill Rodopi.

Pandey, S. (2021). Archetypal criticism: a study of Northop Frye and Maud Bodkin. *International Journal of English Language, Literature, and Translation Studies, 8*(4), 56–9.

Pascoe, B. (2018). *Dark Emu: Aboriginal Australia and the birth of agriculture*. Magabala. (Original published 2014.)

Pascoe, B. (2024). *Black duck: A year at Yumburra*. Thames & Hudson.

Paterson, B. (2018). *Saltbush Bill, J.P., and other verses*. Project Gutenberg. Retrieved June 1 2024 from https://www.gutenberg.org/files/1317/1317-h/1317-h.htm (Original published 1917.)

Payne, S. (2014–2017). *George Alexander Anstey*. The Info List. https://theinfolist.com/php/SummaryGet.php?FindGo=George_Alexander_Anstey

Pelizzon, A., & Kennedy, J. (2019). "Welcome to Country" and "Acknowledgment of Country": (Re)conciliatory protest. *Contention, 7*(1), 13–28. https://doi.org/10.3167/cont.2019.070103

Perera, S., & Pugliese, J. (2023). Never settler enough: The double economy of terror and deaths in custody in Australia. *Filozofski Vestnik, 44*(2). https://doi.org/10.3986/fv.44.2.14

Phillips, L., & Bunda, T. (2018). *Research through, with and as storying*. Taylor & Francis. https://doi.org/10.4324/9781315109190

Pisa, J., & Hruska, V. (2023). Disentangling the 'capacity to act': Variegated resources of individuals exerting change agency. *European Planning Studies*, 1–19. https://doi.org/10.1080/09654313.2023.2258165

Poetry Foundation. (2024a). Ghazal [definition]. https://www.poetryfoundation.org/learn/glossary-terms/ghazal

Poetry Foundation. (2024b). Pantoum [definition]. https://www.poetryfoundation.org/learn/glossary-terms/pantoum

Polak, I. (2020). Native apocalypse in Claire G. Coleman's The Old Lie. *Humanities, 9*(69), 1–13. https://doi.org/10.3390/h9030069

Powers, R. (2018). *The overstory*. Penguin.

Pritchard, E. (2022). 'Breathing through its spectacles': The queer trees of Frank O'Hara. *Cambridge Quarterly, 51*(2), 144–156. https://doi.org/10.1093/camqtly/bfac017

Rademaker, L. (2020). Eaglehawk and Crow: Aboriginal knowledges, imperial networks and the evolution of religion. *Journal of Colonialism & Colonial History*, *21*(3). https://doi.org/10.1353/cch.2020.0027

Raglan, L. (1949). *The hero: A study in tradition, myth and drama*. The Thinker's Library. (Original published 1936.)

Rancière, J. (2011). The thinking of dissensus: Politics and aesthetics. In P. Bowman & R. Stamp (Eds.). *Reading Rancière: Critical dissensus* (pp. 1–17). Bloomsbury.

Rank, O. (2015). *The myth of the birth of the hero: A psychological exploration of myth* (G. C. Richter & E. J. Lieberman, Trans.). Hopkins Press. (Original published 1909.)

Rapti, V., & Gordon, E. (2021). Introduction. In Rapti, V., & Gordon, E. (Eds.), *Ludics: Play as Humanistic Inquiry* (pp. 1–17). Palgrave Macmillan. https://doi.org/10.1007/978-981-15-7435-1_1

Rashed, M. A. (2023). Mad pride and the creation of culture. *Royal Institute of Philosophy Supplement*, *94*(1), 201–217. https://doi.org/10.1017/S1358246123000188

Razum, O. (Ed.). (2022). *Refugee camps in Europe and Australia: An interdisciplinary critique*. Springer.

Reconciliation Australia (2021). *Demonstrating inclusive and respectful language*. Reconciliation Australia. https://www.reconciliation.org.au/wp-content/uploads/2021/10/inclusive-and-respectful-language.pdf

Reischer, E., & Koo, K. S. (2004). The body beautiful: Symbolism and agency in the social world. *Annual Review of Anthropology*, *33*, 297–317. http://www.jstor.org/stable/25064855

Reysen, S., Packard, G. A., & Plante, C. N. (2024). Sexism and racism negatively predict preference for diverse characters in Star Wars fans. *Psychology of Popular Media*, *13*(2), 256–261. https://doi.org/10.1037/ppm0000462

Rhys, J. (1966). *Wide Sargasso sea*. WW Norton.

Richardson, E., Grube, V., & Horwat, J. (2023). Comic artists' navigation of trauma, affect, and representation: Drawn images as entanglement of body, material, memory. *Journal of Literary & Cultural Disability Studies*, *17*(3), 349–368. https://doi.org/10.3828/jlcds.2023.26

Riley, C. (2015). The Intersections between early feminist polemic and publishing: How books changed lives in the second wave. *Women*, *26*(4), 384–401. https://doi.org/10.1080/09574042.2015.1106258

Rimstead, R., & Beneventi, D. A. (2019). Introduction: Reading space through conflict. In D. A Beneventi & R. Rimstead (Eds.). *Contested spaces, counter-narratives, and culture from below in Canada and Québec* (pp. 3–38). University of Toronto Press. https://doi.org/10.3138/9781442629912-002

Rutter, R. (1987). William Caxton and literary patronage. *Studies in Philology*, *84*(4), 440–470.

Robinson, T. (2003). The Seanchaí and the database. *Irish Pages*, *2*(1), 43–53.

Rodas, J. M. (2018). *Autistic disturbances: Theorizing autism poetics from the DSM to Robinson Crusoe*. University of Michigan Press. https://doi.org/10.3998/mpub.9365350

Rodriguez Gonzalez, C. (2016). The rhythms of the city: The performance of time and space in Suhayl Saadi's Psychoraag, *Journal of Commonwealth Literature*, *51*(1), 92–109.

Romagnoli, A. S., & Pagnucci, G. S. (2013). *Enter the superheroes: American values, culture, and the canon of superhero literature*. Scarecrow Press.

Rose, D. B. (2017). Shimmer: When all you love is being trashed. In A. Tsing, H. Swanson, E. Gan, & N. Bubant (Eds.), *Arts of living on a damaged planet* (pp. 51–63). University of Minnesota.

Rose, S. (2009). Who invented the printing press? *Agora, 44*(3), 17.

Rosenthal, O. E. (2022). Academic colonialism and marginalization: on the contentious postcolonial-decolonial debate in Latin American studies. *Postcolonial Studies, 25*(1), 17–34. https://doi.org/10.1080/13688790.2022.2030576

Ross, A. S., & Rivers, D. J. (2019). "Froome with his SKY bodyguards, layers of armour": The 'sport is war' conceptual metaphor in grand tour cycling commentary. *Communication & Sport, 7*(2), 176–197. https://doi.org/10.1177/2167479517752431

Rozema, R. (2019). Books-in-action: The new neurodiverse canon [Review]. *English Journal, 109*(2), 102–104. https://doi.org/10.58680/ej201930367

Rymhs, D. (2019). For king and country?: War and Indigenous masculinity. In D. A Beneventi & R. Rimstead (Eds.). *Contested spaces, counter-narratives, and culture from below in Canada and Québec* (pp. 163–187). University of Toronto Press. https://doi.org/10.3138/9781442629912-010

Sadri, H. (2020). The return journey in Alison Bechdel's Fun Home. *The Journal of Popular Culture, 53*(1), 111–128.

Said, E. (1979). *Orientalism*. Vintage.

Sainsbury, D. (2017). Constraints, concealment, and buried texts: Reading Walter Abish with Georges Perec and the Oulipo. *Comparative Literature, 69*(3), 303–314. https://doi.org/10.1215/00104124-4164426

Sanchez, R. (2020). Deafness and modernism. In A. Hall (Ed.). *The Routledge companion to literature and disability* (pp. 193–202). Routledge. https://doi.org/10.4324/9781315173047-20

Sanders, M. A. (2011). Toward a modernist poetics. In G. Maryemma & J. W. Ward (Eds.). *The Cambridge history of African American literature* (pp. 220–238). Cambridge University Press. https://doi.org/10.1017/CHOL9780521872171.013

Sanders, J., & van Krieken, K. (2018). Exploring narrative structure and hero enactment in brand stories. *Frontiers in Psychology, 9*, 1645–1645. https://doi.org/10.3389/fpsyg.2018.01645

Sandywell, B. (2011). *Dictionary of visual discourse: A dialectical lexicon of terms*. Routledge

Saunders, M. (Ed.) (2022). *This all come back now: An anthology of First Nations speculative fiction*. University of Queensland Press. Promotional Webpage: https://www.uqp.com.au/books/this-all-come-back-now

Saunders, P. (2020). Cripping Kairos: The risky rhetorical performance of autism disclosure for the college student. *Disability Studies Quarterly, 40*(2). https://dsq-sds.org/index.php/dsq/article/view/7072

Schalk, S. (2018). *Bodyminds reimagined: (Dis)ability, race, and gender in Black women's speculative fiction*. Duke University Press. https://doi.org/10.1515/9780822371830

Sen, U. (2017). Developing terra nullius: Colonialism, nationalism, and Indigeneity in the Andaman Islands. *Comparative Studies in Society and History, 59*(4), 944–973. https://doi.org/10.1017/S0010417517000330

Senier, S. (2020). Disability in Indigenous literature. In A. Hall (Ed.), *The Routledge companion to literature and disability* (pp. 9–20). Routledge. https://doi.org/10.4324/9781315173047-3

Shahjahan, R. A. (2015). Being "lazy" and slowing down: Toward decolonizing time, our body, and pedagogy. *Educational Philosophy and Theory, 47*(5), 488–501. https://doi.org/10.1080/00131857.2014.880645

Shaw, G. (2021). *Pygmalion* [play script]. William Collins. (Original premiered 1913.)

Shelley, M. (1993). *Frankenstein*. Project Gutenberg. https://www.gutenberg.org/files/84/84-h/84-h.htm (Original published 1818).

Shihab, N. F. M. (2019). Écriture feminine in the narration level of Jeanette Winterson's The Powerbook. *Teknosastik, 15*(2), 69–75. https://doi.org/10.33365/ts.v15i2.30

Sholette, G. (2021). *The art of activism and the activism of art.* Lund Humphries.

Shyrock, R. (2019). The symbolist movement: Anarchism and the avant-garde in fin de siècle France. In C. Kosuch (Ed.), *Anarchism and the avant-garde: Radical arts and politics in perspective* (pp. 13–36). Brill Rodopi.

Siegelman, E. Y. (2005). An anti-hero's journey. *The San Francisco Jung Institute Library Journal, 24*(2), 47–57. https://doi.org/10.1525/jung.1.2005.24.2.47

Simon, E. (1987). *Through my eyes.* Collins Dove.

Sinfield, A. (1994). *Cultural politics – Queer reading* (2nd ed.). University of Pennsylvania Press, Inc. https://doi.org/10.9783/9781512820539

Smith, L. T. (2021). *Decolonizing methodologies: Research and Indigenous peoples* (3rd edn.). Bloomsbury. https://doi.org/10.5040/9781350225282

Smith, B., & Sparkes, A. C. (2005). Men, sport, spinal cord injury, and narratives of hope. *Social Science & Medicine, 61*(5), 1095–1105. https://doi.org/10.1016/j.socscimed. 2005.01.011

Somerville, A. (2021, February 14). Canons don't only belong to dead white Englishmen. We have a Māori canon too. *The Guardian.* https://www.theguardian.com/world/2021/feb/14/ canons-dont-only-belong-to-dead-white-englishmen-we-have-a-maori-canon-too

Stapleton, K., & Wilson, J. (2017). Telling the story: Meaning making in a community narrative. *Journal of Pragmatics, 108*(2017), 60–80. https://doi.org/10.1016/j. pragma.2016.11.003

Streitmatter, R. (1995). Creating a venue for the "love that dare not speak Its name": Origins of the gay and lesbian press. *Journalism & Mass Communication Quarterly, 72*(2), 436–447.

Stroude, A. (2022). What if time was not money? Towards a pluriversal understanding of time for sustainable consumption. *Consumption and Society, 1*(2): 358–374.

Subramaniyaswami, S. (1996). *Loving Ganeśa: Hinduism's endearing elephant-faced god.* Motilal Banarsidass Publishers.

Sugden, J., & Tomlinson, A. (2013). *Power games.* Routledge. https://doi. org/10.4324/9781315012698

Swartz, D. (2011). Bourdieu, Pierre. In R. Dalleo (Ed.). *Encyclopedia of power* (pp. 74–76). Sage.

Taplin, R. L., & Symon, D. E. (2008). Remnant horticultural plants at the site of the former Newman's Nursery, 1854—1932. *Journal of the Adelaide Botanic Gardens, 22,* 73–96.

Thomas, S. (1988). Aboriginal subjection and affirmation. *Meanjin, 47*(4), 755–761.

Thompson, J. (2015). "In that time …" in a galaxy far, far away: Epic myth-understandings and myth-appropriation in Star Wars. In J. T. Eberl & K. S. Decker (Eds.). *The ultimate Star Wars and philosophy: You must unlearn what you have learned* (pp. 261–273). John Wiley & Sons. https://doi.org/10.1002/9781119038092.ch23

Thomson, A. (2023). Colonial texts on Aboriginal land: The dominance of the canon in Australian English classrooms. *Australian Educational Researcher.* https://doi.org/ 10.1007/s13384-023-00643-7

Todd, Z. (2015). Indigenizing the Anthropocene. In H. Davis & E. Turpin (Eds.), *Art in the Anthropocene: Encounters among aesthetics, politics, environments and epistemologies* (pp. 241–254). Open Humanities Press.

Tomasena, J. M. (2019). Negotiating collaborations: BookTubers, the publishing industry, and YouTube's ecosystem. *Social Media + Society, 5*(4), 1–12. https://doi.org/10.1177/ 2056305119894004

Toth, H. G., & Nicholls, B. (2020). A dialectical literary canon? *African Identities*, *18*(1–2), 41–63. https://doi.org/10.1080/14725843.2020.1773761

Tracey, G. Morgan, R., & Schraffenberger, J. (2023). *Elements of creative writing.* University of Northern Iowa. https://open.umn.edu/opentextbooks/textbooks/1483

Turner, N. (2010). *Post-war British women novelists and the canon.* Continuum. https://doi.org/10.5040/9781472542700

Unaipon, D. (2006). *Legendary tales of the Australian Aborigines.* Melbourne University Press. (Original published 1930 under the name of George Ramsay Smith.)

UQP. (2022). *This all come back now: An anthology of First Nations speculative fiction* [publisher webpage]. UQP. https://www.uqp.com.au/books/this-all-come-back-now

Valéry, P. (1954). Poetry and abstract thought (C. Guenther, Trans.). *The Kenyon Review*, *16*(2), 208–233.

Vandrick, S. (2015). No "knapsack of invisible privilege" for ESL university students. *Journal of Language, Identity, and Education*, *14*(1), 54–59. https://doi.org/10.1080/15348458.2015.988574

Varney, J. (2020). *Leadership as meaning-making: The hero's journey to transformation.* Productivity Press. https://doi.org/10.4324/9781003133001

Verma, A. (2022). In solidarity. In A. Verma (Ed.). *Anti-racism in higher education* (pp. 197–202). Policy Press. https://doi.org/10.2307/j.ctv2nv8pp2.25

Viljoen, J. (2023, December 28). Black Panther, Wakanda Forever and the problem with Hollywood – an African perspective. *The Conversation.* https://theconversation.com/black-panther-wakanda-forever-and-the-problem-with-hollywood-an-african-perspective-219232

Vincent, E., Neale, T., & McKinnon, C. (2014). Indigenous cultural studies: Intersections between cultural studies and Indigenous studies. In T. Neale, E. Vincent, & C. McKinnon (Eds.), *History, power, text: cultural studies and Indigenous studies* (pp. 11–36). UTS ePRESS.

Vint, S. (2021). *Biopolitical futures in twenty-first-century speculative fiction.* Cambridge University Press.

Vogler, C. (2007). *The writer's journey: Mythic structure for writers* (3rd edn.). Michael Wiese. (Original published 1998.)

Von Eschen, P. M. (1997). *Race against empire: Black Americans and anticolonialism, 1937–1957.* Cornell University Press. https://doi.org/10.7591/9780801471711

Vyasa. (1999). *Mahabharata: The greatest spiritual epic of all time* (K. Dharma, Trans.). Torchlight Publishing. (Original written approx. 200 BCE.)

Vyasa. (2015). *Bhagvad Gita as it is* (A.C. Bhaktivedanta Swami Prabhupada, Trans.). Bhaktivedanta Book Trust. (Original written approx. 200 BCE.)

Wachsmuth, D., & Angelo, H. (2018). Green and gray: New ideologies of nature in urban sustainability policy. *Annals of the American Association of Geographers*, *108*(4), 1038–1056. https://doi.org/10.1080/24694452.2017.1417819

Walker, Alice. (1982). *The color purple.* Harcourt Brace Jovanovich.

Walker, Amelia. (2010). *All you need to teach poetry Ages 10+.* Macmillan.

Walker, Amelia. (2022). Ecopoetry, pedagogical encounters, and holding absence present: Ideas for classrooms. In A. Sorby & S. Kleppe (Eds.). *Poetry and Sustainability in Education* (pp. 185–208). Springer. https://doi.org/10.1007/978-3-030-95576-2_9

Walker, A., Wisdom, T., Marks, S., Pearce, S., & Challans, B. (2017). Editorial: To speak and/as connect-beyond the silencing of violence, and the violence that is silence. *Writing from Below*, *3*(2), n.p. https://writingfrombelow.org/articulations-of-violence/editorial/

Walker, B. G., & Bodnaruk, C. (1997). Review of *Feminist fairy tales*. *Herizons*, *11*(2), 39–39. Herizons Magazine, Inc.

Wark, M. (2023). *Love and Money, Sex and Death: A Memoir*. Verso.

Warren, A. N., & Ward, N. A. (2022). Negotiating the limits of teacher agency: Constructed constraints vs. capacity to act in preservice teachers' descriptions of teaching emergent bilingual learners. *Critical Discourse Studies*, *19*(5), 539–555. https://doi.org/10.1080/1 7405904.2021.1999289

Wasson, S. (2023). Guest editor's introduction: Pain's plurals and narrative disruption: Communicating pain and honoring Its telling. *Literature and Medicine*, *41*(2), 283–302. https://doi.org/10.1353/lm.2023.a921562

Watson, J. J. (1991). An integral setting tells more than when and where. *The Reading Teacher*, *44*(9), 638–646.

Webb, J. (2009). *Understanding representation*. Sage.

Webb, J. (2012). Seeing, doing, knowing: Poetry and the pursuit of knowledge. *TEXT: Journal of Writing and Writing Courses*, *16*(SI 13), 1–13. https://doi.org/10.52086/001c.31149

Weil, S. (1976). Letter to Joë Bousquet, 13 April 1942 (R. Rosenthal, Trans.). In S. Pétrement (author), *Simone Weil: A life* (p. 462). Pantheon.

Weil, S. (2005). *The need for roots: Prelude to a declaration of duties towards mankind* (A. Wills, Trans.). Routledge. (Original published 1949.)

Weston, D. (2016). Contemporary poetic ecologies and a return to form. *C21 Literature*, *4*(1), 1–24. https://doi.org/10.16995/c21.5

White, P. (1976). *A fringe of leaves*. Jonathan Cape.

Whitman, W. (1891). *Pioneers! O Pioneers!* The Walt Whitman Archives. Retrieved June 1 2024 from https://whitmanarchive.org/item/ppp.00707_00802

Williams, C. (2019). The hero's journey: A mudmap for change. *The Journal of Humanistic Psychology*, *59*(4), 522–539. https://doi.org/10.1177/0022167817705499

Williams, R. (1977). *Marxism and literature*. Oxford University Press.

Wilmer, S. E. (2009). Introduction. In S. E. Wilmer (Ed.), *Native American performance and representation* (pp. 1–16). University of Arizona Press.

Winch, T. J. (2019). *The yield*. Penguin.

Winfield, A. S., Hickerson, H., Doub, D. C., Winfield, A. R., & McPhatter, B. (2024). Between Black mothers and daughters: A critical intergenerational duoethnography on the silence of health disparities and hope of loud healing. *Frontiers in Communication*, *8*(1), 1–21. https://doi.org/10.3389/fcomm.2023.1185919

Withers, D. M. (2021). Honno: The Welsh women's press and the cultural ecology of the Welsh publishing industry, *c.* 1950s to the present. *Women: a cultural review*, *32*(3–4), 354–371, https://doi.org/10.1080/09574042.2021.1973726

WNDB. (2024). *WNDB*. We Need Diverse Books. https://diversebooks.org/about-wndb/

Wood, N. (2022). Realism in eco fiction: Climate change and the short story cycle. *Social Alternatives*, *41*(3), 43–47

Wood, R., Litherland, B., & Reed, E. (2020). Girls being Rey: Ethical cultural consumption, families and popular feminism. *Cultural Studies*, *34*(4), 546–566. https://doi.org/10.1080/09502386.2019.1656759

Woodward, E. (2013). When the ghost gum peels. *Australasian Science*, *34*(4), 20–26.

Wright, A. (2006). *Carpentaria*. Giramondo.

Wyld, F. (Personal communication, Oct 31, 2023). Presentation for the Critically Creative Reading and Writing Collective, University of South Australia, Magill Campus.

Wyld, F. (2025). Academic kinship: I once had a game, or should I say it once had me? In A. Walker, H. Grimmett, & A. Black (Eds.), *Ludic inquiries into power and pedagogy in higher education: How games play us* (pp. 133–142). Routledge.

Yaeger, P. (1999). Race and the cloud of unknowing in "Gone with the Wind." *Southern Cultures, 5*(1), 21–28. https://doi.org/10.1353/scu.1999.0045

Yunkaporta, T. (2020). *Sand talk: How Indigenous thinking can save the world.* Text Publishing Company.

Yunkaporta, Tyson. (2023). *Right story, wrong story : Adventures in Indigenous thinking.* Text Publishing Company.

Zandvliet, D. B. (2016). *The ecology of home.* SensePublishers. https://doi.org/10.1007/978-94-6300-579-1

Zhou, N. (2017, June 8). Thomas Keneally: 'Cultural appropriation is dangerous'. *The Guardian.* https://www.theguardian.com/books/2017/jun/08/thomas-keneally-cultural-appropriation-is-dangerous

Zournazi, M. (2005). A Reflection: Kairos or the foreignness of my tongue. *Life Writing, 2*(1), 141–143. https://doi.org/10.1080/10408340308518279

INDEX

race and racism, 27–30, 41, 45, 73, 82–3,
    96, 102, 123, 166, 171 (*see also*
    cultural racism)
Raglan, Lord, 159
Rancière, Jacques, 127–8
Rank, Otto, 159
realism, 129–30
recuperation, Lefebvre's theory of, 101–2,
    106, 133, 135
register in writing, 49
refugee detention camps in Australia, 19
relationality, 7, 13, 16–17, 147, 197 (*see also*
    kin and kinship)
religion, 30, 69–71, 74–5, 107–8, 159 (*see
    also* Catholicism; Hindu literature)
repetition, poetic device of, 11, 167,
    183–6
re-placing texts, 72–3
re-placing language, 94
representation (*see also* misrepresentation)
    Stuart Hall's theory of, xvi, 41–4
    as re-presentation, xxiv, 41–4
    representative imbalances, xxiv, 58,
        69–70, 74, 77, 79, 87, 92, 101, 112
    media representations, 47
resistance, 33–5
resolution, literary concept of, 162, 164–5,
    182–3
responsibility, 15, 86, 145–6, 179–80, 196
restitution narratives, 164, 170
re-writing texts, creative writing strategy
    of, 92–3
rewriting or redrafting (*see also* editing),
    153
rhizome, Deleuze and Guattari's theory of,
    178
Rhys, Jean, 92
right-wing politics, 17, 109 (*see also*
    conservative politics; fascism)
rising conflict (*see* conflict)
round characters, 50–1

Said, Edward, 27
sanism, 90
science fiction, 95–7
science and literature, 7, 9, 11, 83 (*see also*
    arts/sciences split)
Scottish Australians, 6
screenwriting, 157, 164 (*see also* Hollywood)

seanchaí, 9
s/Self and o/Other, 31 (*see also* o/
    Otherness)
setting, device in literature, 48, 51–2
sexuality, 27–30, 42, 45, 47, 56, 73, 84–5,
    96 (*see also* LGBTQIA+; queer)
Shakespeare, William, and Shakespearean
    literature, 27, 86, 182
Sheba Feminist Press, 102–3
Shelley, Mary, 86, 96
short story cycles, 177, 179–80, 186
signs and signifiers, 42–3, 123
Silliman Workshop creative writing
    program, 113
Simon, Ella, 92
Situationists, the, 24, 126
slang, 149
social class
    inequities of, 27–30, 71, 79, 84–5, 144,
        165–7, 197
    reproduction of, 102, 123
    resistance to inequities, 90, 92–3, 101,
        130, 171
social media activism, 104–7
Songlines, 8
sonnet, poetic form, 181–2
space, 38
speculative fiction, 95–6
Star Wars, 157, 161, 164, 168–9, 171
Story and stories,
    definition challenges, 10, 12
    First Nations Australian concept of
        Story, 8
    Story/narrative split, 8, 11–12
    Story-knowledge connections, 8–9,
        12–13
structural violence and/or discrimination,
    41
style in writing, 110 (*see also* aesthetics)
subaltern, 30
subjectification, 22–3, 122, 178
Sudan People's Liberation Army, 28
symbolic capital (*see under* capital)
symbolic violence, 25–6
symbolism, literary device, 150
    conventional or public symbols, 151
    personal or private symbols, 153
    symbolic imagery, 150
synecdoche, 140, 148–50, 154